AF361427

Reflecting on Leadership in Language Education

Reflective Practice in Language Education
Series Editor: Thomas S. C. Farrell, Brock University

This series covers different issues related to reflective practice in language education and includes an introductory book which introduces these areas. The other books in the series clarify the different approaches that have been taken within reflective practice and outline current themes that have emerged in the research on various topics and methods of reflection that have occurred.

Published:

Reflective Practice in ELT
Thomas S. C. Farrell

Micro-Reflection on Classroom Communication: A FAB Framework
Hansun Zhang Waring and Sarah Chepkirui Creider

Forthcoming:

Cooperative Learning through a Reflective Lens
George M. Jacobs, Anita Lie, and Siti Mina Tamah

English Language Teacher Beliefs
Farahnaz Faez and Michael Karas

Language Teacher Identity and Reflective Practice
Zia Tajeddin

Reflective Practice in TESOL Service-Learning Contexts
Cynthia Macknish

Surviving the Induction Years of Language Teaching: The Importance of Reflective Practice
Thomas S. C. Farrell

Teachers Reflecting on Boredom in the Language Classroom
Mirosław Pawlak, Mariusz Kruk, and Joanna Zawodniak

The Reflective Cycle of the Teaching Practicum
Fiona Farr and Angela Farrell

Using Video to Support Teacher Reflection and Development
Laura Baecher and Steve Mann

Reflecting on Leadership in Language Education

Edited by Andy Curtis

SHEFFIELD UK   BRISTOL CT

Published by Equinox Publishing Ltd.

UK: Office 415, The Workstation, 15 Paternoster Row, Sheffield, South Yorkshire S1 2BX
USA: ISD, 70 Enterprise Drive, Bristol, CT 06010

www.equinoxpub.com

First published 2022

British Library Cataloguing-in-Publication Data
A catalogue record for this book is available from the British Library.

ISBN-13   978 1 80050 138 6   (hardback)
             978 1 80050 139 3   (paperback)
             978 1 80050 140 9   (ePDF)
             978 1 80050 165 2   (ePub)

Library of Congress Cataloging-in-Publication Data

Names: Curtis, Andy, editor.
Title: Reflecting on leadership in language education / edited by Andy
  Curtis.
Description: Bristol, CT : Equinox Publishing Ltd, 2022. | Series:
  Reflective practice in language education | Includes bibliographical
  references and index. | Summary: "Reflecting on Leadership in Language
  Education represents the first time that Reflective Practice has been
  positioned at the forefront of leadership development in language
  education. It is also the first book ever to bring together 300 years of
  Leadership in Language Education (LiLE) experience into a single volume,
  capturing the insights from three centuries of lived LiLE experiences
  for the generations of leaders to come"-- Provided by publisher.
Identifiers: LCCN 2021043390 (print) | LCCN 2021043391 (ebook) | ISBN
  9781800501386 (hardback) | ISBN 9781800501393 (paperback) | ISBN
  9781800501409 (ePDF) | ISBN 9781800501652 (ePub)
Subjects: LCSH: Reflective teaching. | Educational leadership. | Language
  and languages--Study and teaching. | LCGFT: Essays.
Classification: LCC LB1025.3 .R434 2022 (print) | LCC LB1025.3 (ebook) |
  DDC 371.14/4--dc23/eng/20211006
LC record available at https://lccn.loc.gov/2021043390
LC ebook record available at https://lccn.loc.gov/2021043391

Typeset by S.J.I. Services, New Delhi, India

Contents

Series Editor's Preface   vii
Thomas S. C. Farrell

Introduction and Overview: Reflecting on Leadership in Times of Crisis   1
Andy Curtis

Chapter 1: Learning from the Life Stories of Others   14

Introduction to the Question One Responses   14
Andy Curtis

The Question One Responses   19
*Okon Effiong, Christel Broady, Leo Mercado, Andy Curtis,
Marjorie Rosenberg, Rosemary Orlando, Rosa Aronson,
Deborah Healey, Neil Anderson, and Kathleen M. Bailey*

Chapter 2: The Multiplicity of Meanings of RP   34

Introduction to the Question Two Responses   34
Andy Curtis

The Question Two Responses   39
*Okon Effiong, Christel Broady, Leo Mercado, Andy Curtis,
Marjorie Rosenberg, Rosemary Orlando, Rosa Aronson,
Deborah Healey, Neil Anderson, and Kathleen M. Bailey*

Chapter 3: The Challenges of Doing RP   68

Introduction to the Question Three Responses   68
Andy Curtis

The Question Three Reponses   73
*Okon Effiong, Christel Broady, Leo Mercado, Andy Curtis,
Marjorie Rosenberg, Rosemary Orlando, Rosa Aronson,
Deborah Healey, Neil Anderson, and Kathleen M. Bailey*

Chapter 4: Reflecting on Leadership Challenges in Language Education   103

Introduction to the Question Four Responses   103
Andy Curtis

The Question Four Reponses   116
Okon Effiong, Christel Broady, Leo Mercado, Andy Curtis,
Marjorie Rosenberg, Rosemary Orlando, Rosa Aronson,
Deborah Healey, Neil Anderson, and Kathleen M. Bailey

Chapter 5: Recapping and Reflecting Forward   161
Andy Curtis

Index   176

Series Editor's Preface

Andy Curtis' edited book, *Reflecting on Leadership in Language Education*, although consisting of reflections from ten leaders in the field of education also has implications for all leadership issues in this time of global responses and non-responses by leaders worldwide to the current Covid-19 pandemic. This timely book tackles the complex issue of what effective leadership entails in language education and focuses on the reflections of ten prominent language educators who have held various leadership positions that amount to 300 years of lived leadership experiences. The ten wonderful reflective teacher leaders (RTLs) who provide the reflections in this volume are Okon Effiong, Christel Broady, Leo Mercado, Andy Curtis, Marjorie Rosenberg, Rosemary Orlando, Rosa Aronson, Deborah Healey, Neil Anderson, and Kathleen M. Bailey.

After an introduction and overview by the editor, Andy Curtis, the book is organized into a four-part structure to help make each chapter accessible, in terms of being a relatively 'quick read', and to bring a consistency to the tremendously varied RTL experiences shared by the ten authors. Each of the four main chapters has an introduction by Andy Curtis which asks questions, followed by the ten authors' responses. The topic of Chapter 1 is 'Learning from the Life Stories of Others' and the authors relate their leadership experiences to give background and context. In Chapter 2, Andy Curtis asks the contributors what reflective practice (RP) means to them and this is followed by an account of how each one engages in their own RP. The next chapter is concerned with 'The Challenges of Doing RP.' Finally, in Chapter 4, Andy Curtis asks the contributors to reflect on either a major leadership challenge they faced, or a series of closely connected challenges, but to provide the account in as 'anonymized' a manner as possible, to avoid any legal and financial repercussions from potentially disgruntled readers who may recognize themselves, as the editor notes that many of the challenges come down to 'HR matters.' The book also has many reflective breaks (62 in all) throughout and 150 questions/tasks to help readers interact with the text, which makes it similar to all the other books in the series. Each chapter also has four writing prompts to help make them as focused as possible. The concluding chapter provides a recap and a look ahead.

Andy Curtis, himself a very experienced TESOL educator and leader, has put together a highly readable, engaging, and absorbing book that goes to the heart of the subject of leadership in language education. As he concludes from the deep and meaningful reflections of ten excellent leaders in language education:

- It is never too early for a teacher to start thinking about and preparing for an educational leadership role—even if they are not expecting to be in such a role.
- It is never too late to start your leadership journey.
- Coming from humble beginnings, with few, if any, of the privileges enjoyed by the majority of those around you, you can develop resilience, determination, and perseverance—all essential leadership qualities.
- While Accelerated Language Learning may be more myth than method, Accelerated Leadership Learning in language education is possible—but beware of burnout.
- Leaders in language education often follow different paths to those of their peers, and different paths from the ones laid out for them, which can make the journey difficult but all the more rewarding for that.
- Diversity is a strength, but with diversity also come the challenges of (very) different ways of understanding the world around us, and of how we communicate with others.

Pre-service and in-service language teachers, language teacher educators, and teachers and teacher educators beyond language education will find the accounts in this book a useful, engaging, and enlightening window into a largely unresearched area. *Reflecting on Leadership in Language Education* will benefit all teachers and other education stakeholders to become (more) reflective practitioners as well as leaders in their particular profession.

Thomas S. C. Farrell
Series Editor, *Reflective Practice in Language Education*
Professor of Applied Linguistics, Brock University, Canada

Introduction and Overview

Reflecting on Leadership in Times of Crisis

Andy Curtis

As I write this introduction, at the end of 2021, the world is still coping with a global pandemic, courtesy of Covid-19 (COrona VIrus Disease, 2019). The phrase 'global pandemic' underlines the fact that all but a handful of the 200 or so countries in the world have reported cases of Covid-19. Not since 1918—making it pretty much not in living memory—has the world been in such a situation, when the mis-named 'Spanish Flu,' which did not start in Spain and was not the flu, took the lives of at least 50 million people worldwide (some estimates say as many as 100 million died)—an incomprehensible loss of life. At this point, some readers may be wondering: What has this to do with leadership? The short answer: Everything! The answer to that question (and so many others) has emerged courtesy of Covid-19.

During my 20 years as a practitioner of Action Research (Curtis, 2020a), my 25 years in leadership roles, and my 50 years of being led, I have been most impressed by how much truly terrible leadership there is out there, and how long institutions and organizations can continue to survive with such poor leadership. In the same way that some learners learn *in spite* of the teaching rather than because of it, countries and corporations can succeed *in spite* of their leaders, not because of them. But then something bad happens. Something hitherto unimaginably bad, like a global pandemic, and the flaws in the leaders' fabric, as in the parable of the Emperor's New Clothes, are laid bare for all to see or—at least, for all those who are capable of seeing and who want to see. As Matthew Karnitschnig (2020) put it, in a *Politico* piece: 'If the coronavirus outbreak has taught us anything beyond the necessity of careful hygiene, it's that the *first victim of a pandemic is leadership*. At no time in the past 75 years ... have global leaders so utterly failed to deliver' (emphasis added).

The leaders of some self-appointed 'first world' countries, like the USA and the UK, seemed to think that the Covid-19 pandemic was somewhere between a joke, a hoax, and an over-reaction. Those same leaders then went from not taking the pandemic seriously to over-compensating, pulling the classic 'too little, too late' maneuver, favored by poor leaders throughout human history. The death tolls in those countries with poor pandemic leadership may well turn out to be much higher than they would have been under effective leadership. Notice, I do not say 'strong' leadership. Adolf Hitler was a strong leader. But that raises the question: What is effective leadership? Putting that question to Amazon books, Google, or Google Scholar results in millions of 'hits.' Based on that entirely unscientific search, it seems that books with numbers in their title are very popular with the business crowd: for example, Joe Sanfelippo and Tony Sinanis' 2016 book, titled, *Hacking Leadership: 10 Ways Great Leaders Inspire Learning That Teachers, Students, and Parents Love* ('hacking' all manner of things also seems to be very popular in the title of books in that market). Sanfelippo & Sinanis advise their readers to 'Be present and engaged' (p. 17), 'Build relationships' (p. 47), and 'Collaborate and learn' (p. 119). I must confess, if any of those pieces of advice are new to teachers (or parents), I cannot help but wonder what kinds of teachers they are—or were, before seeing the light shone by the likes of Sanfelippo & Sinanis (2016).

> **Reflective Break 1:** I have implied (perhaps somewhat harshly, in which case, I apologize) that the advice given by Sanfelippo & Sinanis (2016) such as 'be present' is—or should be—obvious. But that may not be the case. What kind of advice was given to you when you were a beginning language teacher? If you are an experienced teacher, what advice would you give to a new teacher?

This question of what is effective leadership is, of course, not new. For example, 20 years ago Deborah Blagg and Susan Young (2001), at the Harvard University School of Business asked: 'What makes a good leader?' Their insights include 'Communication is key.' As Blagg & Young note in their introduction: 'A stroll through the business section of any large bookstore these days reveals an astounding array of titles related to leadership in business. There has been an explosion of books, articles, instructional tapes, and CD-ROMs.' That was two decades ago, and although CDs have gone the way of the dodo, the search for an answer to the question of what makes a good leader continues. One thing missing from the handy-dandy, easily-digestible leadership lists and recipes is something we had to recite when I worked in hospitals in England in the 1980s: First, do no harm (for some arcane reason, we had to say it out loud in Latin, from the original Greek: *primum non nocere*). That is sometimes referred as the Hippocratic Oath, attributed to the ancient Greek physician Hippocrates, but which actually comes from another of his works titled, painfully appropriately for today's pandemic plagued world, *Of the Epidemics* (Shmerling, 2015). Poor leadership does a great deal of harm—the poorer, the greater.

To a large extent, the answer to the question: What makes a good leader? appears to be the truthful but largely unsatisfactory answer: It Depends. Different situations require different leadership qualities and characteristics. For example, during global pandemic times, leaders should inspire faith, hope, and trust, rather than engaging in scapegoating, excuse-making, and self-aggrandizement. One of the most commonly identified leadership skills is communicating clearly and concisely, efficiently and effectively. And that is where teachers, as classroom managers, can make great leaders, as their teaching and learning is based on such communication. Joining the dots between 'good' leadership, effective communication, and crises, David Robson (2020), reporting for the BBC, asked: 'Covid-19: What makes a good leader during a crisis?' In reply to his own question, Robson noted that 'A leader's response to a crisis is much more than speeches. Yet the messaging may play a key role in obtaining the public's trust and co-operation,' reiterating the importance of a leader's effective use of language, especially during a global health crisis.

Assuming there is no need to further belabor the critical importance of effective leadership, we can look at how Reflective Practice (RP) and Leadership in Language Education (LiLE) can be brought together. As far as we know (but please let us know if not) this is the first time that the large body of work on RP in Language Education has been bought together with the much smaller body of work on LiLE. This book has, then, been written to help bridge the gap between those two areas—RP and LiLE—based not on theoretical frameworks of the kind found in MBA textbooks, but on a total of approximately *three centuries* of the lived leadership experiences of the ten authors who contributed to this book. Again, as far as we know, this the first time that 300 years of LiLE experience has been brought together in this way, in a single volume. One way of bringing together RP and LiLE is to look at the notion of Reflective Leadership (RL). For example, Adam Fridman wrote in *Inc* about 'Why reflective leadership is the key to a successful purpose transformation' (2017), where he stated: 'For many managers and executives, becoming the kind of leader that can inspire younger workers will require some self-reflection on how transforming ourselves as leaders, can transform those we lead.' Of course, it is not only 'younger workers' who can benefit from having reflective leaders.

In the same vein, Naz Beheshti, writing for *Forbes* about 'How a daily self-reflection practice improves leadership performance' (2018), explained that

'The key is to set aside time where you can be radically honest with yourself' and advised her readers to 'Start by dedicating *two minutes each day* for self-reflection' (emphasis added). And reporting on their study in the *Harvard Business Review*, professors Lanaj, Foulk, & Erez (2018) offered advice on 'How self-reflection can help leaders stay motivated.' They recommended that 'taking *a few minutes* in the morning to think and write about aspects of oneself that make one a good leader is likely to energize leaders and to make them more influential at work' (emphasis added). Another example is Eileen Chadnick's (2018) piece in Canada's *Globe and Mail* titled 'To become a better leader, take some time to reflect.'

> **Reflective Break 2:** How would you answer the question: What makes a 'good' leader? And what do you believe makes a 'bad' leader? Do you think it is possible for 'bad' leaders to become 'good' leaders, and if so, how could that kind of positive transformation be facilitated and supported?

This recurring theme of (very) brief periods of time spent on RP or RL—as little as a few minutes a day—seems to assume some highly accelerated, super-condensed form of RP/RL that can achieve results almost instantly. However, those of us who have been working on our RPs for decades now would say that it certainly takes more than a few minutes a day to reap the benefits of RP, using structured, systematic, and sustained engagement. That may be why many of the leaders in language education that I approached about contributing to this book declined the invitation—because they were too busy leading to be able to take the time to step back, reflect, and write about their leadership work. That is entirely understandable, as I approached some of the busiest and most senior leaders in the world of English language teaching and learning. But it did seem, from the number of leaders who declined the invitation, that while RP is built into the training and development of teachers, it is not built into leadership training for language educators. That anecdotal finding may relate to the general lack of training for teachers moving from the classroom to the boardroom (Curtis 2011, 2013)—i.e., moving from language teaching into leadership roles—with little or no training of the extensive kind they were required to complete successfully before being allowed to teach.

Another reason for this book, in addition to bringing RP, RL, and LiLE together in ways they have not been before, is to address the question of accessibility, in relation to available time and cognitive space. When I speak with leaders in language education, from around the world, I often ask them what they have been reading about leadership, as I am always looking for recommendations for texts for the LiLE courses I teach. However, one of the answers I hear most often is something along the lines of: We don't have the time (or the money) for those hefty tomes written by business gurus. And looking at some of the most widely used texts on leadership training and development courses and programs, I can see their point. An especially timely and relevant text is *Leadership in Turbulent Times* (2018) by Doris Kearns Goodwin, who won the Pulitzer Prize for History in 1995. Her book is an in-depth account of the lives and the leadership of four past Presidents of the USA: Abraham Lincoln, Theodore Roosevelt, Franklin Roosevelt, and Lyndon Johnson, the 16th, 26th, 32nd, and 37th Presidents, respectively. However, *Leadership in Turbulent Times* is nearly 500 pages long—and it only reports on four dead US Presidents, i.e., a very small and very particular group.

Another popular leadership text is Peter Northouse's *Leadership: Theory and Practice* (2016). Northouse starts by stating that, although 'leadership is a highly sought-after and highly valued commodity ... People continue to ask themselves and others what makes good leadership' (p. 1). *Leadership: Theory and Practice* is more than 500 pages long, as is Gary Yukl's *Leadership in Organizations* (2012). However, not all books on leadership are as unwieldy. For example, in the area of RL, Richard Couto's (2007) 200-page *Reflections on Leadership* is much more manageable. Couto's book is based on asking 15 prominent leadership scholars to comment on James MacGregor Burns' 1978 (550-page) book, *Leadership,* which is considered to be a founding text in the field of leadership studies. Two other well-known books in the area of RL also need to be mentioned here. Larry Spears' (1995) *Reflections on Leadership* looked at the influence of Robert Greenleaf (1904–1990), who is seen as the founder of the modern servant leadership movement and who established the Greenleaf Center for Servant Leadership in the 1960s. More recently, Steve Richards' (2019) *The Prime Ministers: Reflections on Leadership* presented a 50-year historical account of nine Prime Ministers of the UK, from Harold Wilson (UK PM from 1964 to 1970 and again from 1974 to 1976) to Theresa May (UK PM from 2016 to 2019). However, it is very important to note that those books, with the word 'reflection' in their title, are not based on employing any of the principles or practices of RP, but instead use the term 'reflection' in the most general, thinking-about and looking-back-historically sense of the word.

Reflective Break 3: Have you read one or more books on leadership in general, or more specifically on LiLE? If so, what are some of the main points about leadership/LiLE that you learned from those books?

The time and the 'head space' needed to read such voluminous leadership texts, especially 'the classics' (mostly it seems written by elderly, white American males who ran US mega-corporations), may be available to full-time MBA course participants, but certainly not to busy language teachers. Therefore, although it seems terribly un-academic to describe a book as being good but too long and too heavy (both in terms of kilograms and content), that is precisely what I have been hearing at international language education conferences, about books on leadership, for many years now. Reader accessibility, therefore, is one of the principles that guided the creation of this book, and one of the features that may make this book unique among books on leadership in general, and more specifically on leadership in language education. However, it is important to state clearly and unequivocally that *quality* matters more than *quantity*, and this book aims to balance the two. The way we have tried to do that balancing act is by limiting each of the ten LiLE accounts to a maximum of around 5,000 words, or approximately 10 printed book pages. Condensing 300 years of lived leadership experiences into fewer than 200 pages may never have been done before—but we wanted to try. By limiting the length, we hope to make the leadership lessons we learned from our RP (often learned the hard way) as accessible as possible, to as many readers as possible, from those new to language education and RP, to seasoned professionals drawing on a lifetime's experience in the classroom.

It is also relevant to note that, in the course of my review of the literature on leadership, I was surprised by how much 'secondary reflection' has been published: for example, Spears (1995) reflecting on the work of Greenleaf. That might even be an example of what could be called 'tertiary reflection,' as Spears asked others to reflect on the work of Greenleaf, to which Spears then responded. Likewise, Couto (2007) asked leadership scholars to reflect on Burns' foundational 1978 work, *Leadership*, to which Couto then responded; and Richards (2019) looked at the leadership of nine PMs of the UK. Although there may be much that can be gleaned from these kinds of secondary and tertiary RP, this book is based on 'primary RP,' in which each teacher leader reflects on their own life and work, giving these accounts an immediacy and even an intimacy that may be lacking in other texts.

The idea of the 'reflective teacher leader' brings us to the matter of how to refer to the language educators in leadership roles in this book: as authors, writers, contributors, etc.? Surprisingly, that descriptor 'reflective teacher leader' does not appear to have been used much in the publicly accessible literature. One of the only papers that uses that term is Leena Furtado and Dawnette Anderson's 2012 paper, 'The reflective teacher leader: An action research model,' published in the *Journal of School Leadership*. We will, then, be using 'RTL' to refer to the ten reflective teacher leaders whose experiential accounts, whose responses and answers to the questions below, form the basis of this book.

NOTES FOR OUR READERS AND ABOUT OUR READERS

Regarding our readership, we envisage a busy classroom language teacher—of English, but the RP principles and practices presented in this book also apply to teachers of other languages, and to teachers of other subjects as well. Whoever and wherever you are, and whatever you are teaching, we believe that all teachers can benefit from being helped to become (more) reflective practitioners. Even those of us in this book who have been practicing RP for many decades are still learning about RP. As a reader, you may be a teacher who has never thought about taking on leadership roles and responsibilities outside the classroom. But perhaps you have started thinking about that possibility because, for example, someone has approached you and said, 'I think you'd be great in this up-coming leadership role.' To that you might have replied, as many of the RTLs in this book did at some stage: 'Who? Me? I have no training or background, or even any great desire to take on such role.' On the other hand, you may already be in a LiLE role looking for personalized professional, first-hand accounts of the lived experiences of those who have, like you, been in LiLE roles for many years. In that case, you will find an accumulated total of around three centuries of such experience, as noted above. We hope and believe that there will be many others in language education who will find these accounts engaging and enlightening—and we look forward to hearing from you.

Regarding notes *for* our readers, something I am often asked about is my use of both first and family names when citing the published works of others, as the usual practice in scholarly works is to give the surname/family name only. The simple reason I often give both names is that these researchers were people long before they were researchers. And when they have retired from their professional roles, they will go back to being regular folk once again. A long-standing concern of mine, from my days as a healthcare scientist working in hospitals in England in the 1980s, has been the way we were trained to give the appearance of 'objectivity' by referring to people, in our writings, by their family name only. Can you imagine how rude that would sound in 'real life'? 'Hey Smith!' or 'Hey Jones!' would not be met with friendly replies! Something else I get asked about is my use of 'we.' Why we? Who we? The simple fact is that nothing ever published— that was worth reading—did not involve other people, reviewing, giving feedback comments, making suggestions, etc. We cannot list everyone, so we list no-one. My use of 'we' here, then, acknowledges all of the contributors in this book—*but without any implication that they agree with anything that I have written herein*— as well as the series editor, Tom Farrell, and everyone at the publishers, Equinox Publishing, involved in bringing this book from fantasy to fruition. My 'we' may even include some of the tens of thousands of language educators that I have met over the last 30 years, whose incidental side-conversations, in-between plenary and keynote presentations, have been shaping my understanding of RP and LiLE for three decades. (Heartfelt thanks to each of you, for all of those conference-sidebar 'aha' moments.)

There are a couple of other things that it would be useful for our readers to know at this point, including our use of American English spelling, grammar, and punctuation as the international standard (for better and for worse), and the use of non-academic sources, such as online news reports and other online sources. The Covid-19 global pandemic led to a parallel pandemic of misinformation (Love, Blumenberg, & Horowitz, 2020), making online sources suspect. However, each of the online sources cited in this book has been checked and found to be a *bona fide* source. That does not mean 'unbiased'—as there will always some bias whenever we form an opinion about anything—but these online sources are, to the best of our knowledge, reliable and trustworthy. (For every online source we cited, there were many more that we rejected as being unverifiable.) It is also one of the goals of this book to consciously avoid the common problem of professional academics writing for each other, often using exclusionary language that can only be understood by other members of their scholarly tribe, and with little or no direct, first-hand experience of what it means to be a busy, classroom language teacher. However, we also wanted to contest the notion of RP as 'navel-gazing' (see Farrell, 2020, p. 54) with the implication of someone dwelling on their own thoughts, feelings, and problems—but taking little or no action. As we will see, RP is many things, but navel-gazing it is not!

There is also the problem of pricing and affordability. For example, at the end of 2021, the journal *Reflective Practice* was charging 45 USD to be able to access *one single article*—for just *24 hours*. I know many teachers in many countries who would have to work long and hard to be able to afford those kinds of prices. That is another important reason for our use of reliable, trustworthy online sources that are freely available to anyone with an internet connection. But we have also not 'dumbed down' any of the content, or 'talked down' to teachers, as many of the teachers I have known have far more wisdom than many of the PhD professors I have known (myself included). Our goal, therefore, has been to find that 'sweet spot' between those two extremes, of being overly-academic at the one end, and being overly-conversational at the other. (Please feel free to let us know how you think we did, in that regard.) As part of that balancing act, you will find, at the end of each chapter of this book, a reference list of sources cited, academic and non-academic, a total of around 200 covering more than 150 years—from Victor Hugo (1862/1992) to Wai Cheong Jacky Pow and Kwok Hung Lai (2021), from Olive

Hapgood (1892) to Oscar Wilde (1893) and Stephen Hawking (1988/2011). That list can, of course, be completely ignored with no ill effect on the reading of this book! However, as Farrell (2020, pp. 145–146) has pointed out, there are those who wish to dismiss RP, for one reason or another, including their claims that RP lacks 'rigor.' But as the works cited in this book show, RP can be as wide-ranging, as well-researched, and as rigorous as any other discipline in education, while at the same time being experiential, purposeful, and practical (which is more than can be said for a significant volume of educational research published in the top tier scholarly journals today).

Lastly, the Reflective Breaks like the ones above (and in the following chapters) are one of the features of this book, and the other books in this series, that may not qualify as 'unique,' but are specifically designed with the title of this series, 'Reflective Practice in Language Education,' in mind. As you will see, the 60-odd Breaks in this book, which contain around 150 questions and/or tasks, can help the readers interact with the text in ways that make it a more meaningful and more personalized experience. Not only reading, but reading and reacting. And as one of the many recurring themes in this book is how powerful it can be to engage in RP with trusted professional friends and colleagues, instead of adding a line at the end of each Break encouraging that kind of collaboration, we are recommending here that you do that. In some of the books in this series, the Breaks are not numbered, but in this book, we decided to number them so that they can be cross-referenced, in line with the fact that RP is 'layered.' RP is not a series of free-standing experiences, but a series of understandings, each of which builds on the ones that came before, and lays the foundation of the ones yet to come (Curtis, 2020b). Following that logic, some of the Breaks explicitly refer to other Breaks, but most of them can be connected with most of the other Breaks.

THE FOUR SETS OF RP AND LILE QUESTIONS

To help make each chapter as succinct and as focused as possible, we asked each author to respond to four writing prompts:

Question One: Please give a brief summary of your first role as a leader in language education and where you are now professionally, in terms of leadership.

Question Two: What do you understand by the term 'Reflective Practice'? What does RP mean to you? What do you think of when you hear or read the phrase 'RP'?

Question Three: How do you engage in RP? What are some of the challenges you have faced when engaging in RP? How did/do you address/meet those challenges?

Question Four: Think of a leadership challenge you faced some time ago. Describe that challenge, how you met/coped with that challenge, and what advice you would give someone facing a similar challenge. Or, instead of giving advice, you can describe what you would do differently now, with the benefit of experience and hindsight, if you faced a similar challenge today.

To summarize: We start with a mini leadership bio, to give the necessary background and context (see Farrell, 2020). Then we ask each contributor what RP means to them; followed by an account of how each RTL engages in their own RP, including the challenges of doing that; and we close with reflections on either a major leadership challenge they faced, or a series of closely connected leadership challenges. All of the authors were advised to make their Question Four accounts as 'anonymized' as possible, to avoid any potential legal and financial repercussions from disgruntled readers who may recognize themselves in the Question Four accounts, as many of the challenges come down to 'HR matters.' Also, this simple four-part structure was designed to help make each account accessible, in terms of being a relatively 'quick read,' and to bring a consistency to the tremendously varied experiences shared by these RTLs. Looking back to the beginnings of the multi-year project that this book became, I can see now that the lengthy prompt for Question Four could have been more concise. But we wanted to strike the balance between encouraging each contributor to reflect freely, while at that same time putting in place parameters that would result in a text that formed a coherent and consistent whole. These four sets of questions are the basis of each of the following four chapters, with a fifth and final chapter recapping and reiterating the RP and LiLE learning points illustrated by these RTL accounts, but also expanding on those points by sharing some short, (very) personal, and previously undisclosed vignettes from my decades in language education and in leadership.

Tragically, the Irish poet and playwright Oscar Wilde (1854–1900) died at the age of just 46. But before he departed, he left us with some of the most beloved works of literature in the English language. One of those is the comedic play, *Lady Windermere's Fan, A Play about a Good Woman*, first performed in London around 1890. In the third act, the Dumby character says: 'Experience is the name every one gives to their mistakes.' With characteristic brevity of wit, Wilde captured the bitter-sweet nature of making mistakes, so we can learn from them and evolve, as individuals and as a species. Wilde's shrewd observation is relevant here because at the heart of all reflection lies experience, as we look back on what we did—a moment ago or decades ago—in some structured, systemic, sustained way that enables us to gain deeper insights into who we are now, how we came to be this way, and who we may become. Given the centrality of experience, that is how we have chosen to arrange the responses to the four sets of prompt questions above. Therefore, each of the four main parts starts with the RTL accounts of those who have the least numbers of year of LiLE experience—but even then, at least a decade or more of such experience—and ends with those who have accumulated the largest number—up to approximately 50 years of LiLE experience.

As it turns out, in this company, I am a relative newbie in terms of LiLE experience—at least when comparing my 25 or so years of experience, which I thought seemed like a lot, with Kathleen Bailey, who has spent nearly 50 years in leadership roles. However, as we know, (almost) nobody wakes up one morning to find themselves transformed—magically 'metamorphed' in some Kafka-esque manner—from a teacher into a leader. Although leadership can happen suddenly and unexpectedly, even then it involves a period of transition; typically, from novice teacher to experienced teacher to teacher-trainer to a supervisory or managerial position, and from there into a fully-fledged leadership role. That transitional journey takes time, making the precise pin-pointing of when we first became leaders unfeasible. Also, sadly, that transition often entails leaving the classroom further and further behind, while we spend more and more time on administrative and organizational matters. However, by design and by choice, some of us have been able to come full circle, and return to where we started, spending most of the time and energy of our later professional years back in classrooms ('real' or 'virtual') with our learners and our colleagues. In that sense, although the leadership pathway is often presented as a hierarchical climb, in our field of language education it is often more circular than linear. As the poet T. S. Eliot (1888–1965) put it so beautifully in his 1940s poem, 'Little Gidding': 'We shall not cease from exploration / And the end of all our exploring / Will be to arrive where we started / And know the place for the first time.' The place may be much the same, but we may be entirely different.

REFERENCES

Beheshti, N. (28 September 2018). How a daily self-reflection practice improves leadership performance. *Forbes*. Retrieved from: https://www.forbes.com/sites/nazbeheshti/2018/09/28/how-a-daily-self-reflection-practice-improves-leadership-performance/?sh=3f2ed9285aad

Blagg, D., & Young, S. (2 April 2001). What makes a good leader? *Harvard Business School*. Retrieved from: https://hbswk.hbs.edu/item/what-makes-a-good-leader

Burns, J. M. (1978). *Leadership*. New York, NY: Harper & Row.

Chadnick, E. (27 December 2018). To become a better leader, take some time to reflect. *Globe and Mail* (Canada). Retrieved from: https://www.theglobeandmail.com/business/careers/leadership/article-to-become-a-better-leader-take-some-time-to-reflect/

Couto, R. A. (Ed.). (2007). *Reflections on Leadership*. Lanham, MD: University Press of America.

Curtis, A. (2011). The Manager as Janitor: Developing a 'ManJan' metaphoric model for ELT professionals. In C. Coombe, L. Stephenson, & S. Abu Rmaileh (Eds.), *Leadership and Management in English Language Teaching* (pp. 23–31). Dubai: TESOL Arabia Publications.

Curtis, A. (2013). A gap in our field: Leadership in language education. *TESOL International Association*. Retrieved from: http://exclusive.multibriefs.com/content/a-gap-in-our-field-leadership-in-language-education

Curtis, A. (2020a). Action research at the interface: Personal-professional reflections on the first 20 years. *International Journal of TESOL Studies, 2*(4), 14–23.

Curtis, A. (2020b). Engaging in reflective practice: A practical guide. In C. Coombe, N. J. Anderson, & L. Stephenson (Eds.), *Professionalizing Your English Language Teaching* (pp. 243–251). Cham, Switzerland: Springer. https://doi.org/10.1007/978-3-030-34762-8_20

Farrell, T. S. C. (2020). *Reflective Practice in ELT*. Sheffield, UK: Equinox Publishing.

Fridman, A. (18 August 2017). Why reflective leadership is the key to a successful purpose transformation. *Inc.* Retrieved from: https://www.inc.com/adam-fridman/why-reflective-leadership-is-the-key-to-a-successf.html

Furtado, L., & Anderson D. (2012). The reflective teacher leader: An action research model. *Journal of School Leadership, 22*(3), 531–568. https://doi.org/10.1177/105268461202200305

Goodwin, D. K. (2018). *Leadership in Turbulent Times*. New York, NY: Blithedale Production.

Hapgood, O. C. (1892). *School Needlework: A Course of Study in Sewing Designed for Use in Schools*. Massachusetts: Ginn & Co.

Hawking, S. (1988/2011). *A Brief History of Time*. London, UK: Bantam Press.

Hugo, V. (1862/1992). *Les Misérables*. Translation by C. E. Wilbour. New York, NY: Random House.

Karnitschnig, M. (16 March 2020). The incompetence pandemic. *Politico*. Retrieved from: https://www.politico.com/news/2020/03/16/coronavirus-pandemic-leadership-131540

Lanaj, K., Foulk, T. A., & Erez, A. (13 September 2018). How self-reflection can help leaders stay motivated. *Harvard Business Review*. Retrieved from: https://hbr.org/2018/09/how-self-reflection-can-help-leaders-stay-motivated

Love, J. S., Blumenberg, A., & Horowitz, Z. (2020). The parallel pandemic: Medical misinformation and COVID-19. *Journal of General Internal Medicine, 35*, 2435–2436. https://doi.org/10.1007/s11606-020-05897-w

Northouse, P. G. (2016, 7th edn.). *Leadership: Theory and Practice*. Thousand Oaks, CA: Sage.

Pow, W., & Lai, K. (2021). Enhancing the quality of student teachers' reflective teaching practice through building a virtual learning community. *Journal of Global Education and Research*, 5(1), 54–71.

Richards, S. (2019). *The Prime Ministers: Reflections on Leadership from Wilson to May*. London, UK: Atlantic Books.

Robson, D. (27 March 2020). Covid-19: What makes a good leader during a crisis? *BBC Worklife*. Retrieved from: https://www.bbc.com/worklife/article/20200326-covid-19-what-makes-a-good-leader-during-a-crisis

Sanfelippo, J., & Sinanis, T. (2016). *Hacking Leadership: 10 Ways Great Leaders Inspire Learning That Teachers, Students, and Parents Love*. Cleveland, OH: Times 10 Publishing.

Shmerling, R. H. (13 October 2015). First, do no harm. *Harvard University Medical School*. Retrieved from:
https://www.health.harvard.edu/blog/first-do-no-harm-201510138421

Spears, L. C. (Ed.). (1995). *Reflections on Leadership: How Robert K. Greenleaf's Theory of Servant-Leadership Influenced Today's Top Management Thinkers*. New York, NY: Wiley.

Wilde, O. (1893). *Lady Windermere's Fan: A Play about a Good Woman*. London, UK: Elkin Matthews Publisher.

Yukl, G. A. (2012, 8th edn.). *Leadership in Organizations*. New York, NY: Pearson.

ABOUT THE AUTHOR

Andy Curtis (PhD) is a Professor in the Graduate School of Education at Anaheim University. From 2015 to 2016, he served as the 50th President of the TESOL International Association. He has (co)authored and (co)edited 200 articles, book chapters and books, he has presented to 50,000 language educators in 100 countries, and his work has been read by 100,000 language educators in 150 countries. He is based in Ontario, Canada, from where he works with learning organizations worldwide.

Chapter 1

Learning from the Life Stories of Others

INTRODUCTION TO THE
QUESTION ONE RESPONSES

Andy Curtis

The Question One prompt for the RTLs was: Please give a brief summary of your first role as a leader in language education and where you are now professionally, in terms of leadership. But before we look at their responses, we will first summarize the main recurring themes—or RTL learning points. It should be possible for readers to add to these six themes, based on their experiences of LiLE, either as a current leader, a future leader, or as someone who reports to someone else in an official leadership role. Each one of these themes could warrant an entire chapter to itself; however, for the sake of clarity and brevity, we will keep this overview of the Question One responses brief.

The Accidental Tourist was a 1985 award-winning novel by the American author Anne Tyler, which was made into an award-winning movie a few years later. Although a romantic dramedy, *The English Teacher*, was released in 2013, it is unlikely that anyone will make a movie about the life of a teacher of English as a second or foreign language. That really is a pity, because, as the accounts in this book show, many of us have lived lives full of drama, complete with international travel, mystery, and even intrigue. One aspect of those lives that we can see in these ten highly condensed biographies is the idea of The Accidental Leader, as many of the contributors had no plans to be in a leadership role. We enjoyed learning and teaching languages, we were interested in different countries and cultures, but we figured maybe that was it. And then came leadership opportunities, some of which we pursued, some of which were dropped into our laps; some of which came early, some much later in our professional lives.

In their book, *The Accidental Leader: What to Do When You're Suddenly in Charge*, Harvey Robbins and Michael Finley ask the question: 'Who gets called to accidental leadership?' (2004, p. xii). One of the examples they give in answer to that question is: 'A teacher who'd never been in charge of anything, but had to take a rotation as a department chair' (Robbins & Finley, 2004, p. xii). Their book is divided into three parts: Managing Oneself; Managing the Technical Side; and Managing People, all of which are also recurring themes in the four main chapters of this book, including some of the biographical summaries. In terms of what we can learn from such bios, even ones as brief as these, first, it is never too early for a teacher to start thinking about and preparing for an educational leadership role—even if they are not expecting to be in such a role. And second, it is never too late to start your leadership journey.

Reflective Break 4: Have you ever taken on a leadership role in TESOL—in the field or in the international association? If yes, did you apply for that position or was it offered to you? If you were offered that position, did you accept it? Why or why not?

Starting from humble beginnings has become something a of cliché, especially in the MBA-type leadership literature. But as these highly compacted bios show, many of us who became leaders at the highest levels of our organizations and associations did indeed come from humble beginnings, for example, as immigrants of one kind or another, as visible minorities, and/or as users of English as a second or foreign language in the world of English language education. London Business School professor, Don Cable, in the *Harvard Business Review*, explains 'How humble leadership really works' (2018). Cable writes about 'the humble mind-set of a servant leader' and he characterizes 'servant leaders' as people who 'have the humility, courage, and insight to admit that they can benefit from the expertise of others who have less power than them.' Although Cable (2018) is writing for a business-oriented readership, he could just as easily have been addressing language educators. For example, he goes on to explain that servant leaders 'actively seek the ideas and unique contributions' of those they serve, while creating 'a culture of learning, and an atmosphere that encourages followers to become the very best they can.' As you read through the brief bios that follow, you will see how coming not from a position of privilege but from a humble beginning can be important in building up our capacity to overcome our disadvantages—what University of Pennsylvania professor Angela Duckworth refers to as 'Grit' or 'The power and passion of perseverance' (2016).

Accelerated learning was more of a fad than an educational methodology, and a look at some of the related book titles gives us a clue as to why it was more the former than the latter. For example, *Accelerated Learning Techniques: Mind Hacking and Memory Improvement: Advanced Strategies to Learn Faster, Be More Productive, Improve Memory, and Unlock Your Full Potential* (Faber, 2019). Many of the books in the accelerated learning market have similarly elongated titles, and they often appear to be self-published, but the main problem is that they over-promise and under-deliver, making claims that are hard to demonstrate or substantiate. Some of the books in that market have made their way into language learning, for example, *Accelerated Spanish: Learn Fluent Spanish with a Proven Accelerated Learning System* (Moser, 2016). However, although such super-fast learning may be more myth than method, as these bios show, there is such a thing as Accelerated Leadership Learning (if I decide to self-publish long-titled books in this area, I will use the acronym 'ALL,' as that seems suitably inclusive). Some of the contributors in this book built up their leadership experience slowly and gradually over time, but many of them use metaphors on the theme of 'in at the deep end,' 'sink or swim,' etc. which relates to the front cover illustration of *The Accidental Leader* book (Robbins & Finley, 2004)—depicting a life buoy. The RTL learning point here is that it is possible to build up a great deal of leadership in language education experience in a relatively short time. But teachers need to be aware of the potential for burnout if they take on too much too soon (Bailey, Curtis, & Nunan, 2001).

The metaphor of the journey may be one of the most widely used in all languages, and in addition to the water-based metaphors we see in these bios, there are also recurring references to journeys. Some contributors write about 'the roller coaster ride' of leadership or about 'moving sideways into leadership,' while others describe literal journeys that took them around the world and eventually brought them back home. Robert Frost's 1915 poem, 'The Road Not Taken,' is perhaps one of the most well-known poems by an American writer in the last hundred years, especially the closing lines:

> *Two roads diverged in a wood, and I—*
> *I took the one less traveled by,*
> *And that has made all the difference.*

Although the meaning of the poem is still being vigorously debated a century later (see, for example, Ward, 2015), an idea that emerges in these bios is that of not following the professional route taken by our peers—the route we were expected to follow, the safe path. Instead, we took the roads less traveled and less certain, and although ELT may be a relatively low-risk profession, forging a new path entails uncertainty and therefore some degree of risk.

Perhaps one of the most striking aspects of these ten compacted biographies is the diversity of voices, experiences, languages, and cultures represented by this group. First, we meet Okon Effiong, Nigerian-born, now living and working in Qatar, who came to the world of TESOL and to LiLE later in life, bringing with him a wealth of experience from other worlds, personal and professional. Next comes Christel Broady's origin story, from which we learn that she was born in Germany and has been living and working in the USA for many years. Christel took her early experiences of poverty and put them to work in becoming an accomplished leader and mentor of future leaders. From Leo Mercado's account we learn that he is from Queens, New York and has spent many years living and working in Peru, which has led him to take an entrepreneurial approach to his work in language education. Then there's myself, officially described on my 1981 UK Census Form as being: First-Generation Post-Colonial Anglo, Indo Afro-Caribbean Pacific. I was given one line to describe my ethnicity 'in as much details as possible', so that is what I came up with to summarize my Indian, Guyanese, and UK multiple ethnicities. (The UK Government rejected my census form, and returned it to me, with a big, angry red line though my description, saying, simply, 'NO!')

After my story, we read that of Marjorie Rosenberg, who was born in the USA, but who has spent most of her adult working life in Austria, and who is a good example of someone who followed a markedly non-traditional path into ELT. In Rosemary Orlando's account, we read about her early experiences in the Caribbean and her current work in Vietnam, while in Rosa Aronson's story we see the circle of professional life, in her role as Executive Director of the TESOL International Association, from which she retired, only to take up the same position again, three years later. And in the last three compacted bios, we learn about the journeys of Deborah Healey, Neil Anderson, and Kathleen Bailey, all past presidents of the TESOL International Association, over a period of more than 20 years (from 1998 to 2020), all of whom were born in and are based in the USA, but who have lived and worked all over the world.

Although most of us who work in the areas of international education believe that Diversity is Good, in fact, as Boston University professor Evan Apfelbaum points out, 'Diversity is Difficult' (Moran, 2018). Based on his research in business contexts, Apfelbaum (interviewed by Moran) concludes that: 'Different backgrounds and opinions lead to better decisions, but getting there isn't easy' (Moran, 2018). One of the consequences of the tremendous diversity represented by the contributors in this book is that the different accounts are written in varying styles and voices, with differing approaches to and perspectives on RP and LiLE, challenging the reader to be able to adapt to this kind of diversity. One way (of many ways) of representing diversity is country-of-birth, and the writers in this volume hail from France, Germany, Nigeria, the USA, and the UK—that is, five countries of origin within just ten authors, which makes for a high degree of diversity. Another way of representing diversity is by country-of-work, i.e., where each author was living and working at the time of writing. By that measure, we can add Austria, Canada, Peru, and Qatar. And in relation to this book breaking new ground, this is the first time (as far as we know) that *more than 300 years* of LiLE experience have been brought together in a single volume. Not only that, but given the fact that these contributors are in their 50s, 60s, and 70s, the ten highly condensed bios that follow represent *more than 500 years* of lived experience, distilled down into the following pages.

To recap, the following compact LiLE bio-statements illustrate the following points:

(i)   It is never too early for a teacher to start thinking about and preparing for an educational leadership role—even if they are not expecting to be in such a role.

(ii) It is never too late to start your leadership journey.

(iii) Coming from humble beginnings, with few, if any, of the privileges enjoyed by the majority of those around you, you can build resilience, determination, and perseverance—all essential leadership qualities.

(iv) Accelerated Language Learning may be more myth than method, but Accelerated Leadership Learning in language education is possible—just beware of burnout.

(v)   Leaders in language education often follow different paths to those of their peers, and different paths from the ones laid out for them, which can make the journey difficult but all the more rewarding for that.

(vi) Diversity is a strength, but with diversity also comes the challenges of (very) different ways of understanding ourselves and the world around us, and the connections between the two.

> **Reflective Break 5:** What is your own definition of 'diversity'? In your teaching-learning context, are you a member of a 'visible minority', for example, because of your gender, race, skin color, age, etc.? If so, how does that affect or influence your work as a language educator? Is your workplace diverse? If so, in what ways is it diverse?

These bios provide the personal-professional context for the following Chapters 2 and 3, based on the following questions: Chapter 2: What do you understand by the term 'Reflective Practice'? What does RP mean to you? What do you think of when you hear or read the phrase 'RP'? And Chapter 3: How do you engage in

RP? What are some of the challenges you have faced when engaging in RP? How did/do you address/meet those challenges?

THE QUESTION ONE RESPONSES

*Okon Effiong, Christel Broady, Leo Mercado, Andy Curtis,
Marjorie Rosenberg, Rosemary Orlando, Rosa Aronson,
Deborah Healey, Neil Anderson, and Kathleen M. Bailey*

To recap, the Question One prompt for these RTLs was: 'Please give a brief summary of your first role as a leader in language education and where you are now professionally, in terms of leadership.' Again, for the purposes of clarity and conciseness, each RTL was asked to keep their mini-bio-statement to no more than around one page.

Okon Effiong: Seeking Professional Development, But Finding Myself in at the Deep End

I was already approaching 50 when I embarked on a doctoral degree in Applied Linguistics in the UK. Coming into the field with a science background, I was determined to attend the annual International TESOL Convention in Boston, USA, in 2010, to gain a better understanding of language teaching. Although, at the time, I never thought of any involvement with the Association other than to attend academic sessions and network with colleagues in the field, the trigger for my leadership journey, unknown to me at the time, happened to be a plenary session in Boston. I sat in the audience listening to a plenary given by three renowned individuals representing global affiliates of the TESOL International Association. The plenary revealed that Africa had only four affiliates—I wondered why a huge continent like Africa with more than 50 countries, and over a billion people, could only have four affiliate countries in an association which had more than a hundred affiliates all over the world. With my lack of understanding of how professional bodies operate, I believed the Association had not done enough to include or attract Africa. Ignorantly, I put all the blame squarely on the Association's shoulders, and thus the armchair critic was awakened.

I returned to England and summoned the courage to write to the TESOL President at the time seeking justification for Africa's poor showing. As a result of the eye-opening response I received from the President, I had to shake off the misconception of the Association not doing enough, and realized that I should therefore seek ways of bringing Africa into the fold. I wrote to the Executive Director of TESOL asking for an opportunity to get involved. What better arm of TESOL was there to serve on than the Diversity Committee where 'Inclusion' was the watchword? The response from the Executive Director was positive and I became a member of the Diversity Committee at the following year's annual international convention. On the committee were seasoned TESOLers who had served on the Board of Directors, so I was in good company and felt safe to learn.

After serving for a year on the Committee, the Past Chair nominated me as Chair-elect. I looked around the room at other members who had more experience and wondered why she had done that. I told her I knew nothing and was not sure if she had made the right choice. She smiled and said that she could recognize talent when she saw it. There was no objection from other committee members, and it suddenly dawned on me that this was a window of opportunity. After all, I was seeking an avenue to promote diversity in the TESOL International Association and to bring more Africans into the Association mainstream.

I served two terms as Chair of the Diversity Committee (2013–2015) and I saw the second mandate as a vote of confidence by the TESOL Executive Committee. In the years that followed, I served as the Committee's sun-setting Past Chair and Chair-elect of the English as a Foreign Language Interest Section (2015–2016) and subsequently served on the Nominating Committee (2017). I went on the serve as President of Qatar TESOL (2014–2015), founded Africa TESOL in 2015 and served as its President for two years (2017–2019), then as its Past President (2020). I am now a member of the TESOL International Association Board of Directors (2020–2023).

Christel Broady: My Path to Leadership

In 1989, I attended Ruhruniversität Bochum in Germany as a non-traditional student coming from poverty after having earned my high school diploma at the age of 25, the first person in my family to do so. After my BA equivalency (Zwischenprüfung), I received a letter that changed my life. I was offered a scholarship and assistantship in the USA with the obligation to teach several undergraduate classes each semester. Once in the USA, I found myself in front of 25 eager students. I was overwhelmed by my new role. Not only did I have to learn how to be a graduate student in another country, but also, and more importantly, I had to simultaneously learn how to be a teacher. The task of teaching, as daunting and intimidating as it first appeared, turned out to shape my professional destiny. My apprehension as a beginner turned into a passion. Therefore, I decided, as well as doing an MA in Literature, to simultaneously earn a US teaching certificate to acquire knowledge about teaching and learning. After receiving my graduate degree, I taught in schools in Missouri and Nebraska and began presenting at regional conferences in several states, my first one in Kansas.

While teaching, I wanted to learn more about learning, theories, and theorists and thus decided to pursue a PhD in Curriculum and Instruction with a specialization in language acquisition. As a result, I was a teaching assistant again, and as I loved returning to teaching university-aged students I decided to become a professor. Later, as chair of an ESL teacher endorsement program, I connected with the local, state, and national professional organizations. Since then, I have served for more than a decade as a state TESOL board member, president, organizer of a state conference, and later, as an organizing committee member for a Southeast TESOL regional convention. At the TESOL International Association, I served as a steering board member of the Video and Digital Media IS (Interest Section), and the CALL (Computer-Assisted Language Learning) IS. I also served on the Elementary Education IS steering board and later became the Chair. In 2018, I became the first German-born member of the TESOL International Association Board of Directors and a member of the Board's Finance Committee.

Of all my leadership roles, being a TESOL board member has impacted me the most as a professional leader. Being elected to represent a worldwide membership brings with it considerable responsibility. I exercise my duties responsibly and with passion for the global diversity of the members. The learning never stops, whether becoming more literate in budget matters, in the revision of existing policies and conceptualizing new ones, or finding the best way of giving voice to and making space for others and myself in the complex, multidimensional, and ever-evolving world of cultures and languages.

Leo Mercado: Getting on the Roller Coaster

As many others have experienced in their own ESL/EFL professional lives, I crossed over to the field after first working in other industries. In my case, it was a consequence of finding myself living in a new country, Peru, where my knowledge of English as a native speaker became an unwitting asset. After my first brief time as an English language teacher and coordinator, I moved on to teaching at a very large binational center that promoted cultural exchange between Peru and the United States. Within three months, I received two promotions: the first as the test center administrator of the first international computerized English language testing site in Peru, and the second as an academic supervisor, when I quickly learned the importance of being approachable with teachers and getting to know them. My first lesson learned is consistent with the notion that being open and making yourself available to talk is vital to building supervisor–teacher relationships (Chamberlin, 2009). Thus, I went from being a stranger who sparked curiosity to becoming a well-known, 'friendly guy' that teachers grew to like and trust. All of this happened between mid-1995 and early 1997.

Over the next few years, my responsibilities grew rapidly. I became an Academic Branch Manager, responsible for more than 140 teachers and almost 10,000 students. This stage in my career left a memorable mark on my professional life. Unfortunately, it was also relatively brief. I was promoted a little after a year to Deputy Academic Director and a year after that to Deputy General Director. Finally, in January 2005, I became the Academic Director of the institution, overseeing 30,000 students and 400 full-time teachers. I was given the responsibility of turning things around after two previous external academic audits had led to disappointing results, coupled with a serious downturn in enrollment. In my new role as academic director, I would initiate a process of dramatic transformational change. It would ultimately lead to major innovations, the center's sustained growth to almost 60,000 monthly enrollments, and its distinction of becoming the first and largest binational center in the world to obtain a renowned international accreditation.

In 2015, my career at the binational center concluded after the successful culmination of an accreditation process with the CEA (Commission on English Language Accreditation). I soon moved on to my next institution, where I started having a spell of déjà vu. I was hired under similar circumstances, my specified role being to initiate a recovery and bring about innovation and strong growth. As in my previous appointment, I began a process of transformational change. Perhaps the achievement I am most proud of was to lead the institution through its first EAQUALS (Evaluation and Accreditation of Quality Language Services) onsite inspection as part of the accreditation process. I have recently started my own consulting firm, from which I continue to support my former institution with their EAQUALS accreditation process, other major projects, and professional development for the teachers there. My goal is to apply 25 years of experience in the field to succeed as an academic entrepreneur. Fortunately, Peru is fertile ground for such ambitions.

Andy Curtis: 'Going' into Teaching but 'Falling' into Leadership

I stumbled into my first leadership role more than 25 years ago, in 1994. I say 'stumbled' because, like many of the language teaching professionals I have met over the years, in many different countries and contexts, I did not expect to be in such a role, and had no formal training or preparation for what lay ahead. That role was as President of the Graduate Students' Association at the University of York, in England, where I completed my master's and where I was working on my PhD. A lasting memory from that time is thinking, on my last day in that one-year role: 'Thank goodness that's over with! Glad I did it, but glad it's done!' And realizing on that last day, with one year's worth of experience under my belt (which felt like a lot at the time), that for the first time I really felt like I knew what I was doing, and what I needed to do. I realize now how heavily, during that year, I had relied on trial-and-error, learning the job whilst doing the job, and fake-it-till-you-make-it.

In the years that followed, from 1998 onwards, I took on a number of leadership roles in language education, initially at polytechnics and universities in Hong Kong, then at a university in Ontario, Canada. But the leadership role that has most shaped me was my year as the 50th President of the TESOL International Association, from 2015 to 2016, preceded by a year as President-elect, and followed by a year as Past President. In addition to all of the first-time events in 2015, marking the Association's first half-century milestone, I was also the first president of Indian origin and the first of Guyanese origin, as well as one of the only presidents born in the UK, rather than the USA, and based in Canada, rather than living and working in America.

My first stint in Hong Kong was from 1995 to 2000, and my second was from 2007 to 2011. When I returned home to Canada, from my second stint, I decided to do as much pro bono international education consulting work as I could, and in the ten years that followed (2011–2021) I worked the equivalent of nine of those years for free. That represents unearned/potential income in the hundreds of thousands of US dollars. But in return, I have had the honor of working with inspiring language teachers doing amazing work with minimal resources, from a school at the edge of the Gobi Desert in Mongolia, to working with the poverty-stricken 'untouchable,' 'lowest of the low' (under)caste, the Dalits, in southern India (where some of my ancestors come from). I have no regrets at all, and I would do it all again, in a heartbeat.

I recently completed a three-year term on the Board of Trustees of The International Research Foundation (TIRF), from 2018 to 2021, where I continued to develop my knowledge, skills and competencies in the areas of leadership in language education. Like the TESOL International Association, TIRF is also a non-profit language education organization, but there are no members or membership dues or conferences, making fund-raising one of the main challenges.

Marjorie Rosenberg: Moving Sideways into Leadership

Coming into a leadership position somehow seemed logical after a number of years of building up to one. Leadership comes with every teaching position, no matter whether we run large online courses, webinars, teacher training workshops, university classes, or one-to-one training sessions. I began teaching classes on general English as a Foreign Language at the Adult Education Centre of the Chamber of Commerce in Graz, Austria in 1981, and I brought many of the skills I had learned while running a small opera company with a former university classmate in the USA. After arriving in New York City armed with a Master of Fine Arts degree in vocal performance in 1975, taking this step afforded us the chance to perform roles we would never have had, not only the chance to sing, but also to learn how to organize and plan productions from start to finish. Later, these leadership skills came with me into the adult classroom and included showing respect and understanding for others, time management, having a clear vision of where we were going, remaining flexible, using imagination, creativity, and critical thinking to solve problems as they arose, and keeping a sense a humor throughout. During those early years in Austria I also had to learn my way around the world of the freelance teacher, which called on many of those skills in order to find and keep work. In 1992, I had the opportunity to begin training as an NLP Practitioner (Neuro-Linguistic Programming) and went on to become an NLP Trainer. What NLP taught me was the nuts and bolts of rapport and communication as well as how to set achievable goals, useful for kick-starting an ELT career as a writer and teacher trainer.

Through a conference run by the British Council in Vienna in the 1990s, I discovered TEA (Teachers of English in Austria) and joined up. In 1998 I took the plunge and joined the board of TEA, taking on responsibilities such as organizing conferences and events and making use of the skills I had learned in New York. As time went on, I felt the call to do more and served as Chair from 2003 to 2005. Some of the tasks involved finding the right people for committee positions, encouraging them, listening actively to their concerns, and delegating work to people. I was confident that I could do it. During this time, I also became more active in the IATEFL BESIG (the Business English Special Interest Group of the International Association of Teachers of English as a Foreign Language), which I had joined in 1995. After attending a number of their conferences, I ran successfully for the position of Events Coordinator in 2008 and when the Joint Coordinators stood down in 2009, I threw my hat in the ring to lead the SIG. This position as head of the largest IATEFL SIG with some 600 members from close to 70 countries around the world was a learning experience right from the start. It was necessary to learn to run meetings efficiently and to assign tasks ensuring we met our goals which also required a great deal of autonomy among the board members.

The culmination of all these years of leadership positions, however, came in 2015 when I took over the position of IATEFL President. I was lucky to be able to work with helpful and supportive colleagues whom I asked often for advice. I was also fortunate to be mentored by past presidents who were extremely generous with their time and advice. This is an experience that can help you to develop and grow if you are ready to do that, and at the time I took over the job I felt that it was important to keep learning, something I have continued to do since my time as President and outgoing Vice President ended in 2018.

Rosemary Orlando: Just Another Day in Paradise?

My first role as a leader in education was at a newly built, very small university on a Caribbean island that was established as part of a joint venture with the US university where I was employed at the time. At the US university, I was a full-time associate professor teaching ESL as well as English Composition and Oral Communication. I was invited to be a visiting professor at the Caribbean university when it first opened in 1989, and then about a year later was brought back in a leadership position. I was hired as the Academic Director responsible for all academic programs including the English Language program. Since I had just been there teaching a year earlier, I was familiar with the location and somewhat with the culture. During my time teaching there as a visiting professor, I had been well-received by the students and the local people as well.

I was excited and very motivated to do a good job in this new leadership position. Looking back, I realize I may have been too 'nice' in my role initially as Director and then as Dean of Academic Affairs. I was young and was conscious of the fact that I was a visitor in their country and did not wish to overstep my remit. However, I was not prepared for the casual approach many of the teachers had towards showing up to teach, or even canceling classes in order to attend to personal or business matters away from the university. My American bosses had certain expectations and demands, so the dichotomy was evident. In hindsight, I should have been stricter with those teachers who did not seem to consider it important to show up to teach on a regular schedule, or to let me know if they were not coming. Had I realized that sooner, I could have guided them in a more direct fashion.

I loved that job but should have been stricter and less tolerant of flagrant disregard of the rules. I got along well with the teachers and students at the university, but looking back, I would have handled things differently. I did some reflecting and writing down of my thoughts at the time, but it was more of a process of learning on the job. I made some mistakes, thankfully none of real consequence, and tried to learn from my missteps, but I was not systematically reflecting. I suppose I was developing some insight from my experience and trying to put that into practice, but not in a formal manner. I was successful in that position, but were I to do it again, I would make some changes. Eventually, the locals decided they wanted to be completely on their own without the partnership of the American university and tried running things without the financial resources and personnel provided to them by the joint venture. Unfortunately, after a devastating hurricane and much damage to the university, it was forced to close down.

In the years that followed, I returned to the US and eventually moved to a new state and went to teach at a different university. I have held leadership positions as the Chair of a department program and also as an administrator for a department with an Intensive English Program (IEP), both undergraduate and graduate bridge programs, and a master's degree program that included an international partnership with a university in Southeast Asia.

Rosa Aronson: Crossing Borders between Countries and Organizations

My first leadership position in language education happened in 2010, when I was selected to serve as Executive Director of the TESOL International Association. Until then, I had spent eight years teaching English as a Foreign Language in France, then 24 years in a variety of roles at the National Association of Secondary School Principals in the United States. Although I didn't know it at the time, both experiences prepared me for the TESOL leadership position.

As a teacher in France, I was immersed in the daily life of a key TESOL constituent, although the TESOL Association was unknown to me then. In the French context, at that time, teaching English was a very isolated activity. There was no collaboration among teachers, no professional development offered by the school or district administration. You were on your own. The school was located in a specially designated zone called ZEP (Zone d'Education Prioritaire, or high-priority educational zone), due to the fact that a majority of the student population came from low-income immigrant families from the Maghreb area in North Africa. My students, whose first language was Arabic, were second-generation immigrants in a very hostile environment. Their knowledge of French was limited, which made the learning of yet another foreign language (English) even more challenging.

In 1985, I began a new life in the United States. I was hired by the National Association of Secondary School Principals (NASSP), a not-for-profit, professional association representing middle level and high school administrators in the US and Canada. My tenure at NASSP spanned more than two decades, including eight positions in five different departments of the organization, from student programs to development, foundation work, advocacy, and policy work. This extended tenure in a North American educational organization provided me with a diverse skill set in leadership and management, all of which prepared me for my next leadership position. By 2010, I was part of the senior leadership team of NASSP, overseeing three major areas of work—student programs, advocacy, and fundraising. My direct supervisor was the Executive Director.

When I joined the TESOL Association in 2010, I was able to draw from my knowledge as a former teacher in an EFL context, as well as the competencies I acquired at NASSP, to equip myself for my new role as Executive Director of an international education organization with a specific focus on second language teaching and learning. In this new role, I was leading a staff of 18 and working with a membership-elected Board of Directors including an Executive Committee comprised of three presidents (past, present, and incoming), a network of over 100 affiliates of the TESOL International Association in over 50 countries, numerous committees and volunteer groups, and a membership of about 11,000 individuals worldwide in around 170 countries.

After seven years at the Association, in 2017, I retired from that position and, in the following years, served twice as an English Language Specialist for the US Department of State's Bureau of English and Cultural Affairs (ECA), providing organizational leadership expertise to English teachers and leaders in Vietnam and Central Asia. In this role, I assisted new or existing language education organizations to establish and strengthen their presence, focus, and relevance as professional associations in their own contexts.

In 2020, I accepted an invitation to return to the TESOL International Association as part-time Interim Executive Director to help the Board of Directors navigate one of the most challenging years in its history caused by the Covid-19 pandemic and its consequences on global economies.

Deborah Healey: When a Door Opens, Walk Through

My first foray into work-related educational leadership was probably in 1984, when I led our administrative computing efforts at my institute's Intensive English Program (IEP), then our educational computing efforts the following year, while teaching nearly full time. I served in a similar position, working with administrative and educational computing, at our USAID (United States Agency for International Development) grant-funded project in Yemen in 1985–1988. I came back to being Technology Coordinator of the institute in 1988. I found I enjoyed using technology and was intrigued by figuring out how to motivate learning with our new tool, the microcomputer. Using computers in language learning was relatively new at that time, and those who were involved became strong advocates. My interest at work crossed over into association involvement, with my joining the brand-new CALL-IS (Computer-Assisted Language Learning Interest Section) in the TESOL Association in 1985. I was an active participant in the CALL-IS, working with my fellow CALLers in copying free software onto 5¼-inch floppy disks for sale at the annual convention. When we started the Electronic Village at the Association's annual convention, for the first few years, I helped procure the loaned computers and set them up for use. I became part of the CALL-IS Steering Committee, then the CALL-IS Chair-elect in 1990 and the Chair in 1991. I stayed part of the CALL-IS in various capacities after that, as software archivist, Steering Committee member, and general supporter of the interest section.

I followed a somewhat parallel path to increasing responsibility in the language institute, moving from Coordinator of Instruction in 1991 to Director from 1999 to 2008. As Director, I had to take a much larger and longer view of the institute, including its context within the university, the local community, the competitive IEP world, and international student mobility; and the strengths and constraints of faculty and staff, students, student workers, and volunteers. As a self-supporting unit, the institute had to live within or expand its budget. I became Director not long after the Asian economic crisis, in the late 1990s, which reduced enrollment by 30%. We were rebuilding when the September 11, 2001 attacks in the US took place, again reducing enrollment. My most rewarding moments were when we were awarded highly competitive grants and when a faculty member who 'just wanted to teach' found she enjoyed being the principal investigator on a grant.

My work as IEP Director was very consuming. Once I left that position, I was able to think more about association work again. I ran for the TESOL Board and was successful, serving from 2014 to 2017. I decided that my work in the institute and in many ways within the TESOL Association could be very helpful for me as TESOL President, so I sent in my Expression of Interest to run for that position. I was nominated and, to my surprise, chosen as President-elect in 2018. I made frequent use of my administrative and leadership experience as TESOL President in 2019–2020, but there was and is always more to see and learn.

Neil Anderson: Falling into TESL

As an undergraduate student I attended Brigham Young University (BYU) in Provo, Utah, USA. As a freshman I was not completely sure what my major would be. As I progressed in my studies, I enrolled in Spanish classes and had an opportunity to teach Spanish. I enjoyed being in the classroom and learning about becoming a good language teacher. I also found myself gravitating towards a major in business management. I formulated a plan to get involved in international business, perhaps in Latin America.

As I began my junior year of studies, I enrolled in an accounting class. The professor gave us a pre-course assessment test on the first day of class, informing us that it would be a strong indicator of our preparedness for the upper-division classes. I looked at each of the problems and panicked. I could not answer the questions. I left the first day of class very discouraged. The experience caused me to engage in deep reflection about what I wanted to accomplish in life. I questioned my assumption that I would become an international business person living in Latin America. I discussed my feelings of discouragement and doubt with my wife. As we talked about my options, she asked if I had given any consideration to studying Teaching English as a Second Language (TESL). She had been accepted into the TESL MA program at BYU prior to our engagement and marriage, but due to a variety of circumstances, she did not enroll in the program. As we discussed my questions, she pointed out that I had liked being in the role of a Spanish language teacher.

We had two very good friends who had received their MA degrees in TESL. I spent time with each of them and then met with an academic advisor at the university. The academic advisor pointed out to me that with two more semesters of coursework, I could graduate with a BA degree in teaching Spanish. So, instead of having two more years of studies to earn a BA in business management, I completed two more semesters and then transitioned into the TESL MA degree. The transition started by questioning the assumptions that I had been operating under. From the day I made the decision to enter the TESL MA degree, I have not questioned my decision. I moved forward with a new vision of my future.

During my MA studies at BYU, I served as the President of the BYU TESL Society. This was my first leadership role within a TESOL context. I loved the opportunity of bringing graduate students together to explore ideas about language teaching and learning outside of our class discussions. Immediately after graduation, I accepted a teaching position at the English Language Center at BYU. This position initially gave me the opportunity to be a program supervisor and a year later to be the language testing coordinator for the program. These roles allowed me to further develop my leadership skills.

Within the first few weeks of being a program supervisor, I knew I wanted to be a teacher educator and to teach at a university, for which I would need to earn a PhD. I also knew I wanted to get as much classroom teaching experience and leadership experience as possible before entering a PhD program, so that I would have a clear purpose to be an effective teacher educator.

Kathleen M. Bailey: My History as an Educational Leader

Many years ago, after preparing to be a secondary school teacher of English literature, I enrolled in a graduate program to become qualified as an ESL teacher. I completed my MA degree and then, through a series of bizarre circumstances, I ended up running the ESL program at the university where I had been a graduate student. This job entailed supervising the teaching assistants (TAs). After working as the coordinator of that ESL program for a few years and undertaking doctoral studies, I was hired for my dream job: chairing a new MA program and training English language teachers at the Middlebury Institute of International Studies (MIIS), a small college in California. I was the Chairperson of that MA program for six years, during which time our full-time faculty grew to five. The students were highly motivated and my colleagues were wonderful, so all in all, that experience was very positive.

A few years later, however, I became the Director of our small Intensive English Program. Although I was professionally prepared for this role, it was a huge struggle. In fact, it was much more difficult than being the coordinator of the large, university-based program that I had run earlier. In this context I had to advertise the program, write contracts for teachers, generate and defend the program budget, and recruit students. In the university situation, all those tasks had been handled by other people. Later, I served again as acting Chairperson of the MIIS MA program while the person who held that position was on sabbatical. By that time, there were eight full-time faculty members and a multifaceted curriculum.

Now, 20 years later, I am in the Chairperson's role once more and wrestling with many issues—some old and some new (clearly, I am a slow learner). Two additional work experiences gave me opportunities to grow as a leader. I served as the Assistant Director of the first TESOL Summer Institute, under the guidance of a wonderful mentor. Five years later I became the Director of the TESOL Summer Institute. In both of these positions, I was able to work with local and invited faculty members and with students from many parts of the world.

Other leadership experiences arose in volunteer opportunities in professional organizations. I served on the TESOL Board of Directors (1992–1995) and again two years later in its presidential line (1997–2001). Some years later, I was elected to the presidential line of AAAL (the American Association for Applied Linguistics)—another long-term commitment (2013–2018). Finally, as of this writing, I have been serving as the President and Chairman of the Board of

Trustees of TIRF (The International Research Foundation for English Language Education) since 2009.

Each of these leadership roles has been challenging, frequently rewarding, and regularly frustrating. I have grown (both personally and professionally) through all of them. For example, in reflecting on what I had learned by being TESOL President, I listed '(1) interpersonal skills; (2) management and leadership skills; (3) professional communications skills; and (4) time management, a micro-skill that cuts across all the others' (Bailey, 2002, p. 32). I believe (I hope) I have done some good for the people and the programs I have served.

> **Reflective Break 6:** Having read these summaries of the RTLs' lived experiences, and building on the Reflective Break 5, write a short summary—no more than one page—of where you are now in your professional life, how you got to this point, and where you would like to be headed in the future.

> **Reflective Break 7:** In many of the mini-bios above, different images, metaphors, and analogies are used to describe these RTLs' journeys. What images, metaphors, or analogies would you use to describe your journey as a language educator, from where you started to where you are now?

REFERENCES

Bailey, K. M. (2002). What I learned from being TESOL President. In J. Edge (Ed.), *Continuing Professional Development: Some of Our Perspectives* (pp. 32–38). Kent, UK: IATEFL.

Bailey, K. M., Curtis, A., & Nunan, D. (2001). *Pursuing Professional Development: The Self as Source*. Boston, MA: Heinle & Heinle.

Cable, D. (April 23, 2018). How humble leadership really works. *Harvard Business Review*. Retrieved from: https://hbr.org/2018/04/how-humble-leadership-really-works

Chamberlin, C. R. (May 2009). Nonverbal behaviors and initial impressions of trustworthiness in teacher-supervisor relationships. *Communication Education*, 9(4), 352–364.

Duckworth, A. (2016). *Grit: The Power of Passion and Perseverance*. New York, NY: Scribner.

Faber, K. (2019). *Accelerated Learning Techniques: Mind Hacking and Memory Improvement: Advanced Strategies to Learn Faster, Be More Productive, Improve Memory, and Unlock Your Full Potential*. CAC Online Publishing.

Moran, B. (July 30, 2018). Diversity is difficult. *The Brink: Boston University*. Retrieved from: http://www.bu.edu/articles/2018/diversity-is-difficult/

Moser, T. (2016). *Accelerated Spanish: Learn Fluent Spanish with a Proven Accelerated Learning System*. Kenmore, WA: Kamel Press.

Robbins, H., & Finley, M. (2004). *The Accidental Leader: What to Do When You're Suddenly in Charge*. San Francisco, CA: Jossey-Bass.

Ward, D. C. (August 10, 2015). What gives Robert Frost's 'The Road Not Taken' its power? *Smithsonian Magazine*. Retrieved from:
https://www.smithsonianmag.com/smithsonian-institution/
what-gives-robert-frosts-road-not-taken-its-power-180956200/

ABOUT THE AUTHORS

Dr Okon Effiong is a lecturer in the Foundation Programme, Qatar University. He is a member of the TESOL Board of Directors and served on its Nominating Committee, Diversity & Inclusion Committee, as Chair-elect of the EFL-Interest Section. He is founder and Past President of Africa TESOL. He was the President of Qatar TESOL.

Dr Christel Broady is Chair of graduate programs, as well as Director of the ESL Program at Georgetown College, Kentucky, USA. An international leader, Christel has served in many leadership roles with TESOL International and affiliates. Her list of domestic and international publications, keynotes, presentations, and awards is extensive.

Leo Mercado has been in the field for more than 25 years, making contributions as a director of studies, e-learning and proficiency testing specialist, project leader, author, and academic entrepreneur. Based in Atlanta, Georgia, USA, he has also successfully led two international accreditation processes, as well as large-scale, nationwide projects at the Ministry of Education level.

Andy Curtis (PhD) is a Professor in the Graduate School of Education at Anaheim University. From 2015 to 2016, he served as the 50th President of the TESOL International Association. He has (co)authored and (co)edited 200 articles, book chapters and books, he has presented to 50,000 language educators in 100 countries, and his work has been read by 100,000 language educators in 150 countries. He is based in Ontario, Canada, from where he works with learning organizations worldwide.

Marjorie Rosenberg has been involved in tertiary and adult education in Austria since 1981. She is an active teacher trainer, conference presenter, and ELT author. Marjorie served as IATEFL President from 2015 to 2017. Her latest project is working as a mentor through a program designed by EVE and Africa TESOL.

Dr Rosemary DePetro Orlando is a Professor at Southern New Hampshire University, USA. She regularly travels to Vietnam National University in Hanoi to teach MS TEFL courses in a university partnership degree program. As a language teacher educator, Rosemary regularly presents at national and international English Language Teaching conferences worldwide.

Dr Rosa Aronson is the Interim Executive Director of the TESOL International Association in Alexandria, Virginia, USA. Her career in Education began as an EFL teacher in France and continued in the USA in professional educational organizations. She has served as an English Language Specialist focusing on organizational leadership. She holds a PhD in Social Foundations of Education from the University of Virginia.

Dr Deborah Healey was the 2020–2021 President of the Board of Directors of the TESOL International Association. An online and face-to-face teacher educator, she writes and presents extensively internationally (Africa, Asia, Latin America, Europe, US) on appropriate use of technology in language teaching. Her doctorate is in Computers in Education.

Dr Neil J. Anderson has been actively involved in leadership roles and reflective practice for over 40 years. He currently teaches at Brigham Young University–Hawaii, USA. Neil served as President of the TESOL International Association for 2001–2002. He received the prestigious James Alatis Award from TESOL in 2014.

Dr Kathleen M. Bailey is a Professor of Applied Linguistics at the Middlebury Institute of International Studies at Monterey (MIIS), California, USA. She completed her MA and her doctorate at the University of California at Los Angeles. Her research interests include teacher education, language assessment, and the teaching of listening and speaking.

Chapter 2

The Multiplicity of Meanings of RP

INTRODUCTION TO THE
QUESTION TWO RESPONSES

Andy Curtis

In the second set of question prompts, the RTLs were asked to respond to these three slightly different versions of the same question: What do you understand by the term 'Reflective Practice'? What does RP mean to you? What do you think of when you hear or read the phrase 'RP'? The reason for the different versions is that, as language educators, we know that presenting the same question multiple times—but each time in a slightly different linguistic and/or grammatical form, with a slightly different focus—can increase the likelihood of eliciting more thorough and thoughtful replies, which accurately describes the accounts in Question Two.

We also know, as language educators, that words and phrases are so much more than just collections of letters and sounds. Within a phrase like 'Reflective Practice' there can be myriad meanings; a continuum, from an emphasis on the reflective part of the phrase, at one end of the continuum, to a focus on the practice part, at the other end. However, once a phrase like 'Reflective Practice' becomes so widespread and so commonly used, there may be a natural tendency to assume that everybody—at least everyone within a particular community of practice—knows what the phrase means. But from that generally correct assumption, it is easy to slide into an assumption that is incorrect, i.e., that not only do we all know what RP means, but that we all share *the same meaning*. However, in the same way that we have moved past the one-size-fits-all model in language education, and in language teacher professional development (Bailey, Curtis, & Nunan, 2001; Farrell, 2020), RP means different things to different people. Therefore, one definition of RP does not fit everyone, which makes it essential to start engaging in RP by asking yourself what you understand by 'Reflective Practice'. Six of the recurring themes that emerged from the ten sets of authors' responses are briefly summarized here. However, it is important to note that readers are encouraged to find additional themes, depending on how their own experiences relate to these authors' experiences.

One of the recurring themes in Question Two is the fact that *RP takes time*, which may seem obvious as anything worthwhile requires time (indeed, even seemingly pointless activities still take time). It is also worth noting, as we will see in Question Three, that finding and making the time needed to engage in meaningful RP is one of the big challenges. The point then becomes whether that time spent on RP is worth it. In her booklet, *Developing Your Intuition: A Guide to Reflective Practice* (which is written with leadership development rather than teacher development as its focus), Talula Cartwright (2004) states: 'Reflective practice may seem time-consuming at the beginning but the time you put in on the front end is well worth the investment. It will pay you back both in time and in the quality of the decisions you make' (p. x). Regarding Cartwright's comment, the first thing to point is out is that RP does not *seem* time-consuming—it *is* time-consuming, and not just at the beginning. Practice Makes Perfect may constitute one of those well-meaning untruths that actually does damage, as perfection may not be a reasonable or achievable goal (Talwar, Yachison, Leduc, & Nagar, 2018). However, practice can lead to more effective and more efficient performance and outcomes, in terms of getting more done, and done well, in less time. When applied to RP, the more time we spend engaged in RP, the deeper we can go and the more we can learn. We will come back to this time challenge in Question Three, but here we will consider two other Question Two themes which are not commonly discussed in relation to RP: Mindfulness and Metacognition.

> **Reflective Break 8:** What do you think of when you hear the following three words and phrases? Reflective Practice? Mindfulness? Metacognition?

Not only do some researchers believe that RP and Mindfulness go together, they even combine the two into what is referred to as Social-Emotional Competence. Elita Virmani and a large group of colleagues at the Collaborative for Understanding the Pedagogy of Infant/toddler Development, or CUPID (how cute is that!), recently reported on how pre-service early childhood professionals' mindfulness, reflective practice beliefs, and individual characteristics shaped their developmentally supportive responses to infants and toddlers. Virmani et al. (2020) found that 'reflective practice beliefs were significantly associated with developmentally supportive responses' and concluded: 'we need to pause to consider the ways in which we, as university educators, engage in meaningful, intentional and trusting relationships with the students in our classrooms' (p. 1063).

Of course, that conclusion applies not only to our relationships with university students, but to all teacher-student relationships.

Highlighting the overlap between RP and mindfulness, Nugent, Moss, Barnes, & Wilks (2011) describe mindfulness as 'a particular type of practice of reflection' (p. 1). In describing mindfulness, Nugent et al. (2011) draw on the work of Professor Jon Kabat-Zinn (2003), who is credited with bringing eastern beliefs, such as Buddhism, to Western medicine, especially in the treatment of stress-related disorders. According to Kabat-Zinn, mindfulness is based on 'examining who we are, with questioning our view of the world and our place in it, and with cultivating some appreciation for the fullness of each moment we are alive. Most of all it has to do with being in touch' (1994, p. 3). The first part of that description may apply to language educators more than the second part, but there does appear to be a clear overlap between RP and mindfulness, as seen, directly and indirectly, in some of the Question Two responses.

As noted above, the fact that *RP takes time* may seem self-evident, but it is none-theless important for teachers to set aside dedicated RP time, so that systematic, deliberate engagement in RP can take place. Likewise, one of the other recurring themes that emerges in both the Question Two and the Question Three responses is the fact that *RP is hard*. RP is neither a quick fix nor an easy answer to the many challenges facing teachers all over the world, from a global pandemic to local short-ages of teaching and learning materials. As Nugent et al. (2011) put it: 'the experi-ence of trying to be reflective is by no means straightforward when we are "on the spot" in the lived moments of our working lives' (p. 10). Nugent et al.'s comment relates to Donald Schön's (1991) distinction between reflection in action during a lesson, and reflection on action after the lesson.

The relationships between RP and Metacognition have been recognized in dif-ferent fields, including nursing education. Joyce Johnson (2013) combined the two to come up with a series of questions for nurses which would be equally helpful for teachers engaging in RP, including: 'What assumptions am I making about this situation? What are my worries and fears? How does this situation make me feel? How can I change or respond differently to a similar situation in the future?' (p. 47). Many of the published works on RP are found in the medical field, which may be because both education and healthcare are considered to be part of 'the helping professions.' Dr Mark Barley (2012), an anesthetist at a hospital in England, gave his perspective on learning from reflective practice and metacognition. However, Barley is critical of 'the concept of reflection ... becoming a fashionable compo-nent' (p. 271) in medicine, and he goes on to complain that: 'Reflective practice has become a "buzz word" in medical curricula' (p. 272). In spite of the misgivings expressed at the beginning of his paper, Barley concludes that: 'Reflective practice and metacognition can give us an awareness of our thought processes; with this insight there is the possibility to reduce our subconscious biases, make "better" decisions and engage in true constructivist experiential learning' (p. 278). And on a personal note, highlighting the connections between RP and metacognition, Barley writes: 'I see many parallels between reflection, metacognition and experiential learning, and personally feel these are useful topics for interested, insightful individuals' (p. 278).

Many of the responses to the Question Two prompts refer to gathering different kinds of data, such as quantitative or qualitative data, data from students and teachers, and self-generated data, such as a teacher's journal entries. The use of data-based or data-driven RP is consistent with a decades-old but still often-cited definition from Jack Richards and Charles Lockhart (1994), who defined RP in this way: 'teachers and student teachers collect data about teaching, examine their attitudes, beliefs, assumptions, and teaching practices, and use the information obtained as a basis for critical reflection about teaching' (p. 1). The tripartite relationship between Attitudes, Beliefs, and Assumptions is a recurring theme in the Question Two responses, perhaps envisaged as the three points of a triangle. A related triangular visualization is the three-part EAR model (Curtis, 2020) which represents the relationships between our Expectations, our Assumptions, and the Reality of the situation that we have expectations of and about which we have made assumptions. With RP, we are able to explore how closely aligned or how far apart are our Attitudes, Beliefs, and Assumptions, and how to narrow the distance between those three, as much as possible.

Again, there are many parallels between language education and medical education, especially nursing. For example, Lisa Ruth-Sahd, a professor of nursing at a US university, presented a critical analysis of data-based studies of RP and their implications for nursing education (Ruth-Sahd, 2003). Looking back, Ruth-Sahd wrote: 'During the past decade, terms and phrases such as reflection, reflective practice, reflective teaching, and the teacher as a reflective, inquiring professional have become part of the discourse of nursing education classrooms' (2003, p. 488). Ruth-Sahd reviewed dozens of data-based studies of RP published between 1993 and 2001, and identified a number of recurring findings related to the benefits of RP, including: 'Integration of theoretical concepts to practice ... Increased learning from experience ... Enhanced self-esteem through learning ... Acceptance of professional responsibility and continual professional growth' (2003, p. 490). In addition, Ruth-Sahd found that data-based studies of RP also showed evidence of 'Enhanced critical thinking and judgment making in complex and uncertain situations, based on experience and prior knowledge ... Empowerment of practitioners ... Increased social and political emancipation ... Improvement in practice by promoting greater self-awareness' (2003, p. 490). Such a long list of benefits from data-based RP supports the many references to data-gathering in the RTLs' Question Two responses.

A recurring characteristic of the Question Two responses is the use of different metaphors, analogies, and images by contributors to write about what RP means to each of them. In the same way that water-based metaphors surface in descriptions of what RP means to these contributors, so too do vision-based descriptions. Several of the RTLs refer to the importance of stepping back when writing about what RP means to them. The idea of taking a step (or several steps) back relates to the English phrase 'can't see the wood (or forest) for the trees,' which means that we often cannot understand a situation because we are too deeply immersed in it. In order for us to see more clearly whatever it is we are looking at, it may be necessary to move further away and view it from a more distant perspective. Many Question Two responses refer to seeing both the big picture and the fine detail: for example, Neil Anderson describes views varying from telescopic to microscopic, while I use the photographic metaphor of zooming in and zooming out. As noted in Chapter 1, exploration of each one of these themes could fill an entire chapter. But for the sake of clarity and focus, the RTLs were asked to keep their Question Two responses to no more than a couple of pages each.

To summarize, the RTLs' Question Two responses illustrate the following points:

(i)   RP means different things to different people. Therefore, before engaging in RP, it is essential for teachers to be clear on what they mean and what they understand by the term 'RP.'

(ii) RP requires the conscious, deliberate setting aside of time for more meaningful RP to be possible.

(iii) RP should not be seen as being a quick or easy solution.

(iv) RP can be thought of in relation to metacognition and to mindfulness, as RP can help us become more conscious and self-aware teachers, learners, and leaders.

(v)   Data-gathering of all kinds can help us with our RP.

(vi) It can be helpful to think of RP as a kind of deliberate stepping back, to get a better view, or even as a kind of stepping outside of ourselves, so we can see both the big picture and the close-up detail at the same time.

Reflective Break 9: Write a number beside each of the six points immediately above. Write 1 if you Strongly Disagree with the statement; 2 if you Disagree; 3 if you Agree; and 4 if you Strongly Agree. Can you give reasons for each of your ratings?

THE QUESTION TWO RESPONSES

Okon Effiong, Christel Broady, Leo Mercado, Andy Curtis,
Marjorie Rosenberg, Rosemary Orlando, Rosa Aronson,
Deborah Healey, Neil Anderson, and Kathleen M. Bailey

To recap, the Question Two prompts for these RTLs were: 'What do you under-stand by the term "Reflective Practice"? What does RP mean to you? What do you think of when you hear or read the phrase "RP"?'

Okon Efiong: Reflection and Leadership

Looman (2003) sums up reflective leadership as internal traits leaders need to make long-term plans capable of integrating human potential. My understanding of Reflective Practice (RP) relates to reflective leadership, which looks beyond one's personal agenda. In other words, rather than resumé-building, attention-seeking, or self-aggrandizement, true reflective leaders ought to look beyond themselves and focus more into how best to harness human capital, and how best to develop the human potential of those around them for the good of the organization that they lead. With my science background, I am reminded of the animal kingdom. For example, in the termite colony, the queen lays eggs while the soldier termites carry out their duty of securing the residence and the workers swarm out to find food for the colony. Depending on the needs of the colony, the queen termite produces inhibitory pheromones, and then feeds her pheromone-laden feces to the young ones. The pheromone ensures that the termites in the colony are either workers or soldiers that perform their tasks based on the needs of the queen termite. This is a classic example of biologically programed and predetermined leadership where an individual assumes the role and stays indefinitely in the position.

In my home country, Nigeria, that model of leadership is commonplace in the political arena. There, as elsewhere, political leaders promise heaven on earth while campaigning, but as soon as they win the election, nothing more is heard from them until the next round of elections. Some of these leaders have been on the political scene for 40 or more years with no intention of ever giving up power. Thinking of RP, I do wonder if these leaders make time to reflect on their leadership and succession planning. To understand how their leadership affects those working with or under them, leaders need to reflect on their own behavior. For example, Ollila (2008) reported on 'reflective leadership [which] refers to the process by which leaders reflect on their behavior in order to understand how it affects the behavior of others' (p. 195). RP serves as a reminder that leadership should be about modeling, in terms of leading by example, and setting standards. Weick (1979) had a different perspective of organizational RP, based on the sum total of all the reflections of everybody in the organization. That collective view of reflection relates to the maxim that 'the whole is more than the sum of its parts' and highlights the importance of everyone in an organization engaging in RP and sharing what they learn from that. This suggests that reflective leadership is for not only the leaders but for everyone in the organization, at all levels.

To increase synergy in the team, leaders should work towards maximizing the strengths and minimizing the shortcomings of those who report to them. Reflection paves the way to carrying out internal analyses. Intra- and Interpersonal RP can help leaders identify the strengths and weaknesses of their team, so that the leaders gain a better understanding of the resources and capabilities that could be sources of competitive advantage (Gurel & Tat, 2017). Reflection can also lead to improved understanding of the follower-leader relationship, and consequently help achieve the goals of the organization. Every leader should bear in mind that developing the team's skill sets is crucial for creating high performance organizations. In effect, leaders are project initiators and managers and ongoing self-examination can highlight the connection of daily routines to the strategic goals of the organization. As part of increasing self-awareness, leaders must find or make time to think or reflect, including time for contemplation, examination, and review of oneself (Neale, 2019). Neale adds that carving out time for self-reviewing, as a leader, is essential for leadership development. This reflection includes leaders' reviewing their skill level, strengths and weaknesses, patterns of behavior, and the ways in which they influence others. The result would be increased self-knowledge, authenticity, learning, and improvement in leadership skills and practice.

I see RP as a watchword; a reminder of my leadership in every step I take and in my management processes. For me, RP is a means of asking oneself serious questions about the organization's values, vision, and methods that are in place to achieve its broad goals. I reflect on my management skills that could serve to empower my team members, and I always seek strategies that will motivate my team to continue to do its best to meet our objectives and to advance our goals.

Reflective Break 10: Can you give an example, from your personal or professional life, in which 'the whole is more than the sum of its parts'? In that example, what is the relationship between the parts and the whole?

Christel Broady: My Unintended Leadership Formation

When pondering the point of when reflective leadership first entered my life, I remember that, when I was 16 years old, I spent about a week putting my life goals on paper. Later, when I was older, I realized that the list featured goals I have been holding on to all my life. Palmer (1998/2017) encourages such reflective practices of defining our 'self,' stating that it 'is the question at the heart of my vocation. I believe it is the most fundamental question we can ask' (p. 7). At a young age, I grasped that reflective leadership begins with taking stock of 'what is' in our own circumstances to gain awareness of the reality around us. Being honest with oneself about the conditions of our world, whether in work or in personal life, is the starting point for any formation or change. The reflective practice I engaged in as a young woman was followed by the question of 'what could be.' This process is described by Kouzes & Posner (2012) in Speranza & Pierce (2019): 'self-awareness is imperative for an individual to author a truthful philosophy. Self-awareness includes understanding one's own goals, motivations, strengths, weaknesses, emotions, and morals, and values ... This journey enables one to discover what they truly value and believe in' (p. 167).

Once I had analyzed my life goals, I began to see the world around me with different eyes. I looked for role models of successful leadership, and found them in the autobiography section of the library. While reading about the life stories, struggles, and successes of others, I realized that they all had one common theme: all of them (even those whose success came only after their death) shared an incredible passion for their pursuits. When I grasped this commonality, I began to search for the passion place in my life, and I found it in teaching and learning. Once I noticed that I had arrived at my place, I realized how valuable reflective leadership had been for my journey. It had guided me to a career in which I hoped to make a difference for others. Later, as a teacher, professor, and professional leader, reflective leadership transitioned from focusing on my destiny to leading others. What did not change, however, was my reflective practice, which now was second nature to me. Dewey (1933) confirms that 'reflective practice is intentional, systematic inquiry [that] is disciplined and [that] will ultimately lead to change and professional growth' (in Ghanizadeh, 2017, p. 103).

As I continued the practice of being aware of the world around me, I also noticed that I developed a sense of place for myself. The resulting mindfulness of my role in the world has been an incredible tool for reflection. Mindfulness shapes my reality for the places I occupy in my professional and personal life. As a result, being open to learning opens my space up to the magic of innovation and change. John Smyth (1989) discusses the four essential steps for reflective leaders:

(1) describing a situation, (2) seeking more information about it, (3) confronting what does not work, and (4) reconstructing practice to improve conditions (in Cunningham, 2012, p. 49). As a leader at work and in a professional association, mindfulness is essential. Being open to seeing and hearing the voices around me added an indispensable layer for my reflective leadership practices.

The practice of reflectively describing situations, becoming more informed about them, being honest to myself about problems that need to be addressed, and conceptualizing the necessary redirecting of issues allows me to envision how I could improve my performance and the performance of those around me. Kolb (1984) describes the approach I use as 'a cyclical model which constitutes four stages: concrete experience, reflective observation, abstract conceptualization and active experimentation' (in Matzuo, 2016, p. 308). In my reflective practices, I remove myself from the reality of a situation and look at it through a different lens. Boud, Keough, & Walker (2006) express the approach I use as 'reflection, defined as the practice of "periodically stepping back to ponder the meaning of what has recently transpired to ourselves and others in our immediate environment"' (in Matsuo, 2016, p. 308).

As a leader, I cannot just take inventory and reflect on the current conditions. I am tasked with moving individuals, groups, or associations forward, to develop a vision, to implement a plan on how to reach new objectives, and to oversee in collaboration with others the implementation of plans. Therefore, it is necessary to engage in mindful reflective practice every step of the way. Each stage of my work goals is reached by reflective thought, analyzing how things are going, and a decision to redirect if necessary. As a leader, therefore, I need to engage in constant assessment of my world. Castelli (2016) describes leader mindfulness as 'a state of awareness or the conscious practice that promotes awareness' (p. 218). Also, according to George (2012), 'When you are mindful, you're aware of your presence and the ways you impact other people. You're able to both observe and participate in each moment while recognizing the implications of your actions for the longer term' (in Castelli, 2016, p. 219).

Later in life, I realized that reflection without input from others could lead to biased perceptions and misguided action. The wisdom to truly reflect on my place in the world with the help of others is now an essential component of leadership for me. Thun & Kelloway (2011) state:

> personal wisdom is comprised of three components: advanced cognitive, reflective and affective personality attributes. The cognitive component involves superior knowledge, understanding, and acceptance of life and human nature. The reflective component refers to abilities

for self-insight and self-examination and the capacity to perceive events from multiple perspectives. The affective component captures an individual's consideration and empathy for others. (In Castelli, 2016, p. 200)

It is important to me as a leader to ground myself in my lifelong essential values and never lose sight of them while reflecting on my current duties with the help of others. Others' perceptions of me allow me to self-examine the essence of my servant leadership; to not just *be* in the world according to my perception, but to know *how I affect* the world in relationship to others. I close my discussion of what reflective practice means to me with the words of Castelli (2016): 'Reflective leadership requires the conscious activity of purposeful reflection. As an internal thought process, regular and focused practice is necessary. Reflective practice includes self-awareness, mindfulness, and personal wisdom' (p. 218).

> **Reflective Break 11:** Christel writes about the importance of seeing events from different perspectives, one form of which is known as 'triangulation.' In 'triangulation' a clearer and more detailed picture is built up from three different perspectives, for example, seeing an in-class event from the point of view of the learners, the teacher, and a colleague. Think of something unexpected that has happened in your language class, and write about it from three different points of view: your own; how it might have looked/felt to the learners; and how it might have looked/felt to one of your colleagues. Then compare/contrast the different perspectives, looking for similarities and differences.

Leo Mercado: Reflection as a Driving Force

In my experience, most language program administrators and other leaders do not receive sufficient training or orientation when they are called to assume their new roles (Bailey, 2006; Mercado, 2018; Panferov, 2012), some aspects of which may conflict with their previous work as teachers (White, Hockley, van der Horst Jansen, & Laughner, 2008). That transition from classroom teacher to leader in language education can be difficult, especially when attitudes can change unexpectedly on the part of former colleagues and friends, going from warm and friendly to indifferent and even hostile.

As a director of studies and academic manager, knowing there is always something new and better 'on the horizon' that we can reach together if we put our minds to it can be a highly motivating rallying cry for teachers, language program administrators, and almost everyone else at a language teaching organization.

When there is a need to bring about a process of transformational change, achieving 'buy in' among an organization's key stakeholders may seem daunting. Yet such a favorable scenario is possible if leaders emerge and flourish at all levels of the organization, from teachers who become mentors, presenters at academic events, and protagonists in their professional learning communities to academic coordinators and directors. These leaders will succeed if they can relate to others, engage in their own professional development, communicate effectively, and attain the degree of credibility that encourages others to offer their respect and trust. One of the best ways to develop such competences and skills is to master the art of reflective practice. In fact, studies have shown that reflective leaders are often found to make significant contributions to enhancing an organization's performance (Castelli, 2016; Saunila, Tikkamäki, & Ukko, 2015). The positive effects are likely to be compounded if the leader not only engages in individual reflection but also promotes reflection in others, in its various forms.

In mainstream teacher education, reflective practice is often thought of as a means for teachers to engage in professional development in order to improve their ability to lead and manage the teaching and learning process in the classroom. According to Richards & Lockhart (1994, p. 1), in reflective practice, 'teachers and student teachers collect data about teaching, examine their attitudes, beliefs, assumptions, and teaching practices, and use the information obtained as a basis for critical reflection for teaching.' There is no reason why the same cannot apply to leaders in language education, regardless of the role they have assumed or their placement on the organizational chart. Why would we not want to reflect on what we do, how we do it, and what the results are in relation to our actions and decisions? As leaders we must make countless decisions as we carry out our roles, and those decisions will be better if they are based on objective data and thoughtful reflection. In all my years as a leader in administrative positions, I have always relied on data collection of all sorts, engaged in continuous self-assessment, and reviewed my beliefs, attitudes, and my vision for the future. This was so I could change positively as needed in relation to those I served, and so I could meet the high expectations placed upon me as a language program administrator, especially as an academic director and manager.

Reflection also leads to a greater awareness that helps us determine the degree to which we are making progress in developing our own professional competence as ESL/EFL professionals. In relation to that progression, Gebhard & Oprandy (1999) highlight the importance of 'exploration' for teachers as part of a reflective process, which leads to a greater awareness of the intricacies of the teaching and learning cycle. They refer to John Fanselow's idea of exploring one's own teaching practice through observation—a self-assessment of sorts—whereby teachers come to understand the patterns and rules they follow in their classroom by recording themselves as they teach, transcribing what they and their students say, and analyzing outcomes. In addition to this and other forms of self-observation, Bailey, Curtis, & Nunan (2001, p. 39) proposed additional alternatives for reflective exploration that lead to greater awareness, such as engaging in action research, journal writing, team teaching, peer observation, and teaching portfolios. They also remind us that reflective practice goes beyond thinking about what we do, by also engaging in 'critical analysis of our motivation, thinking, and practice.'

These are all practices that can apply equally well to leaders in language education. As one example from my own experience, I used to video-record my post-observation conferences with teachers, with their permission, of course. The purpose was to reflect on how I gave feedback, my body language and tone of voice, and the way I carried out the interaction from beginning to end. I would actually transcribe key segments of the session and go over what I said and how the teacher responded, and vice-versa. I would assess myself and find opportunities for improvement, as well as continuing what seemed to work well. This eventually became a policy for all of my supervisors and branch coordinators once I became the academic director. The purpose was to help them to reflect on how they engaged with teachers during such sessions, and why their feedback sessions could end up being either more or less successful. This was a particularly impacting policy because it helped convince teachers that we were truly trying to improve our competencies and skills as language program administrators (LPAs) in order to better serve them. In relation to those recordings, I have always considered giving feedback as one of the most important and challenging aspects of the work we do as language program administrators. I have seen with my own eyes how much of an influence a coordinator's approach to feedback can have on a teacher's attitudes and morale.

> **Reflective Break 12:** Do you agree or disagree with Leo's comment that: 'most language program administrators and other leaders do not receive sufficient training or orientation when they are called to assume their new roles'? If you are in a leadership role, do you feel that you received enough and the right kind of training, orientation, and support? If you would like to be in leadership role, what kind of leadership training would you need and want?

Andy Curtis: Room(s) to Reflect

Perhaps the most common cognitive and metaphorical image in the human brain (Kounios et al., 2001) for the word 'reflection' is 'mirror'. Erin Cline (2008) found that the 'metaphor of the heart or mind as a mirror' (p. 337) has been important in both classical Chinese and modern European philosophy. But I have never been a big fan of that particular metaphor for RP, perhaps, at least in part, because my first encounter with what mirrors tell us was a negative one, thanks to the evil queen in the Grimm Brothers' fairytale, *Snow White and the Seven Dwarfs*. When the queen asks her sentient looking-glass: 'Mirror, mirror on the wall, who is the fairest of them all?' the magic mirror replies: 'My Queen, you are fairest of them all'—until, one day, the mirror tells the queen that Snow White is now the fairest of them all, at which point the queen decides that Snow White must die.

An important part of the *Snow White* story, though not one I appreciated as a child growing up in England in the 1970s, when I first encountered the tale, was that the magic mirror never lied. But, as it turns out, mirrors can and do distort reality, as I discovered from reading Lewis Carroll's sequel to *Alice's Adventures in Wonderland*, titled *Through the Looking-Glass, and What Alice Found There* (published in the 1860s and the 1870s, respectively), in my Grade 9 English class. Later, while studying Physics in Grade 10, we learned that mirror images are, in fact, distorted, because of the way light rays travel (Hawking, 1998/2011; De Brabandere, 2019). That inaccuracy of image also applies to the way light reflects off water, making another one of the most common connotations of 'reflection'—a body of still water—another example of distorted images. As a result of those early influences, RP has not, in my mind, been associated with mirrors, limpid pools, or any other reflective surfaces.

For me, 'RP' has spatial connotations, related to the idea of making *room to reflect*. RP means stepping back to get a better view, which runs counter to the idea that, if you want the 'best' view, you need to get as close as possible. The most extreme example of that in my own professional life comes from when I worked in hospitals in England in the 1980s, as a Senior Medical Science Officer. In that world, anything worth seeing was magnified a gazillion times, and seen in an electron microscope. It may, then, seem counter-intuitive to believe that being further away can help you see more clearly, but what if the thing you are seeing is your own professional self? Also, while working in hospitals, I heard patients talk about 'out-of-body' experiences (OBEs, Blackmore, 1984), and although those are, of course, not the same as engaging in RP, OBEs do relate to the idea of us stepping outside of ourselves.

Most of my travels over the last 25 years have been based on a circuit, shuttling between the airport, the hotel, and the conference or convention center. But sometimes I am able to spend a little quiet time in a local museum or art gallery. I must confess, I do not go there for the art, which is often beyond my comprehension. I go there to watch the people watching the art. In museums and galleries around the world, I have seen what I believe may be some kind of 'universal' sequence of behaviors. First, the viewer notices the art work, stops strolling by, and starts to move closer to it. Often the viewer then stops moving towards the art work, either because a security guard wakes up and glares at them, or a proximity alarm goes off. Then the viewer usually reverses their direction and starts moving away; walking backwards, but still keeping their eyes on the art work. What they are trying to do is to make sense—in this case, visual sense—of what they are seeing, first by getting up-close, then by moving back, with the photographic metaphor being 'zooming in' for the 'close-up' and 'zooming out' to see 'the big picture', both of which, for me, apply to RP.

Many years ago, I wrote some teacher professional development pages for a textbook series called *World Link* (2005), written by James Morgan and Nancy Douglas, and published by National Geographic/Cengage Learning. One of the diagrams in those TPD pages was a simple triangle, with the three corners labeled 'Me', 'Myself', and 'I'. Looking back, I can see how that might have sounded somewhat narcissistic, but the triangle was based on the idea of 'estrangement', and the phrase that I coined was 'positive self-estrangement'. However, most dictionaries give negative definitions of the verb 'to estrange'. According to *Merriam-Webster*, it means: 'to arouse especially mutual enmity or indifference in (someone) where there had formerly been love, affection, or friendliness'; the *Oxford Dictionary* gives its meaning as: 'cause (someone) to be no longer on friendly terms with someone'; and the *Collins* entry defines 'estrange' as: 'to separate and live apart from (one's spouse)' or 'to antagonize or lose the affection of (someone previously friendly).' Given all the negativity surrounding 'estrange', it may not have been the wisest choice, but not all of the meanings are so negative. A less commonly used meaning is: 'to remove from customary environment or associations' (*Merriam-Webster*). That is what I was going for, i.e., to engage in RP by creating some psychological distance between Me, Myself, and I.

Expanding on the idea of 'estrangement' as a positive and self-initiated approach to RP, I borrowed from the social sciences a research methodology known as 'triangulation'. As the name implies, the idea is that, if you want to get a more complete view of something, you need to see it from (at least) three distinct points-of-view (Flick, 2018). Coming to the present day, many of us feel like we are living through times of black-white, good-bad, right-wrong dichotomies—polarizations being driven and exploited by some of the world's most influential leaders. Therefore, the ability to see things from multiple perspectives, before we decide what to do, may be even more important now than before.

Me, Myself and I was a 30-minute episodic sitcom, made in the USA, which ran for one season only (2017–2018). The premise of the show was described as follows: 'A comedy examines one man's life over a 50-year span. It explores three distinct periods in his life—as a 14-year-old in 1991, a 40-year-old in present day and a 65-year-old in 2042' (imbd.com). That idea of connecting the past, the present, and the future is what RP means to me, based on the idea that, by finding ways of stepping outside of ourselves, we can see more clearly what we—as teachers with our learners—are doing in our classrooms, with each other. In the next section, I describe some of the ways in which I have been able to estrange my professional self from me, to create that room to reflect.

Reflective Break 13: What are some of the 'false dichotomies' that you encounter in your work as a language educator? If you could replace those dichotomies with continua, what would be at either end of each continuum?

Marjorie Rosenberg: Moving across Disciplines from Business to Teaching

When I hear the term 'reflective practice' it combines two aspects which are extremely important to me. I have always found it necessary to reflect, whether it was after a performance, a lesson, a meeting I ran, or a conference I organized. Taking the time to go back and think about what we did, how we did it, who was involved, how it went, and whether or not we achieved our goals is the one of the best ways to learn and improve.

Since I began my career in ELT, I have felt that being a life-long learner contributed greatly to my energy over the last 40 years. I truly believe that one of the things that drives teachers is curiosity, and I have certainly found this to be true when anticipating working with a new group, working on a new writing project, or planning an event within a teacher association. The problems that arise can then be turned into challenges to be met. Reflecting on ourselves and our working styles is also a learning experience. Writing up the statement I sent to IATEFL as a candidate for the role of president made me think about my strengths and weaknesses. One of the strengths that I had never put into words before was the ability to keep an overview of what we were working on while still being able to concentrate on the details. Moving between these is vital when leading an organization, as those who become fixated on the vision may lose touch with the reality of the situation, and those who worry about crossing every 't' and dotting every 'i' may not be able to consider unusual and new ideas or may stop others from thinking outside the box.

Practice is the other keystone of my work. I have always thought of myself as a practitioner; when I run workshops, seminars, and webinars, the most important message I try to get across is the practical aspect of the material. I heard years ago at a seminar that if we give teachers a lovely bouquet, i.e., ready-made materials, it will last for a few days. But if we give them seeds, i.e., practical ideas, to water and help them grow, these can last for many years. I understand that we need to know about the theoretical concepts of teaching, learning, language acquisition, etc.; however, I also find the 'practical' part of what we do to be what encourages many of us to keep going for many years. Looking back over a teaching, writing, volunteer career that spans almost four decades, what I remember is the fun, the people, and the activities we did in class. This is for me what 'practice' is all about. But we also need to teach teachers how to reflect on their practice.

One of the most important things I learned in Michael Grinder's 'New Trends in Learning Styles' course on NLP for teachers, based on his handbook *Righting the Educational Conveyor Belt* (1991) was how to reflect. Grinder said that we need to think back over our day in the third person in order to disassociate from it, which helps us to 'see and hear' what happened without bringing our emotions into it. Once we have looked at the events in our classrooms and listened to them again, we can put some thought into analyzing what we think went well and what needs improvement. Then, when we begin to plan for the future, we use the first person to rehearse our future actions as we need to be completely invested in what we are going to do. This method has worked well for me and for a number of the teachers I have trained over the years; it is simple but elegant and once it becomes routine, it can aid teachers in reflecting on their practice without self-recrimination or feelings of inadequacy.

According to Michael Wallace (1991), training courses are not generally set up to prepare teachers for the situations that arise and require spontaneous decisions. Katie Head and Pauline Taylor in *Readings in Teacher Development* (1997, p. 23) wrote that:

> Teachers develop skill in dealing with these situations through actual classroom experience, and are far more likely to explain their actions in terms of what was happening at the moment of decision, and of the feeling that they had about it, than to refer back to the received wisdom of their past training.

For this reason, Wallace (1991) recommends a reflective approach during the teacher training period as well, which can incorporate the simple idea set out by Michael Grinder. This can help the trainee and the teacher to gain a deeper understanding of what happened, to look at the way it was handled, and to come up with a way to do it differently next time.

It sometimes seems like the education field feels that it somehow 'owns' the idea of reflective practice (see, for example, Bartlett, 1990; Farrell 2007; Schön, 1987). However, this shows up as well in David Kolb's (1984) work on experiential learning, as Kolb sees learning as a continuous process and one that tests the learner's beliefs by looking at them through the lens of experience and insights as well as adapting to an environment that constantly changes. In the business world, project managers work with the concept of 'lessons learned.' This means capturing new learnings throughout a project and its stages, much like a language course. The lessons learned can then be applied to future steps in the project or noted for future projects. The general idea is to learn from both success and failure and, according to Sandra Rowe and Sharon Sikes (2006), to 'implement good processes and practices to successfully complete existing and future work.' They go on to say that 'Lessons learned are the documented information that reflects both the positive and negative experiences of a project,' and that 'Learning occurs on every project.' The process they describe has five steps: identifying recommendations, documenting ideas, analyzing them, storing them, and retrieving them when needed. These ideas can be generated collaboratively and adapted to the world of teaching. Keeping our eyes and ears open to situations which require spontaneous actions, getting recommendations, and writing them down for future reference can be helpful. Taking the time to evaluate these recommendations for their practicality in the classroom and keeping them somewhere they can be quickly and easily retrieved is for me the definition of putting reflection into practice.

> **Reflective Break 14:** In the Reflective Break 11, we looked at the idea of 'triangulation', and Marjorie recommends writing first in the third person, then in the first, as another way of seeing things from a different point of view. Think of a notable moment in your language lesson—which is often something that you were not expecting to happen—and write about it, first in the third person. Put that written description of that unexpected moment away, and a few days later, think and write about that same moment using the first person. Then compare and contrast the two descriptions.

Rosemary Orlando: Practicing Reflecting

Reflection as a way of learning seems like common sense, yet when I introduce it to teachers, it is not necessarily something they have been practicing consciously. Also, I myself had not always practiced a more systematic reflection in my own career as an educator and administrator in terms of really taking a step back, following a process, taking certain steps to examine a problem, and coming up with possible solutions. In the words of Daudelin (1996), 'Reflection is the process of stepping back from an experience to ponder, carefully and persistently, its meaning to the self ... learning is the creation of meaning from past or current events that serves as a guide for future behavior' (p. 39). Viewing reflective practice as a series of steps can help make the process clearer, more useful, and more manageable as well.

For many years, I did not engage consciously in reflective teaching, although I was practicing it without being fully aware of it. One time, while I was teaching ESL in an Intensive English Program (IEP) in a university setting, I realized I needed to keep learning and improving even if I had to depend on myself. A book that I found very helpful, written by Kathleen Bailey, Andy Curtis, and David Nunan, was *Pursuing Professional Development: The Self as Source* (2001). This book was most useful since it offered ways to practice reflective teaching, and beyond, without having to depend on others.

Although I was not aware of the term 'Reflective Practice' as a child, it recently occurred to me that I had been engaging in a type of reflective writing in a diary I received for Christmas when I was about nine years old. In the beginning, I wrote quite faithfully in the diary, putting on the page my thoughts regarding certain goings-on at school or in my family life. I remember thinking that it might come in handy someday to recall what it felt like to be of a certain age and that it might help me to relate to others as I grew older. Most of the entries were of a young, innocent girl reflecting that time period. As the years went on, I only wrote occasionally, but still managed to record my thoughts as I went through adolescence and my early teenage years. I also decided to try and (somewhat) chronicle my senior year in college/university by keeping a new journal. I managed to begin my senior year writing in the journal, but that, too, became more of an occasional entry as opposed to consistent and ongoing reflection. Looking back, I think keeping a journal was helpful to reflect on and figure out aspects of my life at that time. I still have the diary and the senior year journal buried in a box somewhere, but I have not been brave enough in recent years to go back and re-read what I was concerned with all those years ago!

In 2005, I was visiting Singapore for the first time. I had been out walking in the morning, but when it began to rain, I returned to my hotel. My room was still being serviced, so I went down to the beautiful lobby and took out one of the books I had brought along on my trip. I opened Parker J. Palmer's (1998) book *The Courage to Teach: Exploring the Inner Landscape of a Teacher's Life.* As I was perusing the pages, I was drawn to his point about the 'who' in teaching. So many times, educators ask about 'what' you teach, 'where' you teach, 'how' you teach, and so on as a type of 'Day 1' introductory lesson. As Palmer wrote on the first page of his book: 'We teach who we are' (1998/2017, p. 1). By focusing on the 'who,' student teachers are asked to take a step back. I had read many articles about the topic in my position as a faculty member in a master's degree program for teachers on the Teaching of English and as a teacher of undergraduate and graduate students in an IEP.

Taking time to think and reflect without other distractions was extremely valuable and I realized I needed to do more of that in my role of training and developing teachers. So much of our experience as educators and leaders is bound up with and influenced by individual contexts and informed actions. Therefore, one of the challenges of being in a leadership position is deciding what to do and how to do it within particular contexts and settings. As leaders we need to understand that our development is an ongoing and unending process, and it is necessary to engage in active reflection as we adapt to contextual problems and challenges. In this way, leaders can continue to grow and become cognizant of their personal strengths and weaknesses, which is not easy to do or to practice.

> **Reflective Break 15:** Rosemary emphasizes the importance of context. How would you describe your teaching and learning context to another teacher who is unfamiliar with your context? What are some aspects of your context that facilitate RP, and what are some that make it difficult to engage in RP?

Rosa Aronson: Finding Meaning in the Experience

Whether it applies to leadership or any other domain, the phrase 'reflective practice' implies that practice alone is insufficient without the effort of thoughtfully looking back on our practice, analyzing it, and drawing forth appropriate lessons for improved practice. But let's deconstruct the phrase. What is practice? According to the *Merriam-Webster* dictionary, the noun 'practice' has no fewer than eight different meanings organized under three categories: action or performance, exercising proficiency, and/or exercising a profession. All of these definitions apply to language leadership practice. As a leader, you are expected to take action, you seek proficiency in your position, and you exercise a profession. As for the term 'reflective', *Merriam-Webster* attributes five different meanings to it, including the quality of being thoughtful and deliberative, which is the meaning that most resonates with me. Thus, leaders who exercise the particular skill of reflective practice in language education regularly examine and, perhaps, question their day-to-day motivations, decisions, and actions, and the underlying thought patterns we hold that result in these actions. But for what purpose? And in what forms?

To paraphrase John Dewey (1859–1952), an educator, philosopher, and one of the founders of the progressive education movement in the US, we do not learn from experience ... we learn from reflecting on experience. I may spend over two decades fulfilling different roles within an organization, but there is no guarantee that I learned anything from that long tenure unless I reflect on my practice. Therefore, for me, the purpose of reflective practice is to learn from day-to-day experience as a leader in order to become more effective and successful.

This notion of finding meaning in your experience through reflective habits of mind extends beyond leadership in language education. One can argue that engaging in reflection enriches all aspects of one's life. In his book *Man's Search for Meaning* (1946) Viktor Frankl (1905–1997), an Austrian neurologist and psychologist, who survived Nazi concentration camps as a young man, recounted his experience as a holocaust survivor. His reflection led him to suggest that the purpose of life is not to pursue or enjoy happiness but instead to gain a deeper understanding of one's life experience. Indeed, Frankl further developed this idea into a new theory and approach to helping his patients in psychotherapy. He named it logotherapy, from the Greek word 'logo' (meaning). As leaders in language educational organizations, we also seek meaning in our practice through reflection and contemplation.

In his online article 'How self-reflection can make you a better leader', Harry Kraemer (2016) suggests that self-reflection is a critical component of being a leader. He introduces the idea that self-reflection has to do with how our personal values are aligned with our daily decisions, actions, and interactions. Kraemer recommends a daily practice of setting aside time to answer eight key questions:

- *What did I say I was going to do today in all dimensions of my life?*
- *What did I actually do today?*
- *What am I proud of?*
- *What am I not proud of?*
- *How did I lead people?*
- *How did I follow people?*
- *If I lived today over again, what would I have done differently?*
- *If I have tomorrow (and I am acutely aware that some day I won't), based on what I learned today, what will I do in all dimensions of my life?*

Those guiding questions can provide a useful framework for leaders engaged in self-reflection.

Although leadership feels intensely personal, I believe that engaging exclusively in individual self-reflection may give us an incomplete picture of our work. What sets us aside as leaders is the impact we have on others through our decisions and actions. So, the notion that reflective practice can be a solitary act is, in my view, misguided. Leaders have blind spots. We can't always understand how we affect others, so feedback from external sources is essential to reach an accurate understanding of our practice. This includes direct reports from peers, colleagues from other fields, supervisors, coaches, and other objective observers of our practice. Thus, I believe that reflective practice in language organization leadership has to be a collective effort. By allowing external feedback to be part of their reflective practice, leaders enrich their experience and improve their competencies as managers. Feedback can be provided in the form of short confidential surveys collected by a team of reviewers, in informal face-to-face, online, or telephone conversations, inviting meaningful and actionable suggestions. In my role as executive director of a professional, international language education association, I worked with staff members, board members, other volunteer leaders, members and potential members, and other stakeholders, such as corporate sponsors, exhibitors, government officials, as regular sources of feedback to either confirm or challenge my self-assessment. Their comments helped to draw a broader (and more objective) picture of my performance, and provided a valuable piece that enriched my reflective practice.

As leaders in your institutions, you may work with peers, direct reports, supervisors, sponsors, elected officials, and students and their families, to name a few. Interacting with such different groups of individuals makes leadership a unique role and creates a complex web of communication that poses interesting challenges to the work of reflective practice. How much external feedback should we seek in our reflective practice? Relying too much on external feedback will only dilute the work of reflective practice, but solely trusting our own judgment in the exercise of reflective practice is limiting. There seems to be no magic algorithm for striking the perfect balance. In an online article titled 'How much feedback should leaders seek?' Darcie David (2013) asks:

> Where is that sweet spot effective leaders reach when we have collected the appropriate quantity and quality of advice in order to keep our mission going smoothly, whether we are running a multinational corporation, a not-for-profit agency, boy scout troop or the U.S. government?

This balancing act proved to be one of the challenges I faced in my leadership role at the TESOL International Association. The feedback you receive as a leader is limited by each individual's perspective. Adding this dimension to your reflective practice certainly enriches it, but may also compromise its effectiveness.

Reflective Break 16: Expanding on the questions asked by Harry Kraemer, above, how would you answer the following questions? What do you most enjoy about being a language educator? What do you least enjoy about being a language educator? What changes could you make to your teaching work that would maximize the enjoyment? Is there anything you could do to reduce or minimize the least enjoyable aspects of your work as a language educator?

Deborah Healey: The Pieces Fit Together—Somehow

Most teachers may be familiar with reflecting on teaching. Reflection is nothing new: almost nine decades ago, John Dewey called on teachers to reflect after class as a way of improving their teaching (Dewey, 1933). We engage in informal musings after class about what went well and what to improve next time. This was my primary way of reflecting on teaching, though others might keep a journal to record thoughts in a more consistent way. Formal action/classroom-based research is another option, and I used that in some of my classes where I was trying gamification. The cycle of setting a hypothesis and plan of action, engaging in and recording action, then reflecting and discussing with others makes our usual classroom experimentation much more systematic. Reflective practice in teaching is not just after the fact. Donald Schön (1991) distinguished between 'reflection in action'—thoughtful consideration during a lesson—and 'reflection on action'—reflecting after the class. Reflection in action allows teachers to make changes during the lesson, for example when noticing that students need more explanation before starting a planned activity. Reflection is sufficiently important to Linda Darling-Hammond and Jon Snyder that they urge the use of teacher reflection as a form of alternative assessment of teaching practice, which they refer to as 'authentic assessment' (2000, p. 523). As a teacher educator, I routinely asked learners to use reflection in order to help both my learners and myself build a better understanding of what was going on internally.

Writing a good reflection is not easy. Many of those who express concerns with encouraging pre-service teachers to reflect find that reflections can be superficial. Research by Orla McCormack (2019) indicates that individual reflections are often uncritical, accepting the status quo. Thomas Farrell (in Pang, 2017) feels that pre-service teachers in particular need a framework in order to help them. He suggests a five-stage process to develop a 'reflective portfolio in which their philosophy, principles, theory, practice and beyond practice (critical) reflections will be documented' (p. 177), in that order, so that they can gain a sense of themselves as teachers. Experienced teachers should use the five elements, but do not need to go in any specific order. This is a broader approach that takes background, beliefs, and context into account. Some of my colleagues in the master's program that I taught in used that five-part framework, making it easier for me to ask learners to talk about the principles they were using. Still, it was especially difficult for pre-service teachers to write very reflectively when they had little background in teaching.

Educational leaders can use reflection in similar ways and with similar caveats. Options and actions can be evaluated both during and after making decisions. Planning, reflection, and discussion may take place within a leadership team or with peers in similar settings. For example, Intensive English Program directors in the US have groups such as UCIEP (University and College Intensive English Programs) and English USA that serve as online and face-to-face sounding boards when dealing with common, shared issues. I found the face-to-face meetings in UCIEP particularly useful as an IEP Director. While leaders would be well served by action research, that formal level of planning, action, and reflection is not a common practice. As with teachers, educational leaders could use Farrell's framework and take a longer look at their own philosophy, principles, theory, and actions to result in more effective reflection.

Strategic leadership is another perspective on reflective practice for leaders. For Sarah Klinghammer (2012, p. 79), strategic leadership includes learning

> how to stand back, look carefully at the program, and begin to think strategically—to make decisions based on accurate information about the program, its vision, and its goals. ... the focus should be on identifying the most effective strategies for achieving program goals and creating a plan for implementing them.

Clearly, knowing the organization is key. Strategic leadership is about focusing on long-range as well as short-range goals and continually reformulating the means to achieve them as the situation changes. Strategic leadership is part of any organization's long-term success. Reflection is an essential component in establishing goals, considering the current situation and changes, and developing strategies. Lack of reflection means reaction becomes the primary form of response. Reaction to events is certainly part of leadership, but it should not be a long-term, central driver of action. It is very difficult, in the heat of the moment, to take a breath and think about long-term goals. As Director, I worked at home one day a week. I was accessible by phone and email, but it gave me time to be outside the immediate demands of the office in multiple respects. I used that time for longer-range thinking and activities that took focused attention.

Yet another, related perspective on reflective practice and strategic leadership comes from systems theory. The term 'system theory' is ascribed to Ludwig von

Bertalanffy (1968), and it is relevant to examining any complex organism or activity with interrelated parts. An educational organization would certainly qualify. Each piece of the system is important, but it is the elements and the relationships among them that create the actual system. Systems theory is generally set against 'reductionism'—the tendency to break complexity into small parts and try to explain the whole by reference to each part. Frank Betts (1992) explored ways that systems thinking should be used in educational leadership. Rather than a piecemeal, ineffective approach, Betts wrote that we need 'a paradigm that illuminates the whole, not just the parts; one that is synthetic, rather than analytic; one that integrates, rather than differentiates. This new paradigm is systems thinking' (p. 38).

Analysis—breaking the whole into parts—will be part of thoughtful decision-making and is a step in systems thinking, but analysis of elements is not enough. Whether the issue is student satisfaction in a language program or member retention in an association, each element interacts with others and fits into a larger, expansive whole. Just looking at individual elements does not acknowledge that each element interacts and interconnects with others, and that the end result is also affected by the network within which each element acts. Just looking at individual pieces is much easier and more straightforward, but much is lost when we do not think about interrelationships. Reflection has to take the larger picture of the components and their relationships into account to be valuable in decision-making and overall leadership. This is the approach that I have tried to use most consistently across different leadership settings.

> **Reflective Break 17:** Deborah refers to Tom Farrell's five-step process of 'philosophy, principles, theory, practice and beyond practice (critical) reflections.' Write a short account (no more than a page) summarizing your teaching philosophy as a language educator. What do you believe about language, culture, language teaching, and language learning?

Neil Anderson: Questioning Assumptions through Metacognitive Engagement

Brown & Lee (2015) explain that Reflective Practice (RP) encourages 'teachers [to] critically examine and reflect on their own teaching experiences, leading to improvement and further development' (p. 541). The phrase 'critically examine' is central to my understanding of RP.

Quinn (2012) introduced me to the concept of 'challenging your normal assumptions' (p. 5). His work led me to the creation of a phrase that guides my RP: *question all assumptions*. Quinn (2012, p. 9) asserts:

> deep change is a fundamentally different process because it requires
> people to develop new expectations. As people experience deep
> change, they move from their old assumptions to a new set of assump-
> tions. They start to see, feel, and think differently.

Quinn's description of deep change, as it applies to the discovery of the leader within each of us, facilitates my continuing growth and development of RP and leadership development. Flavell (1976, 1979) engaged in the early aspects of researching and identifying components of metacognition. He wrote that, 'meta-cognition refers to one's knowledge concerning one's own cognitive processes' (1976, p. 232). He proposed a model of cognitive monitoring (1979) which consists of four key elements: metacognitive knowledge, metacognitive experiences, goals (or tasks), and actions (or strategies). Metacognitive knowledge relates to acquired knowledge about cognitive processes, knowledge that can be used to control one's own thinking processes. Metacognitive experiences include cognitive and/or affective experiences associated with learning.

Goals are highlighted as the primary objective of a cognitive activity and actions are the specific steps taken to achieve those goals. When individuals have a greater awareness of these four keys elements of metacognition, they are in a stronger position to engage in RP. In my own work related to metacognition (Anderson, 2008a, 2012), I point out that 'metacognition results in critical but healthy reflection and evaluation of one's thinking which may result in making specific changes in how one learns. Metacognition is not simply thinking back on an event, describing what happened and how one felt about it. It requires a cognitive awareness and engagement with the awareness of one's thinking' (Anderson, 2012, p. 170). Metacognition requires a heightened awareness of cognitive processes. *Questioning all assumptions* and having a heightened awareness through metacognitive engagement perfectly defines RP for me.

In his great work, *Les Misérables*, Victor Hugo (1802–1885) wrote in 1862 [accessed in a 1992 translation]: 'Where the telescope ends, the microscope begins. Which of the two has the grander view?' (p. 767). I appreciate the way that this quote increases my interest in approaching the *questioning of assumptions* through heightened metacognitive awareness. In 2002, I wrote a summary of a plenary address that I delivered as President of the TESOL International Association entitled 'Using telescopes, microscopes, and kaleidoscopes to put metacognition into perspective' (Anderson, 2002). I have also used these metaphorical tools to write about ways to view our leadership (Anderson 2008b).

I see an advantage of examining our thinking about leadership first from the perspective of a figurative telescope. The telescope allows us to locate an item within a larger field of vision. Through a telescopic view of our leadership we can contextualize our experiences by examining the major issues that influence our behaviors, attitudes, and actions. This view allows us to consider factors outside of our leadership experiences that may have an influence on our leadership behaviors. For example, when examining our leadership, do we consider how our relationships with our family members may have an impact on our leadership? Do we consider how our physical health and exercise habits may impact our leadership? Do we consider how our spiritual practices may influence our leadership? By stepping back from our thinking about leadership and keeping the big picture in mind, we are able to gain a new perspective. We can use the telescope to see our leadership practices from the view of all that surrounds them. From this telescopic view we should remember to *question all assumptions* about the larger context of our lives.

After a telescopic view of our thinking and learning about leadership, a second tool for examining ourselves is the figurative microscope. The microscope allows us to examine things that are not visible to the naked eye. So, it provides a close-up view of our thinking about leadership and enables us to carefully examine the details of our leadership experiences. Through this careful examination of the details we can learn things about ourselves and others within our leadership contexts that can improve our skills and abilities as leaders. From this microscopic view, we must also remember to *question all assumptions* about the details of our leadership.

Finally, after examining our thinking about leadership from both the telescopic and microscopic views and engaging in healthy *questioning of all assumptions*, I find it useful to consider a kaleidoscopic view of thinking about leadership. A figurative kaleidoscopic view allows us to perceive the interactions that occur by blending views of leadership. I am always enchanted with the views that I see as I manipulate a kaleidoscope. The shifting patterns and colors help me understand the fragile nature of leadership. As I move the kaleidoscope and look at leadership from its view, I do not see an exact repetition of shapes, patterns, and colors from one time to the next. Each time I look through the kaleidoscope, I see different patterns. That is the way it is with leadership. No two leadership experiences are exactly the same. The view of leadership from the kaleidoscope may give us the most realistic view of what is happening and allow us to carefully *question all assumptions* about our work as leaders.

Telescopes, microscopes, and kaleidoscopes provide three very different perspectives and views of leadership. *Questioning all assumptions* provides a healthy point from which to reflect. When engaged in RP, each of these perspectives and our questioning can lead to a heightened awareness and provide the impetus for change that can lead to increased performance.

> **Reflective Break 18:** As we will see in the Question Three and in the Question Four responses, it is normal and natural to make assumptions, without which it is not possible to make decisions. As a language educator, in order to be able to plan courses and lessons, you have to make some assumptions, for example, about your learners' different competence levels in the target language. The important thing about making assumptions is *testing* those assumptions, to see how small or how big is the gap between your assumptions and the reality of the situation. Which of your assumptions do you make most often, and how do you test those assumption?

Kathleen M. Bailey: What Does Reflective Practice Mean to Me?

For me, the concept of reflective practice has three sources: the literature about the topic, my experience engaging in reflective teaching, and a personal tendency to be introspective. I believe that although our contexts may be varied, whether we are reflecting on our work as teachers, parents, or administrators, reflective practice demands honest self-scrutiny. A widely cited definition of *reflective teaching* is from Richards & Lockhart (1994). They say that in practicing reflective teaching, 'teachers and student teachers collect data about teaching, examine their attitudes, beliefs, assumptions, and teaching practices, and use the information obtained as a basis for critical reflection about teaching' (p. 1). A main challenge with this view is the time needed to collect and to analyze data.

A different definition of *reflective teaching* came from Zeichner & Liston (1996). Their view can be applied to reflective practice in leadership contexts as well as in teaching. For those authors, reflective practice entails 'a recognition, examination, and rumination over the implications of one's beliefs, experiences, attitudes, knowledge, and values as well as the opportunities and constraints provided by the social conditions in which the teacher works' (p. 6). A key distinction was provided by Schön (1983), who contrasted two phases in reflective teaching. Reflection-*in*-action occurs while we are actually teaching, but reflection-*on*-action occurs before or after lessons. The latter 'refers to the ordered, deliberate, and systematic application of logic to a problem in order to resolve it; the process is very much within our control' (Russell & Munby, 1991, p. 164). In contrast, reflection-*in*-action occurs very quickly, while we are concurrently engaged in the action upon which we are reflecting.

Zeichner & Liston (1996) described five 'dimensions of reflection' (p. 47). The first two—rapid reflection and repair—are instances of reflection-*in*-action.

The last three—review, research, and retheorizing and reformulating—all involve reflection-*on*-action. I end by explaining each of the five dimensions.

Rapid reflection is described as 'routine and automatic' (Zeichner & Liston, 1996, p. 45). Teachers are constantly involved in rapid reflection during lessons, and I think most leaders must engage in it regularly as well. It is quick and happens regularly, and can occur almost out of our conscious awareness. *Repair* is also a type of reflection-in-action, but it is more thoughtful than rapid reflection. It involves choosing to change our behavior in some way—either by explaining it or by acting differently. For example, while teaching, if we notice that our students are confused about a task, we may rephrase the instructions or ask them which part of the task they do not understand.

In contrast, *review*, as a type of reflection-*on*-action, occurs before or after teaching or—in the case of leaders—before or after making a decision or taking action of some kind. Review involves not just thinking about but also writing or talking about some aspect of our practice. It is 'often interpersonal and collegial' (Zeichner & Liston, 1996, p. 46), such as having an informal discussion with colleagues. *Research*, the fourth dimension, entails collecting data about our practice and reflecting on what those data have to tell us (e.g., by keeping an introspective journal or soliciting input from employees). The research process may continue for some time and is more systematic than are the first three dimensions. Thus research, in Zeichner & Liston's framework, is related to the definition from Richards & Lockhart (1994) cited above: It entails collecting and analyzing data. Finally, *retheorizing and reformulating* is described as being 'more rigorous than the other dimensions' (Zeichner & Liston, 1996, p. 48). At this level teachers (or leaders) critically examine their own beliefs, but they also consider 'public academic theories' (p. 46). Thus, retheorizing and reformulating is a continuous process that may last for years.

Reflective Break 19: According to Kathi's interpretation of Zeichner & Liston's (1996) five 'dimensions of reflection' (p. 47), 'Repair' is focused on the teacher consciously changing their behavior. If you could change *one thing* about your teaching behavior, what would you change and why? And, if you could have made that change before now, what has been stopping you from making that change?

Reflective Break 20: Having read the ten responses to Question Two, choose one that was of most interest to you. What was it about that particular response that stood out for you? What did you learn about RP from reading that response?

REFERENCES

Anderson, N. J. (2002). Using telescopes, microscopes, and kaleidoscopes to put metacognition into perspective. *TESOL Matters, 12*(4), 1, 4.

Anderson, N. J. (2008a). Metacognition and the good language learner. In C. Griffiths (Ed.), *Lessons from Good Language Learners* (pp. 99–109). Cambridge, UK: Cambridge University Press.

Anderson, N. J. (2008b). The four scopes of effective leadership development. In C. Coombe, M. L. McCloskey, L. Stephenson, & N. J. Anderson (Eds.), *Leadership in English Language Teaching and Learning* (pp. 17–26). Ann Arbor, MI: The University of Michigan Press.

Anderson, N. J. (2012). Metacognition: Awareness in language learning. In S. Mercer, S. Ryan, & M. Williams (Eds.), *Psychology for Language Learning: Insights from Research, Theory and Pedagogy* (pp. 169–187). Basingstoke, UK: Palgrave. https://doi.org/10.1057/9781137032829_12

Bailey, K. M. (2006). *Language Teacher Supervision.* New York, NY: Cambridge University Press. https://doi.org/10.1017/CBO9780511667329

Bailey, K. M., Curtis, A., & Nunan, D. (2001). *Pursuing Professional Development: The Self as Source.* Boston, MA: Heinle & Heinle.

Barlett, L. (1990). Teacher development through reflective teaching. In J. C. Richards & D. Nunan (Eds.), *Second Language Teacher Education* (pp. 202–214). New York, NY: Cambridge University Press.

Barley, M. (2012). Learning from reflective practice and metacognition—An anaesthetist's perspective. *Reflective Practice, 13*(2), 271–280. https://doi.org/10.1080/14623943.2012.657792

Betts, F. (1992). How systems thinking applies to education. *Educational Leadership, 50*(3), 38–41. Retrieved from: http://www.ascd.org/publications/educational-leadership/nov92/vol50/num03/How-Systems-Thinking-Applies-to-Education.aspx

Blackmore, S. J. (1984). A psychological theory of the out-of-body experience. *Journal of Parapsychology, 48*(3), 201–218.

Boud, D., Keogh, R., & Walker, D. (Eds.). (2006). *Reflection: Turning Experience into Learning.* London, UK: Croom Helm.

Brown, H. D., & Lee, H. (2015). *Teaching by Principles: An Interactive Approach to Language Pedagogy* (4th edn.). White Plains, NY: Pearson.

Cartwright, T. (2004). *Developing Your Intuition: A Guide to Reflective Practice.* Greensboro, NC: Center for Creative Leadership.

Castelli, P. A. (2016). Reflective leadership review: A framework for improving organisational performance. *The Journal of Management Development, 35*(2), 217–236. https://doi.org/10.1108/JMD-08-2015-0112

Cline, E. M. (2008). Mirrors, minds, and metaphors. *Philosophy East and West, 58*(3), 337–357. https://doi.org/10.1353/pew.0.0006

Cunningham, C. L. (2012). Critically reflective leadership. *Australian Journal of Teacher Education, 37*(4), 49–61. https://doi.org/10.14221/ajte.2012v37n4.5

Curtis, A. (2020). Featured presentation: Living and learning online in a post-pandemic world. *Qatar University 5th Annual International (Online) ELT Conference: English Language Teaching and 21st Century Skills—Communicate, Collaborate, Create.* November 7 and 8, 2020. http://www.qu.edu.qa/foundation/Conference/Conference-2020/Program

Darling-Hammond, L., & Snyder, J. (2000). Authentic assessment of teaching in context. *Teaching and Teacher Education, 16*(5–6), 523–545. https://doi.org/10.1016/S0742-051X(00)00015-9

Daudelin, M. W. (January 1996). Learning from experience through reflection. *Organizational Dynamics* (pp. 36–48).

David, D. (December 18, 2013). How much feedback should leaders seek? *Customer Think.* Retrieved from: http://customerthink.com/how-much-feedback-should-leaders-seek/

De Brabandere, S. (June 6, 2019). Distorted images. *Scientific American.* Retrieved from: https://www.scientificamerican.com/article/distorted-images/

Dewey, J. (1933). *How We Think: A Restatement of Reflective Thinking to the Educative Process.* Boston, MA: D. C. Heath & Co. (Original work published in 1910.)

Estrange. (2021a). *Collins Dictionary.* Retrieved from: https://www.collinsdictionary.com/dictionary/english/estrange

Estrange. (2021b). *Merriam-Webster Dictionary.* Retrieved from: https://www.merriam-webster.com/dictionary/estrange

Estrange. (2021c). *Oxford English Dictionary.* Retrieved from: https://www.lexico.com/en/definition/estrange

Farrell, T. S. C. (2007). *Reflective Language Teaching: A Guide to Classroom Communication.* Thousand Oaks, CA: Corwin Press/Sage Publications.

Farrell, T. S. C. (2020). *Reflective Practice in ELT.* Sheffield, UK: Equinox Publishing.

Flavell, J. H. (1976). Metacognitive aspects of problem solving. In L. B. Resnick (Ed.), *The Nature of Intelligence* (pp. 231–236). Hillsdale, NJ: Erlbaum.

Flavell, J. H. (1979). Metacognition and cognitive monitoring: A new area of cognitive-developmental inquiry. *American Psychologist, 34,* 906–911. https://doi.org/10.1037/0003-066X.34.10.906

Flick, U. (2018). *Doing Triangulation and Mixed Methods.* Thousand Oaks, CA: Sage. https://doi.org/10.4135/9781529716634

Frankl, V. (1946). *Man's Search for Meaning.* Boston, MA: Beacon Press.

Gebhard, J. G., & Oprandy, R. (1999). *Language Teaching Awareness: A Guide to Exploring Beliefs and Practices.* New York, NY: Cambridge University Press.

George, B. (October 26, 2012). Mindfulness helps you become a better leader. *Harvard Business Review.* Retrieved from: https://hbr.org/2012/10/mindfulness-helps-you-become-a

Ghanizadeh, A. (2017). The interplay between reflective thinking, critical thinking, self-monitoring, and academic achievement in higher education. *Higher Education, 74*(1), 101–114. https://doi.org/10.1007/s10734-016-0031-y

Grinder, M. (1991). *Righting the Educational Conveyor Belt.* Portland, OR: Metamorphous Press.

Gurel, E., & Tat, M. (2017). SWOT analysis: A theoretical review. *The Journal of International Social Research, 10*(51), 994–1006.

Hawking, S. (1988/2011). *A Brief History of Time*. London, UK: Bantam Press.

Head, K., & Taylor, P. (1997). *Readings in Teacher Development*. Oxford, UK: Heinemann.

Hugo, V. (1992 [1862]). *Les Misérables*. Translation by C. E. Wilbour. New York, NY: Random House.

Johnson, J. A. (2013). Reflective learning, reflective practice, and metacognition: The importance in nursing education. *Journal for Nurses in Professional Development*, *29*(1), 46–48. https://doi.org/10.1097/NND.0b013e31827e2f27

Kabat-Zinn, J. (1994). *Wherever You Go, There You Are: Mindfulness Meditation for Everyday Life*. London: Piatkus.

Kabat-Zinn, J. (2003). Mindfulness-based interventions in context: Past, present, and future. *Clinical Psychology: Science and Practice*, *10*(2), 144–156. https://doi.org/10.1093/clipsy.bpg016

Klinghammer, S. J. (2012). Strategic planner. In M. Christison and F. L. Stoller (Eds.), *A Handbook for Language Program Administrators* (pp. 79–98). San Francisco, CA: Alta Books.

Kolb, D. A. (1984). *Experiential Learning*. Englewood Cliffs, NJ: Prentice Hall.

Kounios, J., Smith, R. W., Yang, W., Bachman, P., & D'Esposito, M. (2001). Cognitive association formation in human memory revealed by spatiotemporal brain imaging. *Neuron*, *29*(1), 297–306. https://doi.org/10.1016/S0896-6273(01)00199-4

Kouzes, J. M., & Posner, B. Z. (2012). *The Leadership Challenge*. San Francisco: CA: Wiley.

Kraemer, H. M. (December 2, 2016). How self-reflection can make you a better leader. *Kellogg Insight*. Retrieved from: https://insight.kellogg.northwestern.edu/article/how-self-reflection-can-make-you-a-better-leader

Looman, M. D. (2003). Reflective leadership: Strategic planning from the heart and soul. *Consulting Psychology Journal: Practice and Research*, *55*(4), 215–221. https://doi.org/10.1037/1061-4087.55.4.215

Matsuo, M. (2016). Reflective leadership and team learning: An exploratory study. *Journal of Workplace Learning*, *28*(5), 307–321. https://doi.org/10.1108/JWL-12-2015-0089

McCormack, O. (March 23, 2019). How research on reflection has changed my view on reflective practice. Retrieved from: https://info-ted.eu/how-research-on-reflection-has-changed-my-view-on-reflective-practice/

Me, Myself and I. (n.d.). Internet Movie Database (imdb). Retrieved from: https://www.imdb.com/title/tt6477194/

Mercado, L. A. (2018). Supervision of early-career teachers. In J. I. Liontas, T. and M. DelliCarpini (Eds.), *The TESOL Encyclopedia of English Language Teaching*. https://doi.org/10.1002/9781118784235.eelt0140

Morgan, J., & Douglas, N. (2005). *World Link* (1st edn.). Boston, MA: National Geographic/Cengage Learning.

Neale, P. (2019). Self-reflection in leadership—Part 1: Ambitions, values and personality. Retrieved from: https://unabridgedleadership.com/self-reflection-in-leadership/

Nugent, P., Moss, D., Barnes, R., & Wilks, J. (2011). Clear(ing) space: Mindfulness-based reflective practice. *Reflective Practice*, *12*(1), 1–13. https://doi.org/10.1080/14623943.2011.541088

Ollila, S. (2008). Creativity and innovativeness through reflective project leadership. *Creativity and Innovation Management, 9*(3), 195–200. https://doi.org/10.1111/1467-8691.00172

Palmer, P. J. (1998/2017). *The Courage to Teach: Exploring the Inner Landscape of a Teacher's Life*. San Francisco, CA: Jossey-Bass.

Panferov, S. (2012). Transitioning from teacher to language program administrator. In M. A. Christison & F. A. Stoller (Eds.), *A Handbook for Language Program Administrators*, 2nd edn. (pp. 3–18). Miami, FL: ALTA Books.

Pang, A. (2017). Reflective teaching and practice: Interview with Thomas Farrell. *RELC Journal, 48*(2), 174–179. https://doi.org/10.1177/0033688217707632

Quinn, R. E. (2012). *The Deep Change Field Guide: A Personal Course to Discovering the Leader Within*. San Francisco, CA: Jossey-Bass.

Richards, J. C., & Lockhart, C. (1994). *Reflective Teaching in Second Language Classrooms*. Cambridge, UK: Cambridge University Press. https://doi.org/10.1017/CBO9780511667169

Rowe, S. F., & Sikes, S. (2006). Lessons learned: Taking it to the next level. Paper presented at PMI Global Congress 2006. Newtown Square, PA: Project Management Institute. Retrieved from: https://www.pmi.org/learning/library/lessons-learned-next-level-communicating-7991

Russell, T., & Munby, H. (1991). Reframing: The role of experience in developing teachers' professional knowledge. In D. A. Schön (Ed.), *The Reflective Turn: Case Studies in and on Educational Practice* (pp. 164–187). New York, NY: Teachers College Press.

Ruth-Sahd, L. (2003). Reflective practice: A critical analysis of data-based studies and implications for nursing education. *Journal of Nursing Education, 42*(11), 488–497. https://doi.org/10.3928/0148-4834-20031101-07

Saunila, M., Tikkamäki, K., & Ukko, J. (2015). Managing performance and learning through reflective practices. *Journal of Organizational Effectiveness: People and Performance, 2*(4), 370–390. https://doi.org/10.1108/JOEPP-05-2015-0017

Schön, D. A. (1983). *The Reflective Practitioner: How Professionals Think in Action*. New York, NY: Basic Books.

Schön, D. A. (1987). *Educating the Reflective Practitioner: Towards a New Design for Teaching and Learning in the Professions*. San Francisco, CA: Josey-Bass Publishers.

Schön, D. A. (1991). *The Reflective Turn: Case Studies in and on Educational Practice*. New York: Teachers Press, Columbia University.

Smyth, J. (1989). Developing and sustaining critical reflection in teacher education. *Journal of Teacher Education, 40*(2), 77–106.

Speranza, C. R., & Pierce, A. (2019). Development of a personal leadership philosophy: An experiential and reflective opportunity in the graduate classroom. *Journal of Leadership Education, 18*(3), 167–174.

Talwar, V., Yachison, S., Leduc, K., & Nagar, P. M. (2018). Practice makes perfect? The impact of coaching and moral stories on children's lie-telling. *International Journal of Behavioral Development, 42*(4), 416–424. https://doi.org/10.1177/0165025417728583

Thun, B., & Kelloway, E. K. (2011). Virtuous leaders: Assessing character strengths in the workplace. *Canadian Journal of Administrative Sciences*, 28(3), 270–283.

Virmani, E. A., Hatton-Bowers, H., Lombardi, C. M., Decker, K. B., King, E. K., Plata-Potter, S. I., & Vallotton, C. D. (2020). How are preservice early childhood professionals' mindfulness, reflective practice beliefs, and individual characteristics associated with their developmentally supportive responses to infants and toddlers? *Early Education and Development*, 31(7), 1052–1070.
https://doi.org/10.1080/10409289.2020.1798718

von Bertalanffy, L. (1968). *General System Theory: Foundations, Development, Applications*. New York, NY: George Braziller Publishers.

Wallace, M. J. (1991). *Training Foreign Language Teachers: A Reflective Approach*. Cambridge, UK: Cambridge University Press.

Weick, K. (1979). *The Social Psychology of Organizing* (2nd edition). McGraw-Hill Inc, New York, USA.

White, R., Hockley, A., van der Horst Jansen, J., & Laughner, M. S. (2008). *From Teacher to Manager: Managing Language Teaching Organizations*. Cambridge, UK: Cambridge University Press.

Zeichner, K. M., & Liston, D. P. (1996). *Reflective Teaching: An Introduction*. Mahwah, NJ: Lawrence Erlbaum.

ABOUT THE AUTHORS

Dr Okon Effiong is a lecturer in the Foundation Programme, Qatar University. He is a member of the TESOL Board of Directors and served on its Nominating Committee, Diversity & Inclusion Committee, as Chair-elect of the EFL-Interest Section. He is founder and Past President of Africa TESOL. He was the President of Qatar TESOL.

Dr Christel Broady is Chair of graduate programs, as well as Director of the ESL Program at Georgetown College, Kentucky, USA. An international leader, Christel has served in many leadership roles with TESOL International and affiliates. Her list of domestic and international publications, keynotes, presentations, and awards is extensive.

Leo Mercado has been in the field for more than 25 years, making contributions as a director of studies, e-learning and proficiency testing specialist, project leader, author, and academic entrepreneur. Based in Atlanta, Georgia, USA, he has also successfully led two international accreditation processes, as well as large-scale, nationwide projects at the Ministry of Education level.

Andy Curtis (PhD) is a Professor in the Graduate School of Education at Anaheim University. From 2015 to 2016, he served as the 50th President of the TESOL International Association. He has (co)authored and (co)edited 200 articles, book chapters and books, he has presented to 50,000 language educators in 100 countries, and his work has been read by 100,000 language educators in 150 countries. He is based in Ontario, Canada, from where he works with learning organizations worldwide.

Marjorie Rosenberg has been involved in tertiary and adult education in Austria since 1981. She is an active teacher trainer, conference presenter, and ELT author. Marjorie served as IATEFL President from 2015 to 2017. Her latest project is working as a mentor through a program designed by EVE and Africa TESOL.

Dr Rosemary DePetro Orlando is a Professor at Southern New Hampshire University, USA. She regularly travels to Vietnam National University in Hanoi to teach MS TEFL courses in a university partnership degree program. As a language teacher educator, Rosemary regularly presents at national and international English Language Teaching conferences worldwide.

Dr Rosa Aronson is the Interim Executive Director of the TESOL International Association in Alexandria, Virginia, USA. Her career in Education began as an EFL teacher in France and continued in the USA in professional educational organizations. She has served as an English Language Specialist focusing on organizational leadership. She holds a PhD in Social Foundations of Education from the University of Virginia.

Dr Deborah Healey was the 2020–2021 President of the Board of Directors of the TESOL International Association. An online and face-to-face teacher educator, she writes and presents extensively internationally (Africa, Asia, Latin America, Europe, US) on appropriate use of technology in language teaching. Her doctorate is in Computers in Education.

Dr Neil J. Anderson has been actively involved in leadership roles and reflective practice for over 40 years. He currently teaches at Brigham Young University–Hawaii, USA. Neil served as President of the TESOL International Association for 2001–2002. He received the prestigious James Alatis Award from TESOL in 2014.

Dr Kathleen M. Bailey is a Professor of Applied Linguistics at the Middlebury Institute of International Studies at Monterey (MIIS), California, USA. She completed her MA and her doctorate at the University of California at Los Angeles. Her research interests include teacher education, language assessment, and the teaching of listening and speaking.

Chapter 3

The Challenges of Doing RP

INTRODUCTION TO THE
QUESTION THREE RESPONSES

Andy Curtis

In the third set of question prompts, the RTLs were asked to respond to these questions: How do you engage in RP? What are some of the challenges you have faced when engaging in RP? How did/do you address/meet those challenges? Unlike the Question Two prompts, these are three different questions, but in common with the Question Two responses, six more recurring themes were found in the RTLs' responses, which are briefly summarized below. Each theme, as noted in the earlier chapters, could be the basis of an entire chapter. And again, readers are encouraged to find additional themes, by relating their experiences to those of these RTLs.

Time is mentioned in all ten of the responses to the Question Three prompts. We will, therefore, take the time to consider this essential aspect of RP in more detail. Often those mentions are in relation to the challenge of finding or making the time to engage in RP, as well as descriptions of looking back over time, which can be an essential aspect of RP. Some of the reflective teacher leaders, as part of their RP, refer to the first time they encountered a particular situation, which they compare and contrast with the next time they had a similar encounter. Other Question Three responses describe the tasks and activities that busy classroom language teachers have to spend time on, which can leave little time for much else, as well as describing challenging timelines, time constraints, and other chronological concerns, which are reflected in the ways in which we think and talk about time.

It has been more than 40 years since George Lakoff and Mark Johnson published the first edition of their book, *Metaphors We Live By* (1980), but it is still being cited (Baş, 2020). The first of the 30 or so short chapters in Lakoff &

Johnson's book looks at the 'argument is war' metaphor, with examples such as: 'He *attacked every weak point* in my argument ... I *demolished* his argument ... He *shot down* all my arguments' (Lakoff & Johnson, 1980, p. 4, original emphases). Leaving aside the use of only male pronouns (which was common at that time) the second chapter is about the metaphors in English related to time, especially 'time is money', with no fewer than 16 examples listed, including: 'You're *wasting* my time ... You're *running out* of time ... You don't *use* your time *profitably*' (Lakoff & Johnson, 1980, pp. 7–8, original emphases).

We are still trying to figure out how we humans make sense of and articulate our perceptions of this thing we call 'Time.' For example, in Vyvyan Evans' 2013 book, *Language and Time*, she points out that the ways in which we think and talk about time have been 'a recurring topic of study [in] experimental psychology [for] over a century' (Evans, 2013, p. xv). However, in spite of all that time and all those studies, Evans observes that 'it is striking how much remains to be understood about time in language and thought' (p. xv). It is not clear if there are such things as universal metaphors, which exist in the same way in all human languages and cultures. But Alverson (1994) compared the metaphors of time in five distinct languages—English, Mandarin Chinese, Hindi, and the African language Sesotho—and found far more similarities than differences in their metaphorical ways of thinking and talking about time.

Reflective Break 21: If, in addition to English, you know another language (or languages) well, how do the metaphors related to time compare in English with your other language(s)? Does the 'time is money' metaphor exist in your other language(s) as well? If so, what are some of the similarities and differences between the 'time is money' metaphors in English and in your other language(s)?

These considerations about time bring us to the question of whether time spent on RP is worth it, to which the short answer is Yes, as the accounts in this book clearly illustrate! But the question also requires a longer answer, as there is the consideration of *how much* time should be spent on RP, the answer to which is: It Depends. The first factor is how much time the teacher has available, but if a teacher believes that they have no time at all to engage in RP, then it may be necessary for them to review their schedule, to ensure that they can make some time for RP. A general, approximate guide that teachers may find helpful is the 10 percent rule of thumb, in which a teacher sets aside a minimum of 10 percent of their teaching time for RP. For example, if they teach 10 hours a week, they would set aside one hour for systematic, structured RP, and two hours for 20 hours per week of teaching. It is, of course, possible to spend more than 10 percent of teaching time on RP, but to spend less than that is not desirable—and may even be detrimental to a teacher's professional development.

As the Question Three responses show, for some teachers, in addition to the time crunch, other challenges include, initially, not knowing how to engage in RP, or where to begin, or what the difference is between simply thinking about our teaching and engaging in RP. One source of support identified in some of the Question Three responses was reading clear, concise accounts of other teachers' reflective practices, such as those in Bailey, Curtis, & Nunan's *Pursuing Professional Development: The Self as Source* (2001) and Parker Palmer's *The Courage to Teach: Exploring the Inner Landscape of a Teacher's Life* (1998/2017), for example. Palmer begins his book by stating: 'We teach who we are' (p. 1). And as noted in Question Two, it can be helpful to step outside of our familiar comfort zone and read accounts from other fields, outside of education, such as healthcare, as both fields come under the heading of the helping professions, as noted in Chapter 2.

A good example of giving clear, concise advice about RP is a short piece by Jane Westberg (2001), who was based in a department of family medicine at a US university. In just six pages, Westberg described more than a dozen ways of helping healthcare students to become reflective practitioners. However, Westberg began by stating her concerns regarding the undervaluing of RP: 'In crowded curriculums and busy clinical settings, reflection is too often neglected. In environments where "doing" and "being productive" are central values, those who don't understand how critical reflection is to effective learning and patient care can devalue reflection' (Westberg, 2001, p. 314). That is still a valid concern, 20 years later. The practical advice Westberg gave includes: 'schedule times and places for reflection' (p. 314), as noted above, and 'consider using video-recordings of the learners' work' (p. 314), which relates to the idea of using data-based RP, as discussed in Question Two. Likewise, Steve Walsh and Steve Mann recommend: 'Doing reflective practice ... [using] ... data-based and evidence-led reflection' (Walsh & Mann, 2015, p. 351).

Although Westberg's paper was written with her healthcare students in mind, her suggestions are equally applicable to language educators, as she encouraged her students to reflect specifically on: 'Any new issues or learning goals that emerged ... What they did well ... What they were thinking ... Key decision points and options ... Any assumptions, values, or biases that might have affected their behavior ... What they were feeling ... What they need to work on' (Westberg, 2001, pp. 318–319). Needless to say, it would be overwhelming for a teacher to try to reflect on all of the items on Westberg's lists in every language lesson. But it is possible to choose one or two areas to focus on in each lesson, to developer a deeper understanding and build up a more complete picture of our teaching and learning over time.

In terms of being unsure of how, where, when, or why to begin RP, some of the Question Three accounts highlight the importance of looking for an RP mentor, i.e., someone who may be not only an experienced classroom teacher, but also an experienced reflective practitioner. This is where an RP coach or a mentor can be a source of great support, especially on those teaching days which have been particularly difficult, when the last thing we want to do is to reflect on the day, instead just wanting it to be over, in the hope that tomorrow will be better! Tracey Sempowicz and Peter Hudson, who looked at the mentoring of two pre-service teachers' reflective practices at a university in Australia, begin by stating: 'Reflective practice appears crucial for professional growth; making connections between mentoring practices and mentees' reflections may assist mentors to guide reflective processes' (Sempowicz & Hudson, 2012, p. 52). In their study, the two authors collected and analyzed video, audio, and observational data, which reiterates the point made earlier, about using data to facilitate RP, and they found that the mentors 'modelled reflective practices to their mentees ... which [positively] influenced the mentees' reflective practices and their pedagogical development' (p. 52). In relation to the time challenges discussed above, Sempowicz & Hudson concluded that the mentors 'facilitated time and opportunities for this [RP] to occur' (p. 62).

Although a case-study approach was used by Sempowicz & Hudson, involving just four teachers (two mentors with two mentees), their findings help to show what a positive difference an RP coach or mentor can make. However, for such a mentoring or coaching relationship to work, a high degree of trust between the two parties is essential. For example, in their book *Peer Supervision in Coaching and Mentoring: A Versatile Guide for Reflective Practice* (2018) Turner, Lucas, & Whitaker stress the importance of trust, and explain what happens when there is either a lack of trust to begin with, or if something happens that damages the trust, which usually results in the eventual inevitable breakdown of the mentoring or coaching relationship.

One of the earliest publications that explicitly addressed the importance of lesson planning may be Olive Hapgood's book, *School Needlework: A Course of Study in Sewing Designed for Use in Schools*—published in 1892. Some 130 years later, we are still working on lesson planning (Njika, 2020) during which time lesson objectives, learning goals, learning outcomes, etc. have continued to be an essential part of lesson planning. As some of the Question Three responses show, similar kinds of goal-setting can help focus our RP, and help us to distinguish between simply thinking about our teaching versus engaging in RP, both of which are important, but are not the same. Some of the RTLs in this book had specific goals, for example, Okon Effiong's goal of increasing the presence of teachers of English in Africa in the TESOL International Association. Having such goals enables us to use RP to self-assess how we are doing, in terms of moving towards and reaching those goals, and to ask ourselves what we have done towards achieving or accomplishing a particular goal. Therefore, in the same way that we think of data-based RP, we can also think of goal-oriented RP, which can help us meet the challenge of being overwhelmed, which can be a common reaction when we first start to engage in RP.

In a single language lesson of, say, one hour with 20 students, more than a hundred decisions may be made by the teacher. If the teacher asks a question and five students raise their hands, then in choosing one student to give the answer, the teacher has, in that same moment, decided not to ask the other four students who also raised their hands. Therefore, the teacher has, in effect, made five decisions, which multiply every time students raise their hands, resulting in a kind of decision-making cascade. Added to the teacher's decisions regarding who is or is not called on, there are myriad moment-to-moment decisions made by the teacher about, for example, whether to keep following their lesson-plan, or to omit some parts of the plan, or to rearrange the order of tasks, or to spend more or less time than planned on some activities rather than others, etc.

With so much happening in every lesson and with every class, RP can help us pick out particular instances, for example, if the teacher asked a question and no hands were raised. Amy Colton and Georgea Sparks-Langer presented a conceptual framework that can be used to guide this kind of teacher reflection on teacher decision-making. Emphasizing the relationship between RP and decision-making, Colton & Sparks-Langer (2016) describe teachers as 'reflective decision maker[s] ... thoughtful persons intrinsically motivated to analyze a situation, set goals, plan and monitor actions, evaluate results, and reflect on their own professional thinking' (p. 45). And in connecting RP and goal-setting, as the following Question Three accounts show, it is also necessary to be specific and to think longer- rather than shorter-term. For example, if the RP begins with a very general question, such as, What can be done to motivate my students? then the answers may be equally general, and therefore more difficult to implement. But if the question is more specific, for example, What can be done to help/encourage my students to use more of the spoken target second/foreign language in class?

then more specific potential answers may emerge. However, such specificity also needs to be balanced with bigger-picture, longer-term RP, as language learning takes time. As language educators, we know that the marketing of 'learn a foreign language fluently in a month, a week, or even a day' commercial materials is unhelpful and untrue hyperbole. (If only language learning really was that quick and that easy!)

To recap, the following the RTLs' Question Three responses illustrate the importance of the following learning points:

(i)   Set 'dedicated' time aside for RP, with no distractions, so your RP can be focused.

(ii) Read the published RP accounts of other teachers, but also read RP accounts from outside of education and language education, in other helping professions.

(iii) Gather data/feedback on what is happening in your classrooms and lessons, for example, audio/video recordings, journal entries, teaching portfolios, etc.

(iv) Look for RP mentors whom you trust and who can help you figure out how, where, and when to engage in the kind of RP that works best for you.

(v)   Learn to set RP goals and to ask RP questions, in the same way as you do in your regular lesson and course planning and preparation.

(vi) In your RP, balance seeing the moment-to-moment interactions in your classroom with seeing the big picture and thinking long term.

> **Reflective Break 23:** As a language educator, have you been a coach or a mentor to another teacher? What did you learn from the experience? If you are already an experienced reflective practitioner, what advice would you give to a teacher who is new to RP?

THE QUESTION THREE RESPONSES

Okon Effiong, Christel Broady, Leo Mercado, Andy Curtis,
Marjorie Rosenberg, Rosemary Orlando, Rosa Aronson,
Deborah Healey, Neil Anderson, and Kathleen M. Bailey

Here it might be helpful to have a reminder of the Question Three prompts: 'How do you engage in RP? What are some of the challenges you have faced when engaging in RP? How did/do you address/meet those challenges?'

Okon Effiong: Leadership Pipeline Laced with Obstacles

Leadership experience can sometimes start at an early age and be carried on into adulthood. However, my journey into leadership began very late. In describing how I engage in RP, I look back on my time with the Diversity Committee of the TESOL International Association. Despite my work as a Chair on a TESOL committee, I did not feel like I was a leader. Rather, I saw my role as a contributor and my effort as service to the profession. As Chair-elect, I served under a very capable Chair and learnt from her and other committee members. My confidence grew by the day and I was able to carry out my responsibilities to the satisfaction of all concerned. I went on to become the Chair of the Diversity Committee the following year. With hindsight, I can see that the reality was that I headed a TESOL committee and should therefore have felt like a leader. However, I have that feeling only now. I was attending business meetings and luncheons organized for leaders, submitting reports, and participating in brainstorming initiatives with committee members. The transition from armchair critic to committee Chair seemed over at this stage. Not really! At that point, I was beginning to think more of my initial motivation to join the Association's leadership ranks, which was to get Africa more involved. In addition, I had a better understanding of how that kind professional body operates, especially one with huge global influence. The process of forming and leading a continental body became my preoccupation. I needed a pathway to achieve this and the opportunity at a national level presented itself.

I attended the 2014 Qatar TESOL conference and sat next to a senior TESOL colleague who had served on the Diversity Committee with me. When the nomination was open, she nudged me to run for the presidency of Qatar TESOL. I said 'No way!' The question was, how could I contest the presidency as a first-time attendee at that particular conference? Nobody knew me, the office of the presidency sounded high above me, and I felt I stood no chance. As I processed my TESOL colleague's suggestion, I did not think that I had done enough work at the TESOL International Association to warrant such an ambitious attempt and such a bold move. However, my colleague countered that nobody would know me if they did not hear or see my name on the ballot. She advised me to put my name on the ballot, saying that by the following year, a few individuals would remember my name and perhaps vote for me then.

With nothing to lose, I put forward my name for the presidency of Qatar TESOL, and assumed I stood maybe a 5 percent chance of winning at best, and even then, only if colleagues from my institution voted for me. On the election morning, I had to sell myself by actively canvassing for votes among any of the delegates who cared to stop and listen to me. To my surprise, and I believe to the surprise of many delegates, especially the confident veterans who had run the board for years, I was elected to the presidency. This was completely unexpected, but I was very pleased nonetheless, and I began to feel the leadership trait coursing through my veins. Becoming president meant I was leading a national affiliate of the TESOL International Association.

In my approach to reflective practice, experience precedes theory. The board of the national English language teacher association that I served on comprised 12 members, with seven individuals from one particular country, while the remaining were of five different nationalities, namely, Nigeria, Iran, Pakistan, Lebanon, and the USA. As president, I adopted a consultative approach to carrying out my duties of organizing conferences and expanding the membership base. My leadership style was to discuss my ideas individually with members to get them to buy into my vision of the affiliate association before bringing my motion to the board meeting. That way, I would get the support needed to pursue the goals of the association. My frustration and disappointment came to the surface when the 'group of seven' pursued a particular course of action that I did not agree with. However unpopular or unproductive it might have been, the motion would receive the majority votes and they would have their way. My frustration knew no bounds. I was being stonewalled and my dream of transforming the association was fading.

Eventually, I chose to resign after a year without serving out my term, because of the frustration and failure to take the association to the level I envisaged. This was, of course, not a good outcome, but I felt that it was the most honorable approach to address the challenge I faced as a leader. In addition, I wanted to avoid being associated with the negative actions of the board I headed. Sadly, in less than two years after my departure, Qatar TESOL had expired in the hands of the 'group of seven'. Before my tenure, individuals from North America dominated the Qatar TESOL Board and they would always win the election to their different offices. To their credit, they were organizing successful conferences in their institution year in year out, and would occasionally move the conference venue to another establishment. However, the feeling was that there was a clique running the association and that the board membership did not reflect the diverse nature of the professionals in the country. This probably explains why I won the presidency.

From being an armchair critic of the TESOL International Association to holding different leadership positions at national and continental levels, I have learnt many lessons in leadership and people management. Furthermore, the transformation to committee Chair and association leader has been a wonderful experience that has influenced the way I relate to people irrespective of whether we are working as a group or interacting socially. Over the years, I have inculcated traits that have become part of my personality. For example, my overall tolerance has become far more elastic than what it was prior to 2010. I have learnt conflict resolution by seeking the middle ground when there are opposing views. Another lesson learnt is that even when everyone is 'losing it,' and becoming upset, the leaders need to stay cool and calm. This is in line with a quote by reproductive rights activist Faye Wattleton: 'The only safe ship in a storm is leadership.' Playing different leadership roles over a ten-year period has provided me with networking opportunities in different parts of the world, which has also increased my willingness to serve in higher-level capacities. The most rewarding aspect of this is my ability to mentor younger colleagues to assume leadership positions in professional bodies, both on the national and the international stage. In the inner recesses of my heart, I never had—and still do not have—any personal ambition to lead for financial rewards or recognition, but only to give service for the common good. This may explain my preference for the term 'backend personality' that I have used to describe my publicity- and camera-shy nature.

> **Reflective Break 24:** If you have yet to take on such a role, how would you rate your desire to be a leader in language education: Very High; High; Low; Very Low? Can you give reasons for your rating? And if you are already a leader in language education, what advice would you give to a teacher is new to those roles and responsibilities?

Christel Broady: Proactive and Reactive Reflection—Tools for Professional Growth

As a first-generation academician and professional, reflection and reflective practice are at the core of my professional development. Since I lacked academic and professional role models at home and in school, I had to seek out mentors and models of effective leadership practices. I felt that this outside view on the professional world privileged me because of the distance between those whom I observed and myself. I was able to acquire a keen understanding of the different domains of professional practices in distinctly different areas of government, private industry, academia, and a professional association.

In each professional domain, I was met by the challenge of understanding the specific rules of effective practices from others and developing my version of them. The way I pursued learning about them was to observe, ask questions, and reflect on what I noticed. During my experiences, I took copious notes and later organized these in ways such that I could look back at them as needed. I have maintained this habit of taking notes and collecting information to this day. In contrast to my early years of note-taking on paper, the task seems easy today because of the many tools digital technology offers. However, I was aware that my method of learning about leadership merely by observing others provided an incomplete picture. Still, in the days before the internet and easy access to endless information, I did not know how to close my information gap. Therefore, I often felt insecure and unsure of my leadership concepts.

Despite my self-doubt, I arrived in positions of leadership; I became the Chair of an academic department. Because of the lack of other resources and knowledge preparing me, I drew from my observations and insights and implemented what I discerned to be the best practices. I was aware, however, that I copied other leaders and that I had not developed my own leadership identity yet. Pellicer (2008) describes this experience well:

> Primarily, we all learn to function in various roles by emulating others whom we regard as being successful in those roles. We learn by doing what we have seen others do in a particular situation and making adjustments in our future behaviors based on trial and error. When we experience a new role for the first time, we have to be content with acting as we think a competent person would do in that particular role in that particular situation. (Pellicer, 2008, pp. 180–181)

Like all leaders, there were times where my leadership did not work as planned. In these cases, the experiences were the door to opportunities. I had to be open to acknowledging when things did not go well and taking inventory of them. Then, after identifying the facts, I had to analyze the reasons for failure and find solutions. I decided that this process had to be immediate and could not be postponed. Therefore, I decided to take notes of challenging situations. Once a week, I gathered my notes and, with the distance of being removed from the circumstances, looked at them with a fresh set of eyes. I analyzed what had led to the situations and reflected on possible consequences. I considered several possible scenarios for each case and decided whether any actions were needed or if it was better not to do anything. If an action was needed, I carefully developed a plan and put it in effect.

In my weekly reflections, I put much time into analyzing what I could do to make my unit run more smoothly. I had to admit to myself that I had significant shortcomings in the areas of data collection and management, data use, how to create surveys and how to interpret them, how to organize digital media and information, and share it with others. At times, this data management skill shortcoming was the cause of challenges. From attending accreditation meetings, I was aware that data are at the heart of good department leadership. Still, I had to admit to myself that I had never thought about a deliberate plan for gaining such skills. I had to acknowledge that I was intimidated by the reality of data-driven decision-making since I had no background in this area.

After acknowledging the problem, I had to consider how I could fix it. I had to develop a deliberate plan to overcome my apprehension towards the world of data. I began this process by seeking out resources that informed me more about the value of data use for effective administrative practices and for the ability to measure the overall effectiveness of operations. Having more information about the reasons for being an effective data manager helped me to seek out the much-needed training. Based on digital leadership training, I also learned to communicate more effectively with others in synchronous or asynchronous ways, which helped me to establish channels of communication, providing me with essential information for my reflective administrative planning.

In the process of my reflections, I pondered how the new and conventional communication channels could be useful to seek information from others to add more viewpoints to issues. To gain such insights, I began to use anonymous Google Forms to allow my department members to provide regular feedback to me. I also asked my colleagues how I could assist them in the improvement of their work. By continuing to do so, I signal to my colleagues that I accept the responsibility of assisting them in fulfilling their obligations and that I am committed to them and their needs. By seeking feedback, I also communicate that each person's success depends on the way they express their needs to others. I try to make them aware of their responsibility to reflect on their practices and to share with me what goes well and what needs improvement. This approach is described by Gallagher & Thordarson (2018, p. 43) as defining the 'true problem.'

As I have learned to be a more effective listener to others, I have gained the opportunity to reflect on how other participants in my unit contribute to a shared understanding of action. The practice of listening to others, valuing their input, and engaging in reflection about their reality makes it much easier for me to conceptualize change and be a better steward of the organization. I have also learned that my effective leadership depends on the willingness of my colleagues to share and contribute their opinions, for which I feel and express gratitude. I therefore agree with Max De Pree (2003), who states that 'the first responsibility of a leader is to define reality. The last one is to say thank you. In between the two, the leader must become a servant and a debtor' (p. 1).

Reflective Break 25: Christel refers to 'data-driven decision-making.' What do you think are some of the pros and cons of that kind of decision-making? Decision-making can also be experientially based. What do you think are some of the pros and cons of that kind of decision-making? In addition to data and experience, are there other forms of knowledge on which to base decision-making? If so, what are they and have you used any of those alternatives?

Leo Mercado: Looking at Oneself

Throughout my career, I have always been an avid promoter of reflective teaching practices. They have come to represent solid pillars for the professional development programs I have instituted in my leadership roles. Teacher-led workshops and other experience-sharing events, self-observation, peer observation, recording feedback sessions, teaching journals, academic focus groups, collaborative action planning, and a host of many other alternatives have, I believe, brought professional learning and a sense of engagement to many of the several thousand teachers I have had the privilege to serve over the years. I have always had a clear idea about what I hoped to accomplish, especially since the progressive implementation of large-scale, comprehensive professional development programs for teachers was also done with the goal of one day meeting the highest standards required by international accreditation agencies. I have always tried to look far ahead, focusing on the teachers' growth and learning from a strategic, long-term perspective. Yet, I have never had the chance to really think deeply about my own reflective practices, until now.

Human relationships are very important to me, most especially the ones I try to cultivate with my teachers and staff wherever I go. In the case of teachers, I have always tried to be there for them and asked the same of the coordinators and other language program administrators I have had the pleasure to work with as teammates. Yet, it can be easier said than done. Sometimes, we get so wrapped up in finishing tasks and meeting schedules, we do not have enough time to think about the significance of every action or decision we take, and how it may affect others. In fact, I have seen many a supervisor or coordinator get fixated on carrying out administrative duties and procedures, while forgetting to make time for something as simple but truly valuable as visiting the teachers' room or lounge to say hello. Consequently, it is possible that at times we may not be fully aware of how those we are supposed to serve may feel about us. Teachers are a special and most important case in point. In my experience, there are language program administrators that teachers love, those that they are relatively indifferent to, and those that are actively disliked. But we may not be aware of those feelings; worse yet, we may be entirely oblivious to the reasons for them, whether good or bad. The only way to develop those relationships is to foster open communication that encourages all stakeholders to ask questions, express their concerns, offer ideas, and request information. Then we need to reflect on what they are telling us, about ourselves and about how things are really going. Over time, we should strive to improve the quality and the quantity of effective communication taking place, which is most likely to succeed with input from teachers and other organizational stakeholders (Mercado, 2018).

We should also seek other ways to obtain the information we need, whether it be through surveys, questionnaires, discussion sessions, or some informal one-to-one, face-to-face time.

One time, I called an academic 'rap session,' which was a type of meeting aimed at discussing topics proposed by teachers, in response to reports that the teachers at one of the branches were upset over a new student satisfaction survey we had launched a couple of months before. When I arrived, some of them looked like they wanted to kill me! They seemed to be extremely upset, and I had no idea why they would feel that way. After a few minutes, things began to make sense. There was a particular question on the survey that teachers were getting negative responses to repeatedly, and it had to do with technology that the teachers were expected to use—but which had not been working at the branch for several months. That technological breakdown had not been reported, so the anxiety and anger began to build up until it reached a boiling point. It was negatively affecting the teachers' student feedback scores, which were eventually included as part of the teachers' formal appraisals. After full and frank discussion, I communicated my decision to review the survey and change that question. Fortunately, everyone appeared to be happy with that decision.

This one story—and there are countless others like it—taught me I that needed to reflect more often, looking at myself as a leader and thinking about the ways in which different decisions, actions, behaviors, and attitudes can lead to different results, ideally ones that are most likely to be welcomed by most people. As with teachers, benefits from individual reflection and consequent action on the part of a leader can be magnified through collaboration with others, which in the end serves the goals and objectives of an institution (Richards & Farrell, 2005). In this case, a seemingly imminent revolt turned into a friendly exchange of ideas and newly won respect for me.

One of my ideas was to develop a self-assessment checklist. It is based on an instrument I created for novice teachers who were asked to engage in self-observation at one of my former institutions (Mercado & Mann, 2014). As opposed to the teacher's instrument, which focused on classroom teaching and student behaviors, my chart focuses on the following:

(i)   Important decisions, with multiple slots for descriptions and my assessment of the outcomes

(ii) Significant interactions with other organizational stakeholders, with descriptions of what was discussed and its impact

(iii) Identification of challenges in terms of their impact on my work and the academic department's goals and objectives, along with how I dealt with those challenges

(iv) How the week went for me from an affective perspective

(v) How I would rate myself in terms of what I had accomplished versus what I had not done, or not done as well as I would have liked

(vi) A list of lessons learned.

This self-assessment instrument has proven to be an invaluable tool for me. Although it is very different from a teaching journal, it still resembles one in a way because it allows me to write about significant incidents and events that relate to my work, as well as my thoughts and feelings about those events. What I enjoy and find most helpful in this case is that I oblige myself to write about the leadership lessons I have learned. Much like a teaching journal does, my notes serve as a place to put the pieces of a jigsaw puzzle together, encouraging me to ask questions and find the answers so that the different pieces of my work that week can be brought together into a big picture (Bailey, Curtis, & Nunan, 2001).

> **Reflective Break 26:** Look again at Leo's six-part leadership 'self-assessment checklist.' If you are already in a leadership role, what items would you include on your checklist? Would you use any of Leo's items? If so which ones and why?

Andy Curtis: Seeing Ourselves as Others See Us

In 2001, Kathleen Bailey, David Nunan, and I published a book in the *Teacher Source* series (edited by Donald Freeman and published by Heinle & Heinle). The book, *Pursuing Professional Development: The Self as Source*, was written to help teachers, especially language teachers, understand and take part in different kinds of professional development activities. One of the opening book chapters is titled 'Reflective teaching: Looking closely.' The following chapters present the theories and practices of using teaching journals, case studies, action research, peer observation, team teaching, mentoring and coaching, teaching portfolios (Curtis, 1999; Curtis, 2017), and other ways of doing professional development. Each of the three of us took the lead on different chapters, and one of the chapters that I took the lead on was on using video, titled 'Seeing ourselves as others see us.' Even now, nearly 20 years later, that chapter stands out in my memory, as seeing myself on video is still a challenging experience. Have you ever seen a recording of yourself teaching? Most of the teachers I know have, and all of them describe the discomfort that comes with seeing and hearing ourselves on camera.

Interestingly, in legal English, the phrase 'in camera' means: 'in private, without the public, newspaper reporters, etc. being there' (*Cambridge Dictionary*), and one of the benefits of recording our teaching is that we can see the recording in private, without anyone else being around. That is, as long as we *choose* to make the recording rather than it being *required*. As with most teacher professional development activities, when we decide to engage in such activities, we put more into them and get more out of them than when those activities are imposed upon us. The same may be especially true for video recordings, because if the recording is required, then whoever required it will also want to see it, which relates to the differences between 'developmental' and 'judgmental' in terms of the purpose of the recording. For the purposes of RP, the recording needs to be self-initiated and developmental, so we can be free to act as 'naturally' as possible in the classroom, given that a camera is pointed at us (Curtis & Cheng, 1998).

In a piece for the Psychology section of the UK newspaper, *The Guardian*, Norwegian cognitive neuroscientist Dr Philip Jaekl wrote about 'The real reason the sound of your own voice makes you cringe' (Jaekl, 2018). He asked and answered: 'Does the sound of your own voice make you want to cover your ears? You are not alone.' There is even a phrase to describe that cringing reaction: 'voice confrontation,' studies of which have been published for more than 50 years. For example, of particular relevance to the work of language educators is Holzman, Berger, & Rousey's (1967) study, which found that bilingual students 'listening to their own voices in their native and later learned languages showed greater affective reactions, more speech disturbances, and more defensive negation to hearing their native speaking voices' (p. 423). Jaekl (2018) summarized the usual explanation for us cringing when we hear our recorded voices, i.e., because we hear our own voice inside our own head, via the bones of the inner ear, but only we hear our voice like that. Everybody else hears something different. He also referred to the work of other scientists who suggest that another reason might be pitch, and the fact that we often sound higher-pitched than we think we do. Whatever the reasons, the fact remains that, in recordings of ourselves, we do not look and sound the way we think we look and sound. But the good news is that this discomfort is what can make such recordings ideal for 'positive self-estrangement' as our immediate reaction, when we first see and hear ourselves on camera, is something along the lines of: 'That's not me. It looks and sounds something like me. But I don't look or sound like that in "real life".' Although that reaction is not, of course, an out-of-body experience, it is very much a 'that's somebody else' kind of experience, thereby creating some distance between Me, Myself, and I.

One way of dealing with that reaction is to allow some kind of acclimatization period, during which we do not attempt to take any notes about our teaching while viewing the recording, but instead just sit there and get used to how we look and sound when we are being recorded. It is also important that the recording not be a 'one-off,' but that recordings are made a number of times, so we can get used to the presence of a camera in the room. And it is not only the teacher who can be distracted by the presence of a recording device, but also the learners, so both parties need time to get used to the camera before anything resembling 'usual' behavior can take place. One of the biggest changes between when I first started recording my teaching, in the 1990s, and today, is in the technology. In her book, *Seeing Ourselves through Technology* (2014), Jill Rettberg wrote about *How We Use Selfies, Blogs and Wearable Devices to See and Shape Ourselves*, going all the way back to 1524, when the Italian painter known as 'Parmigianino' (Francesco Mazzola, 1503–1540) painted his *Self-Portrait in a Convex Mirror*. Needless to say, computer tablets, smart phones, and other devices have made recording easy and unobtrusive, as well as improving the sound and picture quality, which can help us more effectively reflect on what we and our learners are (not) doing and what is (not) happening in our classrooms.

Reflective Break 27: Have you ever seen a video recording of yourself teaching? If so, what did you learn about yourself, your teaching, and your learners from viewing that recording? If you have not yet done so, make a recording of yourself the next time you teach. Initially, seeing the recording may be a deeply discomforting experience! But if you keep watching and listening, you will learn some new things about yourself, your teaching, and your learners.

Marjorie Rosenberg: Reflecting Using NLP Techniques

Any answer to the question, 'What is reflective practice?' must include a number of factors. Perhaps the first one is time. When I began in the profession in the 1980s, I was a freelancer, both working at an adult education center and running courses for the center in companies. This meant not only traveling from one place to another, but also teaching 50-hour weeks. Adding on the time needed to prepare lessons, create activities, and simply pack up the wealth of materials needed for a day of work took all my time and energy. I was lucky, however, that my evening classes were held at a venue which had only a few classrooms and a cafe which stayed open when our classes were over. It soon became routine to sit with the other trainers at the end of the course and chat, usually about what we had done in class, what worked, what didn't work, what we felt we needed, etc. At the time I had not heard of the term 'reflective practice' but realize now that what we were doing was a way of reflecting on our practice. The ideas we exchanged, the support we gave each other, and the recounting of classroom stories to sympathetic ears was invaluable and greatly appreciated, something I was lucky to experience later in the form of staff rooms at both a teacher training institute in the UK and at tertiary educational institutions in Austria. This was especially interesting at the Language

Department of the University of Graz where there were teachers teaching different languages from a variety of countries and cultures, creating one of the most effective and fascinating opportunities for reflection that I have ever had. Having colleagues from a variety of backgrounds offered the opportunity to look at lessons from different points of view and discuss not only what we did in class but also what we could do differently the next time.

After a decade in the field, I was introduced to the concept of NLP (Neuro-Linguistic Programming) at a seminar I attended and in 1992 I became an NLP Practitioner. In the course we learned how to establish rapport by accepting others for who they are, how to set realistic goals, how to recognize different styles of learning, and how to work with timelines and reflect on the past, the present, and possible futures. I began holding teacher training sessions using the NLP techniques I learned in my initial training as well as the course with Michael Grinder, and teamed up with a colleague who was using NLP in an Austrian grammar school. I decided to continue my NLP training and in the mid-1990s completed both the NLP Master Practitioner and the NLP Trainer course at NLP University in California (now housed within the University of California, Santa Cruz), in addition to attending the above-mentioned course on NLP for teachers with Michael Grinder. One of the first eye-openers for me was discovering that most people tend to be visual, auditory, or kinesthetic learners. This gave me the chance to reflect on my own journey in language learning and helped me to put what I had discovered into practice. Once I was clear on the fact that learners processed and stored information differently, I began to change the way I was teaching and expanded my repertoire to include all my learners.

When I became more comfortable with the NLP techniques, I began to think about where I wanted my ELT career to go and began to see myself as a teacher, teacher trainer, writer, and leader. As supervision is an important part of reflection in NLP, I spent time with my colleague and worked through the 'Well-formed outcome' model of NLP with her, by reflecting carefully on each of the specific questions of the model. The questions include: Can you define the goal in positive terms? Is reaching the goal under your control? What resources do you need? When and where do you want to achieve the goal? What effect will it have on other aspects of your life? When will you take the first step? The last question includes what is called 'future pacing' by imagining oneself taking the first step towards an action, which led to my initial foray into a leadership role in ELT, namely joining the TEA (Teachers of English in Austria) committee, and a few years later becoming its Chair. Working with TEA prepared me for the challenge of joining the IATEFL BESIG (Business English Special Interest Group) committee and a year later becoming the committee's Coordinator.

What helped during some challenging committee meetings was looking back at the Disney strategy, which I had learned in my Master Practitioner NLP course. According to those who worked for Walt Disney, he had three different personalities—the 'realist,' the 'dreamer,' and the 'critic'—which he eventually merged to create the movies he is still famous for. Business experts looked at this model and realized that not everyone had all three of these personality elements, but that many people tended to exhibit one more than the others, which influenced how they responded in meetings. I realized I needed to take the time to think about this and reflect on our meetings, which helped me to see where my fellow Trustees on the Board of IATEFL fit into the model. Taking that approach made it easier to work with them and come to decisions we could all be happy about. Combined with that approach was looking at different beliefs people had, which often originated in their mental model of the world, and accepting that many of their actions came from deep-rooted beliefs. This was an important part of my reflection and helped me to move beyond the negative feelings brought up by someone with a different thinking pattern than I had, and to accept that their ideas and comments were simply their reality. Finding ways to combine these three personality types eventually led to ideas we could implement, as a Board of Trustees, but it was first necessary to reflect on what was going on in the meetings, and then plan on how to best deal with it when it happened.

Another area of my reflection dealt with communication. In NLP we learn that communication may come across differently to different people and our intentions do not always elicit the response we had hoped for. This led me back to the importance of rapport and the necessity to build rapport before, during, and after meetings. Finding ways to create a common goal that we could all work towards was, after all, the ultimate aim. I also became aware that asking others for advice could constitute a form of reflection, as other people see what we do differently than we see ourselves. I consciously asked for help from people I found difficult to deal with, and then reflected on what they told me. Their advice helped me enormously and I could feel within myself how my management skills improved from meeting to meeting, although it was always a challenge to put emotions aside and stay neutral.

Reflective Break 28: Marjorie identifies a number of different learning styles, such as visual, auditory, and kinesthetic (seeing, hearing, and touching). How would you describe your preferred learning styles? How do your preferred learning styles shape your preferred teaching styles?

Rosemary Orlando: Advocate, Reflect, Repeat

Reflection can be a highly personal undertaking and requires some discipline and time to get it right. When I first began engaging in this, I thought it meant to sit after class was finished and decide if I thought the lessons went well or not. If not, how could I improve next time? I came to realize reflective teaching is much more than that. Richards & Lockhart (1994) described the reflective approach to teaching as '...one in which teachers...collect data about teaching, examine their attitudes, beliefs, assumptions, and teaching practices, and use the information obtained as a basis for critical reflection about teaching' (p. 1). They went on to state that 'if teachers are actively involved in reflecting on what is happening in their own classrooms, they are in a position to discover whether there is a gap between what they teach and what their learners learn' (p. 4). As I started to better understand that teacher professional development evolved from more knowledge about one's own classroom practices, I began to see how important reflection is, not just as a classroom teacher but also as a professional educator and administrator. I now try to include the process of reflective teaching as part of my course responsibilities when teaching and share that process with the student teachers I work with both in the US and overseas.

As an administrator, including reflection in my day-to-day responsibilities seemed to take on the form of insomnia more than formal reflection! As I lay awake many a night thinking over the day's meetings, aggravations, problems, and other responsibilities, I started to realize I needed a deeper, more probing and systematic process. I needed to think about some of the challenges that go along with being in a leadership position. I was not writing down my thoughts as a practice and so I might not have been learning from my mistakes as I should have, or learning how to approach different people in different ways depending on their mood or disposition. Employees tend to bring their worries to work with them and some of them expect their bosses/supervisors to manage those problems too. Dealing with all the different personalities and personal problems of faculty and staff can be exhausting, and yet one must try and be motivating and supportive of all who work together within a department as well as in the rest of the institution. Being reflective helped me in my dealings with those I supervised as well as those who were above me in the chain of command and with whom I interacted.

One part of the job as a leader in English language education is to regularly explain what teaching English is all about and how it is a worthwhile and professional aspect of education within a department and university. I found that one of the challenges as a professor teaching in a university IEP and then again as an administrator was dealing with a type of elitism or underlying snobbery shown towards faculty teaching in the department that housed ESL classes. It was not always evident, but after being a faculty member for many years, I had experience with this and was not surprised when I could detect it in meetings or discussions surrounding our department. It was not everyone, of course, but as various supervisors came and went, I became aware of the subtle signs that perhaps our faculty and our curriculum were not considered to be on par with other programs at the university.

I can recall years ago approaching the former Dean of the School of Arts and Sciences, of which my department was a part, and explaining that I had submitted a proposal and hoped it would be accepted to present at the annual International TESOL Association convention. I was very fortunate over many years to have my proposals accepted by TESOL and I presented regularly at the annual convention. The Dean, who has long since retired, could be rather patronizing at times and said that faculty from other departments such as Sociology and Humanities submitted proposals to professional conferences that had very low acceptance rates, and that it was probably very easy for a proposal submitted to TESOL to be accepted since it was a different kind of field. I explained that the acceptance rate for TESOL was only about 25 percent, but her point had been made that it was not a 'real' conference. I was only too aware that it was an ongoing process to always be defending our field and explaining at meetings what we were all about, since others tried to define us as being of a rather simple nature. By engaging in RP and organizing my thoughts, I dealt with this challenge by calmly and effectively explaining again and again what my department did and who our teachers were in terms of professional education and engagement. They were not singing songs about the alphabet or simply teaching study skills. They were professionals who knew what they were doing to prepare the university students for further study as fulltime undergraduate and graduate students.

In addition to reading books and articles on this topic in the field of education, I often turn to the business world to see how they might deal with some of the same troubles and what solutions they offer. Very similar to education but written in more business-focused language, I found this information to be helpful:

> Spontaneous reflection is often stimulated by the nagging, unresolved problems or challenges that are a normal part of any manager's job. Reflection then progresses through four distinct stages: (a) articulation of a problem, (b) analysis of that problem, (c) formulation and testing of a tentative theory to explain the problem, and (d) action (or deciding whether to act). (Daudelin, 1996, pp. 39–40)

I have come to realize that being an effective leader in English language education requires intelligent inquiry, time, experience, reflective assessment, and an understanding of the culture of a particular institution. I have witnessed many leaders come and go when they refused to accept or understand some of these complex realities. Leadership roles are demanding and exhausting. Good leaders have a responsibility to seek out solitude to reflect, learn, improve their skills, and carry on. It is critical for success to learn from past or current work situations and adapt these lessons to new situations.

> **Reflective Break 29:** Rosemary refers to Richards & Lockhart's (1994) statement that 'if teachers are actively involved in reflecting on what is happening in their own classrooms, they are in a position to discover whether there is a gap between what they teach and what their learners learn' (p. 4). Such gaps are normal and natural, and perfect alignment is nearly impossible and extremely rare. So, what are some of the gaps between what you teach and what your students learn? How could those gaps be narrowed?

Rosa Aronson: Cultivating Your Internal Compass

In my position as Executive Director of the TESOL International Association, engaging in reflective practice was a critical component of my work, yet, as many leaders know, one of its most challenging aspects. Lack of time, competing priorities, emergencies, human resources issues, and conflict management, were among the obstacles I faced in my reflective practice. Lack of time is a very familiar challenge to any leader, especially in organizations that seek to address global issues, such as second/foreign language teaching and learning. I found that my best reflective time was early in the morning, when no one had arrived in the office yet. The hours between 6:00 and 8:00 AM became my reflective practice time. It started with driving the 40 minutes it took me to reach the office. At that time of the day, the notoriously bad traffic around the Washington DC area was usually quiet and allowed me to focus on the day ahead. That habit was not all about RP, but it did give me the alone space and time I needed as an introvert to prepare for the rest of the day. To my surprise (and delight) I discovered that the time spent on planes traveling from one city to another, or from one continent to another, as part of my duties, was an exceptional time to engage in reflective practice. Unable to sleep on long flights, I had uninterrupted time to think, analyze, and assess recent or future decisions and dilemmas. My writing was also more productive. I realized there was also something liberating about flying literally 'above' the reality of my day-to-day duties. The geographical distance created by traveling created a fertile ground for reflection.

As a leader and manager in an organization that was approaching 50 years of existence, I quickly became aware of the need to navigate two different approaches to the management of the TESOL Association as a professional organization. One was to honor and respect the organizational tradition and history, while the other was an urgent need to adapt to rapidly changing environments in society affecting the future of the TESOL Association. In my previous positions, I had experienced some of these challenges, but now, I felt them more intensely. The field of language education had become very different from when the organization was established. English as a second, new, foreign, or additional language was rapidly becoming a *lingua franca* across many countries and regions of the world. With this expansion, the TESOL Association, claiming to represent all related professionals (and even students) in that field, was becoming a complex, multilevel organization, with different—and sometimes competing—internal interests. By 2010, no fewer than 21 special interest groups (called Interest Sections) had formed within the organization, each wanting a share of the TESOL Association's resources. One of my roles was to manage the welfare of these member groups, all dedicated to the overall mission of TESOL but from different angles. By being an inclusive organization, we had welcomed and even invited these Interest Sections into the fold, whether their identity was central to the mission of the organization or not.

As Priya Parker states in her book *The Art of Gathering: How We Meet and Why It Matters*, 'It wasn't always the big-tent groups, being everything to everyone, that most attracted people. It was often the groups that were narrower and more specific' (2018, p. 18). If you subscribe to the idea that an association is a gathering of individuals holding the same ideals, then being clear on the specificity of your organization's purpose can clash with a culture of inclusivity, and such a culture had prevailed for a long time within the TESOL Association. That clash became a recurring challenge in many aspects of the management of the Association, from how to allocate limited resources to choosing the most significant policy issues to address. This dynamic required all leaders of the Association to make difficult choices, knowing that we would be subjected to the criticism that we were compromising the all-inclusive nature of the Association.

This particular challenge required me to reach beyond my own analysis and personal reflection. I was fortunate to cultivate a strong relationship with members of the Executive Committee, particularly the Presidents of the Association, in the form of regularly scheduled conversations and meetings. These leaders often became trusted advisors and provided a sounding board for the ideas, decisions, and challenges I encountered in my position. This connection was particularly valuable, as these leaders usually had a long history of engagement with the Association, and therefore offered useful insights and feedback. As leaders and managers in their own institutions or organizations, they knew the importance of engaging in RP and were often able to help me reflect on my own practice. I worked with seven presidents during my tenure at TESOL. Each one had a unique approach to leadership born of different cultural contexts and individual histories. Those conversations certainly enriched my reflective practice but, with annual elections, the revolving door of leadership also presented challenges to the continuity needed in organizational decision-making. Overall, however, this reflective strategy proved effective, as it called on me to adapt to new leaders and forced me to answer deep questions such as:

- Why had a certain initiative been undertaken?
- Was it still relevant and justified?
- Should the Association modify the current course of action?
- Was this initiative still aligned with the mission of the Association?

In the last few years of my tenure at the TESOL Association, I decided to personally invest in a professional coach. This strategy proved to be very effective in sustaining my reflective practice. This person had previously served as president in another (non-language related) educational association and filled the role of an objective observer, sounding board, and confidant, who helped me navigate the challenges I faced as a leader. I also valued feedback from my husband, who had served in an executive position, and although he could not be completely objective in his responses, he often helped me process and assess challenging events and situations in a way that helped me recalibrate those events in a positive and productive light. Finally, my long-standing yoga practice proved to be a beneficial strategy in meeting the challenges that we, as leaders, face in our reflective practice. This particular discipline delivers both physical and mental benefits. The habit of cultivating mindfulness lends itself well to the life of a leader. Whether you plan to serve in a leadership position or are already there, give yourself the gift of daily time and reflection. Set aside a time at the beginning or the end of your day to answer some of the questions suggested by Harry Kraemer (see my contribution to Chapter 2), to plan the day ahead, process the events of the day, or simply check in with yourself.

Reflective Break 30: Have you been in a situation like Rosa's, in which an organization's history and traditions can be an impediment to moving forward and making changes? If so, how were the two—the old and the new—reconciled? If they were not reconciled, what happened?

Deborah Healey: A System—and Leadership—Is More Than the Sum of Its Parts

Each leadership position I have held has been different, and in each, reflection has helped me see the larger picture—the system at work. At an Intensive English Program (IEP) at a state university in the US, I took on the role of technology coordinator initially in the mid-1980s. On the administrative computing side, I worked with a consultant to gather information about office record-keeping and reporting to create an automated student record-keeping system that would replace our ineffective paper-based system. I needed to reflect on and understand the overall goal of the system and how all of the pieces worked together. I developed a very strong sense of how important each element of the office was to the overall success of the institute, which was my first foray into systems thinking—seeing how each piece related to others to create the whole. On the educational computing side, my job was to train our teachers about using technology such as email and word-processing for their own personal and professional purposes and how to use educational software with students. I needed to understand what motivated each individual teacher and what would help the institute overall. Similarly, setting up a computer lab at our project in North Yemen required careful consideration of local resources (including crazy voltage swings) and interest in developing creative solutions.

After I returned from Yemen, I became Coordinator of Instruction for the institute and later Director. I had no great interest in being Director, especially during the Asian economic crisis. Finances were very tight in our self-supporting unit. The first year of my initial three-year term was spent trying to hold things together (very reactive) while searching for more ways to generate revenue, including grant writing (strategic and proactive). A cycle of trying a change, evaluating it, discussing it, then trying again helped us slowly get back on an even keel. My second three-year term was marked by the after-effects of the World Trade Center attacks on September 11, 2001: another drop in enrollment, followed by more recruiting, including rebuilding our contacts for short-term groups; marketing, including online; and grant-writing.

With reflection, I had become much more aware of the larger context in which the institute was operating and more attuned to how each member of the faculty and staff could be involved in recruiting and retaining students, as well as working on grants and short-term programs. We started feeling that we were doing quite well in achieving our overall goal of stability through multiple revenue streams, and I thought that I had a good grasp on the system in which we operated. External factors were international student mobility in general, sponsors and recruitment agents, the ebb and flow of currency values that affected affordability, and competition in the institute market. Internal factors included university politics, especially our relationship to our host department and school and Faculty Senate support; the excellent skill base of our instructors; a curriculum process that allowed for flexibility and stability; and the mixture of students, from near-zero proficiency to part-time university level, and from a wide range of countries. I could be proactive with systems thinking and the strategic leadership that it enabled, especially when I could make enough time for consistent reflection. For example, one day working at home most weeks was invaluable.

Within the TESOL International Association, I was the incoming Chair and Chair of the CALL-IS from 1990 to 1992. The Chair position required focused attention, especially leading up to and during the annual convention. I was more reactive than reflective most of the time; it was only after I left the Chair position that I was able to take a longer-term, more holistic view of how the CALL-IS operated within TESOL. Part of the short-term mindset is structural. Even though there is an incoming Chair year, the Chair position is significantly different in terms of demands and expectations. In 1994–1995, I became part of the TESOL Organizational Technology Task Force (OTTF) and the TESOL Technology in the Classroom Task Force (TCTF). In those task forces, a broad view of the role of technology in the organization and in ELT pedagogy, respectively, was required. In retrospect, both task forces were just a little too early; in another two years, the world wide web would change how organizations interacted internally and externally and open many new avenues for teaching and administrative functions. Still, we were looking as far ahead as we could, taking as much context into account as possible.

In 2014, after returning to teaching full time rather than being mired in administration, I ran for the TESOL Board of Directors and was elected. My previous experience with different TESOL Association entities and my administrative experience in the language institute were helpful in understanding Association-wide issues. Being on the Board, though, is different from other roles. I was reflecting on what I was doing and how it helped, but it took at least a year before I started consistently reading information and making decisions from the viewpoint of the Association as a whole. My perspective as a former Interest Section leader never disappeared, but I shifted to a systems view. I was finally, at least to some extent, using Farrell's process, reflecting on how philosophy, principles, and theory fit what I was doing and evaluating my actions in that larger framework. Having three years on the Board gave me the time I needed as well.

In 2019, I became President-elect of the TESOL International Association and part of TESOL's Executive Committee (ExCom), consisting of the President-elect,

President, Past President, and Executive Director. The ExCom holds an online meeting monthly to discuss Association issues with a focus on achieving strategic goals. Being part of the ExCom requires consistent systems thinking, looking at where the Association is, where it should be, and how it is getting there. I used reflection most of the time to consider how decisions fit with goals and strategies and how best to communicate with everyone involved. I became President of the Association in March 2019. As President, I had a strong role to play in guiding the Association and serving as a spokesperson. It was abundantly clear, though, that being president of a large, international member association like TESOL is more like being on the bridge of an ocean liner than piloting a speedboat.

The Executive Director is in charge of managing the Association and ensuring that progress toward goals is happening, as well as speaking on behalf of the Association. But there are no quick changes of course in an association with 15 staff members and whose 11,000 members are in over 150 countries. Nine professional councils and more than 20 different interest sections participate in governance. There are also 13 professional learning networks and about 120 external affiliates. Commercial sponsors help fund the annual conference (drawing around 5,000 people from all over the world), and government and other stakeholders are involved at a range of levels with an interest in what the Association chooses to do and say. All of the elements can affect outcomes; anyone can create at least a minor disruption. When I reflect on a change in the Association's governance structure five years ago that I participated in, I see that it is still setting off waves of effects that were not predictable when the change was instituted. The inability to fully predict or control change is the reality of an open system, but RP has helped me be creative in responding and moving forward.

> **Reflective Break 31:** Are you working in a language teaching organization that has experienced the kinds of changing fortunes that Deborah describes? If so, how did you and your organization adapt to those large-scale, external changes that were beyond your control?

Neil Anderson: Making My Thinking Visible

I engage in RP in three ways: thinking and analyzing my leadership; making my thinking visible through writing; and making my thinking visible through verbalizing my experiences with trusted colleagues. Each of these three ways of engaging in RP provides me with different perspectives on my growth and development as a leader and provides a way for me to *question my assumptions*. Thinking and analyzing my leadership is where I typically begin when I engage in RP. This quiet, solitary act allows me to sort out my thinking and begin to identify ways that my actions have been successful and ways to improve. Thinking and analyzing my leadership allows me to use the telescope, microscope, and kaleidoscope to examine my leadership experiences. I believe that I have increased in my capacity to engage in healthy self-assessment of my leadership through heightened metacognitive awareness and *questioning all assumptions*. I find that the proximity in time between my metacognitive engagement and RP to a leadership situation that I am processing is very important. The further the distance in time between my thinking and analysis of an event, the less effective I am.

One challenge that I face as I engage in thinking and analyzing my leadership and *questioning all assumptions* is to assure myself that my thinking is healthy and not superficial or hypercritical. In a previous publication (Anderson, 2012), I have written about the role of healthy self-assessment as being a central part of metacognitive awareness. I describe self-assessment as a continuum with superficial self-assessment on one end and hypercritical self-assessment on the other. At the center of the continuum is healthy self-assessment. When we are engaged in RP, we should assure ourselves that we are not *superficial* in the self-assessment of our actions. Superficial thinking and analysis are often reflected in a belief that our performance is nearly flawless. In these situations, we often *overestimate* our performance, which may be the result of our having underestimated the difficulty of the task we are engaged in. At the other end of the self-assessment continuum, we can fall into the trap of being *hypercritical* of our performance. We tell ourselves all the reasons why we believe we are not performing well. In these situations, we often *underestimate* our performance.

One thing that I do to assure myself that my *questioning of all assumptions* is neither superficial nor hypercritical is to ask myself, *What evidence do I have of my performance that leads me to the conclusions that I am drawing about myself as a leader?* This question allows me examine evidence of leadership abilities and to avoid being superficial and/or hypercritical. A second way that I engage in RP is through writing, which is an extremely valuable tool for me as a teacher, learner, and a leader. After I have engaged in RP through careful thought and after I have *questioned all assumptions* through my thinking, I find it advantageous to put my thoughts into writing. There are two ways in which I use writing in my application of RP. First, by keeping a leadership journal and second, by writing for publication. Bailey, Curtis, & Nunan (2001) is one source that provided an introduction for me on the advantages of keeping a reflective journal. The audience for our teaching journal can be ourselves, or we can write with the intention of sharing our writing with others. I prefer to use the journaling experience as a private time to write. I can articulate in writing all of the things that I have carefully analyzed and thought about. I can articulate the assumptions that influence my thinking. I can pose questions about my assumptions. The journal allows me to provide the evidence that supports or refutes my assumptions.

In addition to keeping a private, reflective journal, I find that writing for publication is an additional way for me to engage in RP. When I received the invitation from Andy Curtis, the editor of this book, to contribute to each chapter, I was initially hesitant because of other projects that I am currently involved with. As I write this, I am also involved in co-editing a book entitled *Professionalizing Your English Language Teaching* with Christine Coombe and Lauren Stephenson (2020). I have found that both writing projects have allowed me to be fully immersed in RP as I write about improving my leadership skills, and as I write and edit chapters with my colleagues on professionalizing English language teaching. The reason that writing for publication is a valuable RP tool is because such writing moves beyond being a tool for individual use to making thinking visible for others. You might also find these two types of writing activities enhance your reflections on your leadership.

Finally, after carefully thinking about and analyzing a leadership situation and then capturing my thoughts through writing, I sometimes find it valuable to talk to a family member and/or a trusted colleague. In each of the positions that I have held over the past 40 years, I have always had at least one trusted individual with whom I could open up and discuss my thinking. These individuals have served as role models in multiple ways and thus I have come to trust and appreciate insights that they can provide me. They have often helped me discover hidden assumptions that are influencing my actions.

In a recent conversation with a trusted colleague, we discussed a meeting that we had attended together. I had been extremely bold and verbal in the meeting about my position on the subject we were discussing. I immediately recognized that not everyone in the room shared my persepctive. Rather than pause and assess the situation, I continued to be bold and somewhat agressive. As a result I offended colleagues in the meeting. It was not until the next day that my trusted colleague helped me realize where I had failed to pause and to recognize that my assumptions were driving my thinking, rather than a more rational point of view taking into consideration the viewpoints of others. This was a growth opportunity for me as a leader. Thus, thinking about and analyzing leadership, writing in a leadership journal and for publication, and/or verbalizing my thinking with a trusted colleague are three ways that I have consistently engaged in RP over my career as a TESOL leader and professional. These tools have provided ways to heighten my awareness of my practices, allowed me to *question all assumptions*, and identified things that I want to continue doing and things that I want to improve.

Kathleen M. Bailey: How Do I Engage in Reflective Practice?

I have often systematically and actively engaged in reflective teaching (e.g., by keeping a teaching journal—see Bailey, 2001), but I have not been as systematically reflective in my non-teaching leadership roles. While I have engaged in all five of the dimensions described in Chapter 2, as a reflective teacher, my reflective practice as a leader has been much more limited and sporadic. It has typically involved only rapid reflection, repair, and review, though I have been influenced by what I've read about leadership from time to time. In that sense, we could say that I have occasionally practiced reflective leadership at the level of retheorizing and reformulating, but until recently, those efforts have been infrequent and short-lived. (Recently, I was able to teach a seminar on leadership in language education for the first time, and as a result, I engaged much more systematically in reflective practice about leadership.)

Earlier on, in my Question Two response, I shared the five dimensions of reflective teaching put forth by Zeichner & Liston (1996): (1) rapid reflection, (2) repair (both types of reflection-*in*-action), (3) review, (4) research, and (5) retheorizing and reformulating (the last three being types of reflection-*on*-action). At this point, as a result of writing these RTL accounts, I feel compelled to suggest a sixth type: *rumination.* The literal meaning of the verb *to ruminate* refers to animals such as cattle, deer, buffalo, and camels chewing their cud as part of the digestive process. Collectively, these animals are called *ruminants.* They regurgitate some previously ingested food (the 'cud') and chew on it over a period of time. The figurative meaning of *ruminate* is to contemplate or ponder, but I believe it has connections of revisiting an old or unresolved issue as well.

As part of reflective practice, I would place rumination after *review* (reflection-*on*-action at a given point of time) and before *research* (reflection-*on*-action over time involving systematic data collection). Rumination as a reflective practice would fall between these two dimensions, because (unlike review) it takes place over time but (unlike research) it doesn't entail data collection. It is just repeatedly returning to an issue and rethinking the options. As I was re-reading the draft of my Question Three response, I was surprised to see that Zeichner & Liston (1996) actually use the word *rumination* in their definition of reflective practice. I hope that, as is the case with the ruminants, the process of ruminating will eventually prove to be useful (informative if not nutritious).

These days much of my reflective practice as a leader involves simply communicating with my team members and with trusted colleagues, via email or text or phone or face-to-face communication. In this sense, Zeichner & Liston's (1996) category of review is convenient and often helpful to me. Focusing specifically on leadership, I try to practice both reflection-*in*-action and reflection-*on*-action (Schön, 1983). For example, while I am working with my team members, I usually explain not only what I need them to do, but also why I am asking for their help. That is, I want to distribute tasks appropriately and equitably, but I also want to be clear about the reasons for doing so.

Part of my current work involves academic and career advising for my graduate students—all of whom are language teachers in training, though they come to our MA program with a wide range of experience. In this context, much of my work with the trainees is done through email, but the most important interactions occur either face-to-face or synchronously through Zoom. In those contexts, I have learned a few valuable lessons by reflecting on successes, difficulties, and outright failures as an advisor—a role which I see as an important part of leadership. One lesson is that I need to constantly work to be a good listener. When time is short and students are troubled, the tendency (or at least *my* tendency) is to rush in and try to solve the problem, whatever it may be. But my view of a problem may not coincide with the student's view of the problem, so I have learned to try to slow down, to listen carefully, to articulate my understanding of the issues, and to identify the student's goals instead of rushing ahead to do what I assume needs to be done.

Another lesson is that after listening to the student's view of the issue and expressing my understanding of that view, I ask the student what he or she wants from our interaction. I literally ask the question, 'What do you want from me?' I don't ask it in the accusing, self-protective, vehement assertion with strong contrastive stress on the word *me*. That utterance would tell my interlocutor there is nothing I can do. Instead, I ask this question quietly with an emphasis on the word *you*—literally asking the student what it is he or she thinks I can do. The answer is sometimes surprising. Often my advisees will have thought out their own solutions, and just want to know if what they plan to do will meet the program's requirements. At other times, students have said they just want to talk to someone. On other occasions, upon hearing the students' goals, I have actually been able to suggest reasonable plans of actions to help them achieve those goals. A key issue here is achieving a balance among control, efficiency, and effectiveness. In order to achieve that balance, a leader has to trust. For me personally (and, I would venture to say, for many other leaders too) it is a huge challenge to trust other people to do what needs to be done (1) on time and (2) to my standards.

The leadership challenge I will share with you later, in my Question Four response, involves a decision of whether or not to delegate, or to force someone to carry out his responsibility, or to do the job myself. It also raises the issue of time management, which is a matter of some concern to many leaders (see, e.g., Christison & Stoller, 1997; Murphy & Brogan, 2008).

> **Reflective Break 33:** Like many of the other Question Two and Question Three responses, Kathleen's response highlights the importance of trust, in her case, in relation to trusting those to whom you have delegated some responsibility. What do you think are some of the ways in which trust between teachers, colleagues, and students can be built up? And what are some of the ways in which that trust can be damaged or broken?

> **Reflective Break 34:** Having read the responses above, and if you already engage in RP, how would you answer these three questions: How do you engage in RP? What are some of the challenges you have faced when engaging in RP? How did/do you address/meet those challenges?

REFERENCES

Alverson, H. (1994). *Semantics and Experience: Universal Metaphors of Time in English, Mandarin, Hindi, and Sesotho.* Baltimore, MD: Johns Hopkins University Press.

Anderson, N. J. (2012). Metacognition: Awareness in language learning. In S. Mercer, S. Ryan, & M. Williams (Eds.), *Psychology for Language Learning: Insights from Research, Theory and Pedagogy* (pp. 169–187). Basingstoke, UK: Palgrave. https://doi.org/10.1057/9781137032829_12

Bailey, K. M. (2001). What my EFL students taught me. *The PAC Journal, 1*(1), 7–31.

Bailey, K. M., Curtis, A., & Nunan, D. (2001). *Pursuing Professional Development: The Self as Source.* Boston, MA: Heinle & Heinle.

Baş, G. (2020). Teacher beliefs about educational reforms: A metaphor analysis. *International Journal of Educational Reform, 30*(1), 21–28. https://doi.org/10.1177/1056787920933352

Christison, M., & Stoller, F. L. (1997). Time management principles for language program administrators. In M. Christison & F. L. Stoller (Eds.), *A Handbook for Language Program Administrators* (pp. 235–250). Palm Springs, CA: Alta Books.

Colton, A. B., & Sparks-Langer, G. M. (2016). A conceptual framework to guide the development of teacher reflection and decision making. *Journal of Teacher Education, 44*(1), 45–54. https://doi.org/10.1177/0022487193044001007

Coombe, C., Anderson, N. J., & Stephenson, L. (2020). *Professionalizing Your English Language Teaching*. Cham, Switzerland: Springer. https://doi.org/10.1007/978-3-030-34762-8

Curtis, A. (1999). Connecting the hand, the head and the heart: Reflective practice and action research in the classroom. *The Language Teacher, 23*(6), 19. http://jalt-publications.org/tlt/articles/2543-connecting-hand-head-and-heart-reflective-practice-and-action-research-classroom

Curtis, A. (2017). Portfolios. In *The TESOL Encyclopedia of English Language Teaching* (Eds. J. Liontas & M. DelliCarpini). Wiley Online Library. https://doi.org/10.1002/9781118784235.eelt0326

Curtis, A., & Cheng, L. (1998). Video as a source of data in classroom observation. *Thai TESOL Bulletin, 11*(2), 31–38.

Daudelin, M. W. (1996, January). Learning from experience through reflection. *Organizational Dynamics* (pp. 36–48). Retrieved from: questsandsummits.com/Learning

De Pree, M. (2003). *Leading without Power: Finding Hope in Serving Community*. New York, NY: John Wiley & Sons.

Evans, V. (2013). *Language and Time: A Cognitive Linguistics Approach*. New York, NY: Cambridge University Press. https://doi.org/10.1017/CBO9781107340626

Gallagher, A., & Thordarson, K. (2018). *Design Thinking for School Leaders: Five Roles and Mindsets That Ignite Positive Change*. Alexandria, VA: ASCD.

Hapgood, O. C. (1892). *School Needlework: A Course of Study in Sewing Designed for Use in Schools*. Massachusetts: Ginn & Co.

Holzman, P. S., Berger, A., & Rousey, C. (1967). Voice confrontation: A bilingual study. *Journal of Personality and Social Psychology, 7*(4), 423–428. https://doi.org/10.1037/h0025233

In camera. (n.d.). *Cambridge Dictionary*. Retrieved from: https://dictionary.cambridge.org/dictionary/english/in-camera

Jaekl, P. (July 12, 2018). The real reason the sound of your own voice makes you cringe. *The Guardian*. Retrieved from: https://www.theguardian.com/science/2018/jul/12/the-real-reason-the-sound-of-your-own-voice-makes-you-cringe

Lakoff, G., & Johnson, M. (1980). *Metaphors We Live By*. Chicago, IL: University of Chicago Press.

Mercado, L. A. (2018). Supervision of early-career teachers. In *The TESOL Encyclopedia of English Language Teaching* (Eds. J. I. Liontas, T. and M. DelliCarpini). https://doi.org/10.1002/9781118784235.eelt0140

Mercado, L. A., & Mann, S. (2014). Mentoring for teacher evaluation & development. In H. Donaghue & A. Howard (Eds.), *Teacher Evaluation in Second Language Education* (pp. 35–54). London, UK: Bloomsbury Publishing.

Murphy, T. & Brogan, J. (2008). The active professional's balancing act: Time and self-management. In C. Coombe, M. L. McCloskey, L. Stephenson, & N. J. Anderson (Eds.), *Leadership in English Language Teaching and Learning* (pp. 79–89). Ann Arbor, MI: The University of Michigan Press.

Njika, J. A. (2020). Exploring pre-service teachers' perception of interactional activities in lesson planning. *English Language Teaching, 13*(3), 92–99. https://doi.org/10.5539/elt.v13n3p92

Palmer, P. J. (1998/2017). *The Courage to Teach: Exploring the Inner Landscape of a Teacher's Life*. San Francisco, CA: Jossey-Bass.

Parker, P. (2018). *The Art of Gathering: How We Meet and Why It Matters*. New York, NY: Riverhead Books.

Pellicer, L. O. (2008). *Caring Enough to Lead: How Reflective Practice Leads to Moral Leadership*. Thousand Oaks: Corwin Press.

Rettberg, J. W. (2014). *Seeing Ourselves through Technology: How We Use Selfies, Blogs and Wearable Devices to See and Shape Ourselves*. Hampshire, UK: Palgrave Macmillan. https://doi.org/10.1057/9781137476661

Richards, J., & Farrell, T. S. C. (2005). *Professional Development for Language Teachers*. New York, NY: Cambridge University Press. https://doi.org/10.1017/CBO9780511667237

Richards, J. C., & Lockhart, C. (1994). *Reflective Teaching in Second Language Classrooms*. Cambridge, UK: Cambridge University Press. https://doi.org/10.1017/CBO9780511667169

Schön, D. A. (1983). *The Reflective Practitioner: How Professionals Think in Action*. New York, NY: Basic Books.

Sempowicz, T., & Hudson, P. (2012). Mentoring pre-service teachers' reflective practices towards producing teaching outcomes. *International Journal of Evidence Based Coaching and Mentoring, 10*(2), 52–64.

Turner, T., Lucas, M., & Whitaker, C. (2018). *Peer Supervision in Coaching and Mentoring: A Versatile Guide for Reflective Practice*. Oxford, UK: Routledge. https://doi.org/10.4324/9781315162454

Walsh, S., & Mann, S. (2015). Doing reflective practice: a data-led way forward. *ELT Journal, 69*(4), 351–362. https://doi.org/10.1093/elt/ccv018

Westberg, J. (2001). Helping learners become reflective practitioners. *Education for Health: Change in Learning & Practice, 14*(2), 313–321. https://doi.org/10.1080/13576280110059237

Zeichner, K. M., & Liston, D. P. (1996). *Reflective Teaching: An Introduction*. Mahwah, NJ: Lawrence Erlbaum.

ABOUT THE AUTHORS

Dr Okon Effiong is a lecturer in the Foundation Programme, Qatar University. He is a member of the TESOL Board of Directors and served on its Nominating Committee, Diversity & Inclusion Committee, as Chair-elect of the EFL-Interest Section. He is founder and Past President of Africa TESOL. He was the President of Qatar TESOL.

Dr Christel Broady is Chair of graduate programs, as well as Director of the ESL Program at Georgetown College, Kentucky, USA. An international leader, Christel has served in many leadership roles with TESOL International and affiliates. Her list of domestic and international publications, keynotes, presentations, and awards is extensive.

Leo Mercado has been in the field for more than 25 years, making contributions as a director of studies, e-learning and proficiency testing specialist, project leader, author, and academic entrepreneur. Based in Atlanta, Georgia, USA, he has also successfully led two international accreditation processes, as well as large-scale, nationwide projects at the Ministry of Education level.

Andy Curtis (PhD) is a Professor in the Graduate School of Education at Anaheim University. From 2015 to 2016, he served as the 50th President of the TESOL International Association. He has (co)authored and (co)edited 200 articles, book chapters and books, he has presented to 50,000 language educators in 100 countries, and his work has been read by 100,000 language educators in 150 countries. He is based in Ontario, Canada, from where he works with learning organizations worldwide.

Marjorie Rosenberg has been involved in tertiary and adult education in Austria since 1981. She is an active teacher trainer, conference presenter, and ELT author. Marjorie served as IATEFL President from 2015 to 2017. Her latest project is working as a mentor through a program designed by EVE and Africa TESOL.

Dr Rosemary DePetro Orlando is a Professor at Southern New Hampshire University, USA. She regularly travels to Vietnam National University in Hanoi to teach MS TEFL courses in a university partnership degree program. As a language teacher educator, Rosemary regularly presents at national and international English Language Teaching conferences worldwide.

Dr Rosa Aronson is the Interim Executive Director of the TESOL International Association in Alexandria, Virginia, USA. Her career in Education began as an EFL teacher in France and continued in the USA in professional educational organizations. She has served as an English Language Specialist focusing on organizational leadership. She holds a PhD in Social Foundations of Education from the University of Virginia.

Dr Deborah Healey was the 2020–2021 President of the Board of Directors of the TESOL International Association. An online and face-to-face teacher educator, she writes and presents extensively internationally (Africa, Asia, Latin America, Europe, US) on appropriate use of technology in language teaching. Her doctorate is in Computers in Education.

Dr Neil J. Anderson has been actively involved in leadership roles and reflective practice for over 40 years. He currently teaches at Brigham Young University–Hawaii, USA. Neil served as President of the TESOL International Association for 2001–2002. He received the prestigious James Alatis Award from TESOL in 2014.

Dr Kathleen M. Bailey is a Professor of Applied Linguistics at the Middlebury Institute of International Studies at Monterey (MIIS), California, USA. She completed her MA and her doctorate at the University of California at Los Angeles. Her research interests include teacher education, language assessment, and the teaching of listening and speaking.

Chapter 4

Reflecting on Leadership Challenges in Language Education

INTRODUCTION TO THE
QUESTION FOUR RESPONSES

Andy Curtis

The fourth and final set of prompts for the RTLs was: Think of a leadership challenge you faced some time ago. Describe that challenge, how you met/coped with that challenge, and what advice you would give someone facing a similar challenge. Or, instead of giving advice, you can describe what you would do differently, with the benefit of experience and hindsight, if you faced a similar challenge today. As noted in the introductions to Question Two and Question Three, re-presenting the same question in different forms is a common and effective technique used by teachers, perhaps especially language teachers. The first version of the Question Four prompt is focused on giving advice, and the second on describing how the RTL would respond differently had they to face a similar leadership challenge at present. But the difference between those two focuses is really only the difference between giving advice to others and giving advice to oneself.

As with the previous questions in this book, although each of the 12 recurring themes below could form the basis of an entire chapter, for clarity and brevity, the RTLs were asked to keep their Question Four responses to just a few pages each. In spite of that constraint, the richness of these Question Four accounts lend themselves to the discovery of many additional LiLE learning points. Also, in order to set those themes/learning points in the broader context, a brief summary of some of the publicly accessible works on RP, on leadership, and on LiLE is presented. The summary not only gives details of the work that has been carried out in those three areas, but lays a foundation on which a deeper understanding of those themes can be built. The summary also highlights the lack of material available that connects RP and leadership and that links leadership and language education, and gives the readers useful points of reference if they would like to know more about RP, leadership, and/or LiLE.

Reflective Practice, Leadership, and Leadership in Language Education

In the introductory overview to this book, we looked briefly at some of the articles on reflective leadership, and at some of the books that reflect on the lives of leaders in business and politics, but which use the term 'reflection' in the most general, thinking-about, looking-back-historically sense. However, books that are about RP and leadership appear to have been few and far between. One of the first books to bring together RP and leadership appears to be Carl Ashbaugh and Katherine Kasten's *Educational Leadership: Case Studies for Reflective Practice*, published in the early 1990s. The brief case studies, which are as short as a single page and no more than a few pages each, are grouped into four areas: Culture and Climate; Program Design and Delivery; Resources; and External Groups—all of which are topics that appear, directly and indirectly, in these RTL accounts. Another work which also takes a case-study approach to connecting RP and leadership is Deborah Welch's 1998 book, *Reflective Leadership: The Stories of Five Leaders Successfully Building Generative Organizational Culture*. Based on those five narratives, Welch found that all the leaders were disciplined in setting time aside for their RP, and engaged in RP regularly and frequently. Also, each leader used different kinds of RP, combined with intuitive thinking, to critically examine their assumptions, while supplementing their own individual RP with group-based collective RP when making difficult decisions.

One of the other relatively rare books bringing together RP and leadership is *Caring Enough to Lead: How Reflective Practice Leads to Moral Leadership* by Leonard Pellicer, first published in 1999. Pellicer spent 35 years in educational leadership, during which time he served as a high school teacher, a principal, a professor of education leadership, and a dean of a college of education. *Caring Enough to Lead* is based on 20 questions (each of which is a chapter heading) starting with: What is a leader? Why should leaders care about caring? What do I care about? and ending with: Why do I choose to lead? What do leaders owe to those who follow them? Can I care enough to be my own best friend? Pellicer (2008) explained his use of questions based on his belief that 'it is not the responsibility of the leader to dispense the right answers, but rather ... to identify the right question ... then everyone working together can seek the answers to those questions that are *most relevant to them at a particular time under a prevailing set of circumstances*' (p. 4, emphasis added)—i.e., a leader must ask the right question, at the right time, in the right place.

The last part of Pellicer's explanation of his focus on asking the right question, rather than on finding the right answer, highlights the importance of context, which is another one of the recurring themes in the accounts in this book. There are examples in all of the four main chapters of this book in which the authors make it clear that what worked for them, in their particular setting and situation, at that time, would not necessarily work for another teacher leader in another time and place. Although context is generally agreed to be important in education—perhaps especially in language education because of the relationships between language and culture—context is generally given short shrift. Instead, context tends to fade into the background, as part of the landscape or scenery, while its critical importance often remains woefully under-appreciated (Curtis, 2015; Curtis, 2017). Therefore, an essential aspect of RP and LiLE is awareness of the context within which the teaching, learning, and reflection are taking place. Reiterating the importance of both question-asking and context-awareness, Pellicer (2008) states: 'struggling together with the critical questions will do more to define a successful organization than all the answers in the world ... asking critical questions *in the right ways at appropriate times* helps to define one who is caring enough to lead' (p. 4, emphasis added). From Pellicer's point of view, asking critical, context-sensitive questions is a key aspect of being an effective, caring leader, which is one reason that the four main chapters of this book are based on question prompts.

Reflective Break 35: How would you describe the characteristics and personality traits of a caring education leader? If you are in a leadership role, which of those traits describe you and which do not?

Another one of the few books that bring together RP and leadership is Leslie Pereira's largely autobiographical account titled *Between the 'Real' and the 'Imagined': Professional Learning, Reflective Practice and Transformational Leadership* (2008), which describes 'a few defining moments ... five or six ... from forty-two years of experience ... [which] provide very clear indications of my interests and concerns' (p. 20). Based on those 42 years of experience, and the six stories told, Pereira identifies five themes, which are listed as: 'On authority, On knowing, On teaching, On control and On technique' (p. 20). As we saw in Questions One, Two, and Three, the interests and concerns of the RTLs in this book overlap with those of Pereira (2008), and as we will see in the Question Four responses, the leadership challenges faced by many of the contributors have also been 'defining moments' in their personal-professional lives.

> **Reflective Break 36:** Why do you think there are so few books that connect RP and leadership, and even fewer books on LiLE? If you are in a leadership role, have you written about your experiences? If you are in a leadership role, but you have *not* written about your experiences, what has stopped you from doing so?

Given the conspicuous scarcity of books on RP and leadership in the last 30 years, one might assume that there has been little literature on leadership itself. However, that is not the case. In the first nine months of 2020, between January and September, approximately 170 books (in English) on leadership were published (leadershipnow.com)—that equates to a new book on leadership published *every other day*, week after week, month after month. Of those 170 news books on leadership, only one referred to reflection in its title—Marcia Reynold's *Coach the Person, Not the Problem: A Guide to Using Reflective Inquiry* (2020). Echoing Pellicer's (2008) focus on posing the right questions rather than finding the right answers, Reynolds (2020) explains that 'Questions seek answers; inquiry provides insight' (p. i). Reynolds also presents the formula: 'Reflective statements + questions = reflective inquiry' (p. ii), and reiterating Pellicer's point, states that 'Pairing reflective statements with questions frees the coach of the weight of finding the perfect/best/right question' (p. ii).

With such mountains of leadership literature piling up by the day, the lack of books on RP and leadership is puzzling and problematic. In the stampede to tell people how to lead—30 of the 170 new leadership books published between January and September 2020 were titled 'How to ....' (leadershipnow.com) (see, for example, Rubenstein, 2020; Rakowich, 2020; Smith & Ashby, 2020)—the importance of stepping back and reflecting on what one is doing as a leader appears to have been at best overlooked, and at worst, lost. (Likewise, between January and October 2021, approximately 200 new books on leadership were published, leadershipnow.com.) On the one hand, that lack of texts connecting RP and leadership is disappointing and a cause for concern. But, on the other hand, for language educators going into leadership, they can distinguish themselves from other leaders simply by being reflective practitioners. And they can distinguish themselves even more by reading about the reflections of others in LiLE roles, which may eventually lead to them writing about and sharing their own LiLE reflections.

In many ways, the field of Nursing Management has been at the forefront of RP in leadership. For example, in 2010, the *Journal of Nursing Management* (*JNM*) published a 140-page, 14-article special issue on Reflective Leadership. To the best of my knowledge, none of the Language Education journals have published a special issue on that topic. In the introduction to the *JNM* special issue, the guest editor and professor of nursing, Melanie Jasper, explained that she had assumed, initially, that 'the notion of "reflective leadership" was well-documented and thus well-understood ... But, as preparation for the issue progressed ... it became increasingly obvious that reflective leadership is something everyone has heard about, and indeed may practice, but actually is poorly articulated within the literature' (Jasper, 2010, p. 351). What Jasper found instead were 'examples of the execution of reflective leadership, or perhaps interpretations of what it might be, but there is little to be found that identifies the features of the concept, nor provides measures of how it could be assessed' (p. 351).

Many of the articles in the *JNM* special issue were reports on midwifery and working with new mothers, but one of the articles most relevant to education was a case study of a small consulting company that worked for the UK government, reporting directly to the Houses of Parliament (Joyce, 2010, p. 419). Based on interviews and observation, Joyce concluded: 'Understanding the context in which the leader exercises power and influence is crucial ... Indeed, many *failures of leadership* may be linked with misperceptions on the part of staff and the failure of the leader to *recognize the context* within which actions will be understood' (Joyce, 2010, p. 423, emphases added). That finding of Joyce's reiterates the point made above, about the critical importance of understanding the context, as every situation is different. Joyce also notes that 'From self-awareness comes self-management' (p. 421), that 'the positive impact of coaching stems from the empathy and rapport that a leader establishes with employees' (p. 421), and that 'Powerful leaders may be more likely to delegate and to acknowledge the expertise of their staff' (p. 422). All of those leadership traits—contextual understanding, self-awareness, empathetic coaching, and delegating—are highlighted in a number of the Question Four responses.

By its very nature—and perhaps even by definition—RP is 'critical', in the sense of asking difficult questions that make us uncomfortable, such as: What went wrong in that lesson today? Or on the positive flip-side: Why did that lesson go so much better today than when I've taught it before? However, some writers have highlighted the criticality aspect of RP in relation to leadership. For example, in order to learn as much as possible from her first time being a principal in a K-12 USA accredited international school somewhere in South America (the country is not revealed), Christine Cunningham (2012) adapted Stephen Brookfield's (1995) Critical Reflective Practice approach to create what she refers to as Critically Reflective Leadership. Brookfield started by reminding us why we became teachers in the first place: 'Every good teacher wants to change the world for the better' (Brookfield, 1995, p. 1). He also referred to 'narrative disclosure' (p. 3) by which he meant providing 'examples from my life that illustrate points I'm making' (p. 2)—which is the basis of all of the accounts presented in this book. However, Brookfield warned that such disclosure can be misconstrued as arrogance, self-importance, and/or self-indulgence, although his reason for using narrative disclosure is that 'students across the years have told me that this captures their attention and helps them understand a new concept' (p. 2). It is possible that we, as a species, may be in some ways hard-wired for narrative, as the phrase 'Once up a time' appears to exist in some form in all human languages, and it appears that human civilizations throughout history have told stories (Mendoza, 2015).

Not wanting to appear selfish in any of the ways Brookfield described may be one reason why RP and LiLE are so rarely brought together—we cannot reflect on the experiences of other teachers because we are not them! The most or best we can do is to listen closely and carefully to those teachers' accounts, while sympathizing and empathizing—but their experiences are theirs and theirs alone. Therefore, RP is inherently 'self-centered' but not in the self-absorbed way that Brookfield identifies. Rather, RP aims for a deeper understanding of our feelings and thoughts, words and actions, and how those interact with and impact on those around us: the learners, other teachers, and others in our teaching-learning context, such as education administrators and parents. Brookfield defined Critical Reflective Practice as: 'quite simply, the sustained and intentional process of identifying and checking the accuracy and validity of our teaching assumptions' (1995, p. 3). In spite of Brookfield's use of 'quite simply,' there is nothing simple about what he described, which is a complex, cyclical process that is constant and continuous.

> **Reflective Break 37:** Brookfield (1995) used the term 'narrative disclosure', which is really just a fancy way of referring to story-telling. Do you use story-telling in your language classroom? If so, what are those stories about, and what points are you making when you tell those stories in class?

To return to the challenges faced by Cunningham (2012), she starts with a familiar refrain, stating that she 'had no formal training for the leadership role to which I was promoted' (p. 46)—which is one of the most commonly recurring themes in the RTL accounts in this book. Cunningham also found that, although 'Critical Reflective Practice (CRP) has a proven reputation as a method for teacher-researchers in K-12 classrooms ... there have been few published examples of this method being used to document school leaders' work-based practice' (p. 49), and concluded that 'more Critically Reflective Leadership research needs to be undertaken to provide a body of literature about high stakes decision-making by school leaders' (p. 49). In addition, in relation to one of the conspicuous absences mentioned in the Introduction to this book—the lack of leaders in language education who write about their leadership experiences—Cunningham too found that 'there have been too few [school] principals who have written about their practice in a critically reflective manner' (p. 47). That scarcity of LiLE writings is unfortunate, as such writings could be extremely useful in LiLE initial training and ongoing professional development.

The disconnect between published writings on RP and leadership has been highlighted above. However, that disconnect also exists between published work, i.e., work that is publicly accessible, on language education and leadership. Some years ago, I wrote in an article referring to a 'gap' in language education: 'Books in our field on leadership and management are relatively rare, compared with books on methodology in TESOL, and compared with books on leadership and management in other fields, such as health care' (Curtis, 2013). In that article, I briefly introduced four of the (very) few books about leadership in language education. The first is *A Handbook for Language Program Administrators*, edited by MaryAnn Christison and Fredricka Stoller, first published in 1997. Although somewhat dated now, the 350-page, five-part, 21-chapter *Handbook* covers a great deal of useful ground, including chapters on transitioning from being a language teacher to being a language program administrator, dealing with personnel matters, time management, etc. That *Handbook* was followed by *From Teacher to Manager: Managing Language Teaching Organization*, written by Ron White and colleagues (White, Hockley, van der Horst Jansen, & Laughner, 2008), with most of the chapters focused on management rather than leadership—for example, financial, academic, and project management. Two books that did focus more on leadership than management in language education are *Leadership in English Language Teaching and Learning* (Coombe, McCloskey, Stephenson, & Anderson, 2008) and *Leadership in English Language Education: Theoretical Foundations and Practical Skills for Changing Times* (Christison & Murray, 2009). Again, both books are edited collections of useful and helpful chapters written by experienced leaders in language education, although only one of the total of 34 chapters in the two books discusses RP in relation to LiLE (Curtis, 2009).

Reflective Break 38: Before you read further, having read Chapters 1, 2, and 3, what do you think might be some of the recurring themes, or leadership learning points, that emerge from these accounts?

Twelve Recurring Themes Emerging from the RTLs' Reflections on Leadership Challenges

1. Embracing the Fear

Feel the Fear and Do it Anyway was the original title of the best-selling self-help book by Susan Jeffers (1938–2012) first published in 1987. Twenty years later, by 2007, the book's title had grown and expanded to *Feel the Fear and Do It Anyway: Dynamic Techniques for Turning Fear, Indecision and Anger into Power, Action and Love* (Jeffers, 2007). More recently, in the same vein, is Ruth Soukup's equally long-titled *Do It Scared: Finding the Courage to Face Your Fears, Overcome Adversity and Create a Life You Love* (2019). In her book, Soukup describes seven of what she refers to as 'fear archetypes': the procrastinator, rule-follower, people-pleaser, outcast, self-doubter, excuse-maker, and pessimist. Leaving aside the highly lucrative overcoming-fears self-help market, the fact of fear—or the fear factor—can be a powerful inhibitor but also an effective motivator in education (Kaufman, 2016). As a number of the Question Four responses show, many of these RTLs were afraid—for example, they feared making mistakes, making 'bad' decisions, being rejected by their peers, etc. Different leaders feared different things, and experienced self-doubt in different areas, but one thing they all had in common was gradually overcoming and moving past those fears.

2. Staying Focused, Staying Open

One of the most comprehensive international studies of leadership behavior looked at the effectiveness of leaders in 24 countries, including China, India, Russia, and the USA (House et al., 2014). The researchers 'conceptualized and measured nine cultural dimensions' (p. 12), paying particular attention to the work of Geert Hofstede (1928–2020) (1980, 1991) and others in the field of intercultural workplace studies. One of those nine cultural dimensions they called 'Future Orientation' (p. 12), which they defined as 'The extent to which individuals engage (and should engage) in future-oriented behaviors such as planning, investing in the future, and delaying gratification' (p. 12). As teachers, planning and preparing courses and curricula are some of the most time-consuming aspects of our work. However, planning at the organizational and institutional levels is not the same as lesson-planning, although there are some overlaps, for example, setting goals (such as learning outcomes and organizational outcomes). Another leadership challenge in this area, which comes up in several of the accounts in Question Four, is how to balance the forward-focused aspects of leadership in language education with the need to—at the same time—focus on what is happening now and in the immediate future, as much of what happens later is the result of decisions made earlier.

3. Making Mistakes and Avoiding Uncertainty

One of the other nine cultural dimensions of leadership measured by House et al. (2014) is 'Uncertainty Avoidance': 'The greater the desire to avoid uncertainty, the more people will seek orderliness, consistency, structure, formal procedures and laws to cover situations in their daily lives' (p. 13). Although all of those things sought are necessary and important in any organization or institution, one of the natural tendencies that comes through in the Question Four responses is the desire to avoid making mistakes, and one way of doing that is to avoid uncertainty. As noted in the introduction/overview, the Irish poet and playwright Oscar Wilde gave us the line: 'Experience is the name every one gives to their mistakes,' which clearly and concisely expresses how important mistake-making is in learning. Indeed, as language teachers, we reassure our learners that it is okay to make mistakes in our classroom, and some of us even encourage mistake-making as an important part of language learning. However, two key caveats are: (1) Learn something from the mistakes you make, so that you (2) Do not make the same mistake repeatedly. Connecting the Fear Factor to this theme, it is perfectly normal to not want to make mistakes, especially in front of our peers, but we need to remember the line credited to Albert Einstein (1879–1955): Anyone who has never made a mistake has never tried anything new.

4. Being an Outsider

The French daily newspaper, *Le Monde*, ranked Albert Camus' (1913–1960) 1942 novel *L'Étranger* (in English, *The Stranger*) as number one on its list of 100 books of the 20th century. Things do not end well for the main character in *L'Étranger*, the French-Algerian called Meursault, but in real life, most of the RTLs in this book have been outsiders of one kind of another at some time or another. However, all of us have found ways of weaving those negative experiences of being 'strangers in a strange land' into the fabric of who we are, as teachers, as learners, and as leaders, in ways which make us better rather than bitter. In some cases, we have been outsiders because of our gender, skin-color, place of birth, our first language(s) or first culture(s), and in other ways as well (Curtis & Romney, 2006; Curtis, 2018). There is no end to the ways in which we 'other' each other, choosing to focus on our differences rather than our commonalties, egged on by self-serving leaders for their own political and financial gain. That tendency, like our instinctual making of assumptions, does not make us 'bad' people—it simply makes us 'people', perhaps programed to fear those who are unlike us. Not Alike = Do Not Like. Different = Dangerous. We are now living through times of rising linguistic and cultural nationalism (Perkins, 2020), when being different can put us in danger. Hopefully, these times shall pass, but in the meantime, leaders in language education should embrace whatever it is that may make them 'outsiders' or 'strangers.'

5. Working with Coaches and Mentors

Reflecting, coaching, and mentoring were the subject of a 2013 study by Betty Zan and Mary Donegan-Ritter which looked at how those three sets of practices could enhance teacher-child interactions in a year-long education program. Zan & Donegan-Ritter used peer coaching, mentoring, video-based self-reflection, and bimonthly workshops, and found that 'There were significant increases in four dimensions related to behavior management, productivity, language modeling and quality of feedback' (2013, p. 93). In terms of the relationships between the theories and the practices of developing leaders in language education, Julie Gray (2018) notes: 'Over the last two decades there has been a shift in principal preparation programs from a theory-to-practice approach to a knowledge-to-practice approach' (p. 2). Another one of the recurring themes in these Question Four accounts is the critical difference a coach and/or a mentor can make—critical in the sense of being essential, but also in the sense of offering constructive critical feedback that helps with leadership development (Farrell, 2001). As Bailey, Curtis, & Nunan (2001) pointed out, although the two terms—coaching and mentoring—are often used synonymously or interchangeably, there are some important differences, the main one being that coaches are often at the same stage in their professional development as their coaching partner, whereas mentors are usually more experienced than their mentees.

6. Leading and Managing Change and Innovation

As all of the Question Four responses show, managing and leading innovation and change are an inevitable aspect of being a leader in language education. In 2005, Alan Waters and Maria Vilches wrote that: 'As a steady stream of recent papers indicates, ELT curriculum reform projects are *not always as successful as they might be*' (p. 117, emphasis added). It is possible that Waters & Vilches were being diplomatic and discreet in the phrasing of that statement, and in the same way, they later state that: '*there seems to have been something of a failure* ... to learn and successfully apply the lessons of innovation theory and practice, both from outside the

ELT field ... and from within it' (p. 118, emphasis added). To use the same kind of language as that employed by Waters & Vilches, the situation regarding the lack of successful change and innovation may not have advanced all that much in the 15-plus years since their study was published. One of the many lessons learned by the RTLs in this book is that change and innovation are not the same thing—change can be random, unplanned, and negative, whereas innovation is planned, purposeful, and positive. Another lesson is: Expect resistance to whatever change it is you are trying to bring about, as resistance is a problematic and unhelpful but nonetheless normal and natural response to change.

7. Building Trust

Perhaps one of the most important ingredients in any lasting relationship is trust, and many of the Question Four responses illustrate the critical importance of being able to trust and being able to build trust, whether in educational (Bien-Gund & Elrowmeim, 2019), business (Nicholas, 1993; Caldwell & Jeane, 2007), or governmental (Carnevale, 1995) settings. The first person who needs to be trusted is oneself. As discussed above, if we do not trust ourselves, we may become fearful of making mistakes and we may try to avoid uncertainty—to the detriment of our leadership. Once we have built up trust in ourselves, we can start to trust others, who will, in turn, start to trust us. As language teachers, we sometimes see this in our classrooms, when there comes a point in the lesson where the learners want to take the lesson in a different direction to the one the teacher had in mind when they carefully crafted their lesson plan. In that moment, the teacher has to decide whether to trust the students enough to let them lead the rest of the lesson. But trusting means giving up some control, and as some of these Question Four accounts show, although building trust can take a long time, the trust can be quickly and easily damaged if we do not take good care of our professional relationships.

8. Changing Places

A different kind of change to that discussed under Point 6 above is the changing of roles and relationships, as a number of the RTLs in this book have experienced. In some cases, the RTL started off as a junior co-worker, then was promoted above their peers, and eventually found themself in a leadership role. If each of those changes happens at a different institution, there may be less tension, as someone who is new to an organization does not carry with them the same institutional memory or history. But when one is promoted into leadership roles within the organization where one started, especially if those promotions happen relatively quickly, then tensions can arise between one's leadership self and one's colleagues who were formerly peers and co-workers. Studies have shown that relationships between those in leadership roles and those who report to them are critical in creating positive, productive workplaces (Conn, 1990; Arnau-Sabatés & Gilligan, 2020). Therefore, one of the challenges described in some of these Question Four accounts is how to maintain positive professional relationships with staff who used to be our peers but who are now in a subordinate role, in hierarchical institutional structures. One way of re-creating and re-orientating those workplace relations is to build trust, as discussed under Point 7, and by being consistent and transparent in leadership decision-making.

9. Becoming Thick-Skinned

Being criticized and receiving constructive criticism are not the same thing, with the former usually being seen as negative, while the latter is seen more positively. However, the dividing line between those two is thin and easily crossed, as some of the accounts in Question Four show. For example, if someone says, 'Don't take this personally,' but you are the only other person in the room at the time, then it can be difficult not to take it personally, and not to go into some sort of defensive mode as part of our instinctive self-protection strategies. In Deborah Bright's book, *The Truth Doesn't Have to Hurt: How to Use Criticism to Strengthen Relationships, Improve Performance, and Promote Change* (2014), she explains that: 'being on the receiving end of criticism and having to give criticism rank among the top ten most stress-producing challenges in the workplace' (p. 3). Bright is also critical of organizations 'not educating people in the effective use of criticism,' which she describes as 'a major oversight' (p. 16). In English, the expression 'to be thick-skinned' is used to describe someone who does not feel hurt or get upset in response to criticism, and it may be necessary for anyone going into leadership in language education to develop a thick skin, although that can be difficult if the teacher making that transition is more used to being welcomed and positively received.

10. Challenging Assumptions

In the earlier discussion of the Question Two descriptions of what RP means to these RTLs, the importance of challenging assumptions—our own and others'—was highlighted. That is not to say that all assumptions are bad. For example, in *Permission to Speak Freely: How the Best Leaders Cultivate a Culture of Candor* (2017) Doug Crandall and Matt Kincaid advise the reader to 'assume positive intent' (p. 73), which is similar to the idea of giving someone the benefit of the doubt, by not assuming that they are negatively motivated. It may, for example, be possible for someone to propose a solution to a problem that is entirely unworkable, but their intent may nonetheless have been to try to help, not to deliberately make matters worse. Therefore, it is essential that RTLs become aware of the assumptions they are making. Again, that does not mean we should not make assumptions—that would be impossible anyway, as all decision-making involves some assumption-making, as noted in previous parts of this book. The point is to be aware of and limit the number of assumptions we make. We should also be aware of exactly what our assumptions are based on—for example, are they based on data, evidence, and proof, or based on feeling, thoughts, and opinions?

11. Letting Go

'Letting go' could refer to a number of the points above, from letting go of our fears and self-doubt to letting go of our assumptions. But here, we are referring to the challenges of delegation, which entails letting go of our desire to be in charge and in control. Clearly, there is also an element of trust, as we need to trust those to whom we delegate tasks to complete correctly and efficiently. However, delegating requires us to distinguish between someone else getting the job done, and someone else doing it *the way we would have done it*. People do things differently, and those different ways are not necessarily better or worse—just different. This kind of letting go has long been recognized as a challenge. For example, *The Art of Delegating* was first published more than 50 years ago, in 1965. Written by Neely Gardner and John Davis, the slim volume proposed answers to four main questions: What is delegation? (p. 1); When do you delegate? (p. 21); How do you delegate? (p. 40); To whom do you delegate? (p. 69). The answer is: It depends, on a wide range of contextual variables, such as the time frames, the tasks, the knowledge, skills, and abilities of those to whom tasks are being delegated, etc. The most important thing is for leaders to practice stepping back and letting go.

12. Keeping a Sense of Humor

By listing this as the 12th and last of the recurring themes in the Question Four responses, I risk giving the impression that this is the least important. It is not. On the contrary, keeping a sense humor may be a very helpful coping skill, for teachers and for leaders (Baldoni, 2020). For example, Mark Safferstone (1999) reported on a number of studies of workplace humor, including a 'methodologically robust study of 115 managers and their 322 subordinates in a large Canadian financial institution' carried out by Avolio, Howell, & Sosik (1999), who found that 'the use of humor was significantly and positively related to individual and work unit performance' (p. 103). Avolio et al. (1999) also reported that 'managers with active leadership styles were more likely to use humor than those that were more removed from their subordinates' (p. 103). However, having a sense of humor does not mean telling jokes, laughing a lot, or making fun of others. But as some of these Question Four responses show, being able to see the lighter side of difficult workplace situations, especially not taking ourselves so seriously—no matter how seriously we take our work—can be good for our mental health. Often, it is our ego that prevents us from seeing the potential humor in a situation, therefore, to have a sense of humor about ourselves is one way of diminishing the negative impact of our ego.

Reflective Break 39: Reflective Break 38 asked you to anticipate what you thought might be some of the recurring or leadership learning points that emerged from the Question Four responses. How does your before-reading list compare with the 12 points above?

Reflective Break 40: Choose one or two of the 12 themes above that you read with particular interest. What was it about those particular themes that made them especially relevant to you and your context?

THE QUESTION FOUR RESPONSES

Okon Effiong, Christel Broady, Leo Mercado, Andy Curtis,
Marjorie Rosenberg, Rosemary Orlando, Rosa Aronson,
Deborah Healey, Neil Anderson, and Kathleen M. Bailey

Just to recap, the RTLs were asked to 'Think of a leadership challenge you faced some time ago. Describe that challenge, how you met/coped with that challenge, and what advice you would give someone facing a similar challenge. Or, instead of giving advice, you can describe what you would do differently now, with the benefit of experience and hindsight, if you faced a similar challenge today.' And the RTLs were asked to anonymize their accounts, and to keep each of their LiLE 'mini case studies' to just a few pages.

Okon Effiong: Steering Africa TESOL on Course

I can confidently say that prior to my involvement with professional bodies, the only aspect of leadership I had ever experienced had been within the confines of the classroom and I had never conceived of leading any group of individuals outside that domain. The idea of pursuing a leadership pathway never crossed my mind and having found myself in a leadership position, my first challenge was financial. The expectation was that the Association leaders would attend annual conventions, hold meetings, and contribute to building the Association. I was studying full-time and self-funding my doctorate program, which made it financially challenging to attend any international conferences. All the leaders I knew in the Association were earning salaries and could even secure funding from their institutions to attend conventions. I had to continue to work long nights to save up for every TESOL convention until 2012 when I received one of their International Participant's Awards. That same year, I started work and so attending the annual conventions became easier financially. The financial challenge was also met as a result of the excellent support I received from my institution in Qatar, and attending conventions went from being a financial strain to being a pleasure.

My other challenge was self-concept or self-doubt. I wondered how I could make positive contributions to such a huge global organization that I was new to, especially coming from a Science background into the TESOL field. Holding a leadership position in an organization where I assumed rightly or wrongly that I had little knowledge of its modus operandi was a petrifying experience, and working with committee members who had been members of the Association for 20 or more years and seemed to know so much compounded my fears. In spite of all these fears, I was determined to learn and I did. As the saying goes, a journey of a thousand miles begins with a step, and I had already taken a few, so there was no going back. The steeper the learning curve became the more I hung on, and the journey continues to this day.

I never lost sight of the fact that it was my desire to bring Africa into the mainstream of the work of the Association which served as a precursor to the leadership experiences I had later in the Association and in Qatar TESOL. While serving as the Chair of the Diversity Committee, I shared with the Executive Committee my vision of forming a continental body that would bring English language teachers in Africa under one umbrella. Once I had their backing, I decided to reach out to the African affiliates to explore possibilities. By 2014, the number of affiliates had grown and when I emailed ten affiliate leaders in Africa about the idea of forming a continental body, I received positive response from four of them: Sudan, Senegal, Cameroon, and Rwanda. True to form, there was the usual pessimism from the

African leaders because typically any idea that emanates from outside Africa should bring with it some dollars. Even at this conception stage, I received inquiries from some teachers in Africa on what financial support was available to attend conferences in Europe or America. The moment I responded to say the new body had not a single dollar to support teachers to attend conferences outside Africa, that effectively killed their interest.

Living and working outside Africa was problematic in the sense that if I had to run an association from outside the continent, getting people to buy into the idea would not be easy. Some may even have misconstrued my intention. There were doubts on my ability to understand the local context having spent two decades away from Africa, and how I could possibly operate effectively from the Middle East. It was my belief that having teachers who were resident in Africa to run the new body might give it the desired lift. In 2015, I was leading Qatar TESOL and serving the TESOL International Association, and with my finger in so many pies, I opted to serve as the liaison officer of the continental body, to network with entities outside the continent and to elicit their support. In addition, there were technical challenges. For example, hosting online meetings was near impossible due to poor connectivity or the cost of maintaining such technology by teachers whose pay barely met their daily needs. Making international calls by any volunteer teacher in Africa was also out of the question due to the prohibitive cost; hence, communication became a major issue. But I refused to give up.

Compared to established associations with established headquarters, Africa TESOL existed only in my mind. Without the physical infrastructure, it was challenging to run a new body. Depending solely on online operation would have been an option if there were not so many technological challenges in the continent. The next question was where to register the association as a non-profit organization, open a bank account, and fix membership dues with which to run the association. Without the funds to rent a building and recruit a single secretariat staff member, it was impossible to situate the secretariat in any country. However, a close friend and colleague in Qatar who believed in the vision suggested his home country, Sudan, as a base. Though he too was living and working outside Africa he had sufficient influence in his national teachers' association to get their members to support the new body in principle. His country was thus chosen to be the place where the secretariat would be set up. However, credit card transactions in the country were not possible and the international clearinghouses had embargoed foreign currency transactions and transfers. This was a major hindrance to processing future membership dues, and still remains a problem today, as we are yet to have an African country as the headquarters of Africa TESOL. Also, it is of course understandable that if individuals are struggling to pay bills and fees for their wards with their meagre salaries, any extra time they may have in a day must be used to generate additional income to support their family, so they cannot afford to spend time on 'thankless' volunteer tasks like association work.

> **Reflective Break 41:** Volunteering, for example to serve on language education organization committees and boards, can be an effective way to gain valuable leadership experience. However, as Okon points out, such volunteer work can be a 'thankless' task, that also generates little or no additional income. Do you volunteer on a language education committee or board of any kind? If you do, what is it that you bring to that volunteer service, and what do you learn from it?

I liaised with my colleague and friend in Qatar to get the project off the ground. He provided the launch pad with his national association and in February 2016, Africa TESOL was formally launched in Sudan with its first international conference. Both of us are outside Africa, and to minimize criticisms from teachers in Africa, we assigned ourselves roles that would not interfere with the daily running of the association. I was the liaison officer collaborating with entities outside Africa while my friend served as the newsletter editor. Individuals from the four associations who responded positively were the initial steering committee members. This committee had the mandate to chart the future of the new body. The membership of the committee comprised mostly Africa-based teachers, except for the two of us. We held our inaugural conference in Sudan with three past presidents of the TESOL International Association in attendance. The conference was a good start, the local association contributed to its success, and my confidence was high. Although the local officers worked hard to host our first conference, the expectation was that the spirit would permeate the new body and thereafter continue to keep the vision alive. Regrettably, for a whole year, the steering committee only existed on paper and the nominated officers made no effort to reach out to language teacher associations in the continent.

Africa TESOL was becoming moribund in its first year, but I was not going to let my dream die in its infancy. My colleague and I continued to keep the dream alive by planning our second conference in East Africa. Both of us liaised with the Rwanda association to host the second conference. Although we had a constitution with the role for each office clearly specified, it was impossible for only two committed individuals to grow the association. We both tried to rescue the situation at our second conference in Kigali, Rwanda. Rather than conduct an election, we agreed that it was better to ask volunteers to join the new steering committee with each individual submitting a one-year plan of action or presenting an outline of the contributions they would make to the growth of the association. I became Africa TESOL's President in 2017, with my friend as the Vice President. Once again, I found myself in a leadership position of a continental association. I had no intention to preside for long, because I felt the association would benefit more from having individuals living in the continent, who better understood the context, running it. However, at our third convention in Dakar, Senegal, where I had hoped to rotate off, the general assembly voted for me to continue for another year. I thus served as President for two years, and at our fourth convention in 2019 in Abuja, Nigeria, I became Past President and the close friend and colleague who had served as Vice President for two years assumed the presidency.

We now have a very vibrant Board with committed members who reside in Africa. We intend to coach and mentor more colleagues in Africa to be future leaders while those of us outside the continent can play advisory roles and seek collaboration with international entities. At the international level, having served TESOL at the Diversity Committee and Interest Section levels, my ambition grew and I am now serving on its Board of Directors (2020–2023). I had made two consecutive and unsuccessful election attempts to run for the Board. However, a big part of leadership is not giving up, so I will continue my journey.

Reflective Break 42: Okon writes about the difficulties of being a leader from a distance. As a result of the Covid-19 global pandemic, more people have been working online than ever before. Do you work online, and if so, what are some of the challenges of working at a distance? Have there been any unexpected advantages to working from afar?

Christel Broady: Professional Challenges—An Opportunity to Become a Better Leader

Each leader can list instances when, despite their best effort, things go wrong. It is the way leaders react to such situations that either makes them stronger or weakens them. If leaders encounter a problem or a pushback from others, they can respond from a place of power and shut down any discussion. Likely, the result will negatively impact relationships and create a loss of collaborative space for all. The other choice is to get to the bottom of an issue, to find out what went wrong, to acknowledge failure, to learn from it, and to engage in change. As an employee in a new country, I still relied heavily on observations of others and on taking my cues from them. Often, I was unaware of how to find resources. I did not speak the language of leadership, and thus, I was often unable to ask the right questions. In short, I was ill-equipped to determine my leadership formation deliberately. This lack of awareness was the root of the defeat I experienced when I assumed my first leadership position in my professional organization.

Some 15 years ago, a TESOL Interest Section leader asked if they could nominate me as a Chair-elect. I agreed to be on the ballot and, to my surprise, was elected. At the first official meeting, at the next annual convention, I found out that no leader was present. Everyone in the group knew about this since there had been a listserv for our group that had many exchanges before the meeting. In the listserv communication, both of the leaders had conveyed that they could not attend the convention because of emergencies. Apparently, in the exchanges, I had been tasked with taking on the responsibilities of the two absent leaders. Unfortunately, I was unaware of the listserv and, thus, unaware of what had been communicated. At the meeting, all the members expected my leadership. However, I sat at the table with nothing in my hands and nothing to say. I felt deflated, ashamed, and unprofessional. I already had many self-doubts when I agreed to be nominated. And now, in my first leadership experience in my professional organization, I failed. At that moment, I was tempted to give up and to resign from my role.

In my hotel room, I tried to analyze what had gone wrong. I was elected and carried the responsibility for the role I agreed to fill, and I had to learn the ropes. I did not know where to start. Then, I had an idea. I asked around and tried to find leaders in the same type of groups. I had them pointed out to me during the convention and asked them how they prepared for and carried out their responsibilities. Fortunately, my conversation partners were gracious and shared their time and insights. My mindset changed from focusing on the initial negative experience to looking at the leadership role as a positive opportunity. As stated by Jon Gordon (2017): 'Failure is a big part of your path to success. It is not your enemy. It is your partner in growth. It does not define you. It refines you' (p. 173).

I learned about an entire onboarding process that was offered to new leaders. There had been new leader meetings, training, and mentorship opportunities. Materials were distributed, and action plans were shared. I also learned that each group had its bylaws, procedures, definitions for roles, responsibilities for each elected officer, and an entire library of documents. And, importantly, I learned that there was a specific meeting during the conference for first-time leaders like me. I entered the main meeting and was introduced as the leader of my group. Leaders from other groups initiated collaboration on projects like joint sessions at the next convention. This large meeting made me feel part of the organization. Staying in touch with other leaders after the convention and opening communication channels helped me to acquire the necessary skills, and I will be forever indebted to the peers who mentored me.

Now that I knew what to look for and where to find information, I spent much time on catching up with all of the information that I needed. I was able to ask the right questions of the right people, which was key. Before the next convention, I was caught up and prepared for stepping into the role of Chair. I planned some activities to help mend relationships and to gain my group's trust. I also learned that my detailed and purposeful preparation of the meeting afforded me the space to listen to others more purposefully and to hear their concerns more clearly. I was proud that I could use my time during the meeting to help build a community.

> **Reflective Break 43:** Christel writes: 'I did not speak the language of leadership.' What does the language of leadership sound like to you? Can you give some examples of positive, effective leadership language? And can you give some examples of poor, ineffective leadership language?

Many years later, when I was nominated and then elected as a board member of the TESOL International Association, I drew on my first leadership experience of an elected association office. I made sure that immediately after being elected, I established channels of communication with other board members. I participated in the shared communication space, carefully reviewed all materials, policies, and other relevant publications multiple times. I made sure that I understood my roles and my responsibilities. As I studied all of the materials, I identified the questions I had and asked senior board members for clarification. Also, I sought outside professional development opportunities and materials to learn about non-profit board member practices, and pitfalls to avoid. I carefully collected my resources and referred to them as needed. As always, it can be a monumental task to assume a new leadership role, compounded by a new language, a new culture, and a new organization. Preparing for such a position takes time and effort. However, once the responsibilities start, every minute of preparation pays off. Knowledge and preparation allow leaders to get to know each person better and to build relationships. Additionally, prepared leaders have the luxury of being better listeners since discussion points make more sense.

In the end, the dreadful first leadership debacle made me a better leader in the future. More importantly, it made me a committed life-long mentor of emergent leaders in the organization. At this point in my life, and based on my past newbie experiences, I try to identify young professionals with leadership potential and encourage them to consider becoming leaders. And, as I was, they are often surprised when another professional can see leadership potential in them that they may not yet see in themselves. I encourage emergent leaders not to be shy about asking questions and to identify what they need to know *before* they decide to take on a leadership role. I encourage them to attend leadership training, and I share with them the fact that becoming and being a leader is hard work that requires major commitments of time and resources.

Most importantly, I can share my personal experience of how rewarding leadership is, as leaders have the opportunity to shape the future of their profession and to be a voice for other members who may 'invisible.' As Pellicer (2008) states, 'authentic leaders are people who do what they do because of a genuine desire to make things better for others. The fact that a personal sacrifice might be required does not stop them. Simply stated, caring enough to lead' (p. viii). Therefore, I am grateful for my first experience, in spite of how disappointing and disheartening it was. It shaped me into who I am today: a prepared leader who is committed to creating community, who represents other professionals in board decision-making processes, and who can contribute to a stronger professional organization for all.

As I reflect upon my long journey to leadership, I am again reminded of how lucky I was, as a teenager, and as a young woman, not to have had a prescribed path laid out for me, with the usual conditioning for behavior and aspirations. I had the opportunity to construct my own path to professional success and leadership. I transitioned from observing others, trying to be like them, and, thus, role-playing, to becoming an authentic leader. I consider myself even luckier never to have lost my authentic self from the time of poverty and the life of limited educational and professional opportunities. Today, I still carry the same values in me that I had as a child: a fierce commitment to creating opportunities for all people. I will never stop advocating for equal opportunities for all and for having respect for everyone, including for those who are different, such as visible and invisible minorities. The dignity of every person must be preserved and each must be seen in terms of what they can contribute to the world, even if what they do seems small in comparison to what others can do.

> **Reflective Break 44:** Christel highlights the importance of being an active listener. How would you rate your listening skills: Excellent; Very Good; Good; OK; Poor? If your listening skills are at the high end of the scale, how did you develop those skills to that high level? And if your listening skills are at the lower end, what could you do to improve those skills?

Leo Mercado: Flying through the Turbulence

As a leader in language education for more than 25 years, I have encountered innumerable challenges along the way. Some were complex but manageable, while others were truly daunting and tested my mental fortitude. In fact, a couple of them even made me think about leaving the field altogether. Yet, despite the enormity of some of the trials and tribulations, I am still here today. Reflecting on these experiences, it would be difficult for me to look back on a single challenge to write about as having stood out the most. Rather, I will refer to two examples of issues that posed significant challenges and risks at critical times during my career. One of the biggest challenges I have ever had to face was when I became Academic Director for the first time. Although I had held other leadership positions before, this role was one in which I was responsible for the success or failure of the entire academic program, with equal accountability for the people I was called to lead. My actions and decisions would have direct implications for the institution's present and future well-being, as well as for the teachers and students therein.

I assumed the position of Academic Director after two external academic audits had found significant problems with the students' learning outcomes, as well as issues in a variety of other key areas. The institution's highest authorities, the Board of Directors and Executive Director, chose me because of my background in education and business, with master's degrees in both areas, as well as a successful track record in my previous roles. Once officially in position, I began to implement a process of transformational change, which took many teachers and other stakeholders by surprise. The initial reaction on the part of many was: 'This guy is going too fast. He needs to slow down!' I also touched a nerve when I decided to change a coursebook that had been in use for 15 years in its various editions (the third had just been introduced when I became Director.) Many teachers were used to the book, so they were not happy when I announced I would open up a tender and conduct a pilot study to see if there was another book that could be more appropriate. I knew that if the wrong book was chosen, there would be serious implications, most especially with new student enrollment; if the series' first book was found to be too easy or too difficult, it would dissuade new students from enrolling or staying once enrolled. I was also well aware that it could cost me my job before I had even got the seat warm!

In the end, everything worked out, for many reasons, but I want to highlight two of them. First, I engaged in frequent and open communication with all of the institution's stakeholders, especially the teachers. Everyone was informed throughout the transformation process of what was being done and why. As much as possible, people were invited to participate in the process and contribute their ideas. In fact, I made it a policy to start every year with a review of the goals and objectives that were met during the previous term, the ones set for the new year, and what the strategic plan was or how it had changed under the circumstances, highlighting the progress made along the way. Then, every month, the academic department would meet with teachers to follow up on that large meeting, combining academic discussion and professional development with providing the information teachers needed.

The second reason for success was that I focused on inclusion as a fundamental tenet of my approach to leadership. When we changed that textbook after 15 years, I involved all 400+ of the teachers. We had the publishers hold information sessions with them, explaining their proposals, the philosophies behind their books, and the intended benefits for students. I even called for a vote on the part of the teachers to help identify the final participants in the pilot study; teachers were invited to participate in a quick review of the books that were being considered, using specially made forms so the academic department could have a way of receiving feedback from teachers for processing. When the decision was made, I communicated it to everyone, both in person and by way of videoconferencing for those who could not make it to the face-to-face meetings. I wanted to be sure everyone knew why the new book had been chosen and that the decision had been based on objective criteria derived from a long, complex, and professional pilot research study. That inclusion policy would be applied permanently from then on with every other major initiative.

In the end, I was able to change people's minds about me. I went from a crazy 'Dr Frankenstein' in overdrive to a transparent, capable leader who had earned their trust and respect. Years later, when I moved to my next institutional home and began another process of transformational change, I followed the same policy of ample and transparent communication, coupled with inclusion at all levels. This time, we got more done, in less time, and with greater cooperation from teachers. The teachers adapted very quickly, with little resistance and few complaints. The smoothness of that process probably reflects the increased effectiveness of the decision- and policy-making resulting from the lessons I learned from my previous experiences. That seems consistent with studies which show that transparency can be a prime reason for employee happiness or satisfaction and the willingness to collaborate in the workplace (Craig, 2018).

Reflective Break 45: Leo highlights the importance of effective and efficient, clear and concise communication. What do 'effective communication' and 'ineffective communication' look like in your context?

Reflective Break 46: How would you rate your overall communication skills: Excellent; Very Good; Good; OK; Poor? If your communication skills are at the high end of the scale, how did you develop those skills to that high level? And if your communication skills are at the lower end, what could you do to improve those skills?

Another challenge was dealing with office politics, which can come to represent a major source of anxiety and stress when all you want is to enjoy your job to the fullest and avoid conflict. This is the one challenge that has made me think about leaving the field more than once. The fact of the matter is that there are people who are not looking to become leaders but who get chosen for the role anyway, and others for whom there is nothing they wish for more than assuming leadership positions in the organization. This causes competition—often of the unhealthy kind—between co-workers and other negative consequences, such as jealousy, conflict, and sometimes what may even seem like 'open warfare.' Yes, it can get that bad.

Looking back on the conflict-related situations that have arisen during my career, I realize a couple of things. An overly-horizontal approach to managing your staff can 'over-empower,' which means that the line that is supposed to establish authority and respect for an institutional authority can get blurry for some staff members in the office. The other is that competition causes conflict, especially when two or more people are vying for the same role or responsibility. I remember when I was nominated as one of the candidates for the newly created position of Deputy Academic Director, to my great surprise, people began to take sides in favor of one candidate over another. I was a candidate who was surprised by the nomination, but no less deserving. Most flocked to the other person for whatever reason, and few thought I would be offered the position regardless of the merits. In the end, I was the one promoted, which should have meant the end of the conflict. Unfortunately, it did not end there. Far from it.

To keep a very long story relatively short, what I can say is that the threat of conflict is always present. Sometimes, it is quite natural and can even be positive because people can learn from each other, reflect, and grow from the conflict experience—after it has been resolved. In other cases, the conflict can become hostile, but even then, there may still be the potential to learn invaluable lessons. Reflecting on my past, I would say that, for me, at times it has been easier to reach teachers and win their respect than it was to work with fellow staff members in an administrative office. In terms of what I could have done differently, I would say that I would have been less horizontal and asserted myself more as an authority. This does not mean I would change my whole attitude of being approachable and open, but I would also be firm when necessary. In the final analysis, I think my overall success as a leader still justifies most of the decisions I made.

To conclude my leadership reflections on a positive note, I can say that I completed my stint as Academic Director with the ideal team, undoubtedly the best one I have ever had the privilege to lead. Reflecting on why it took me so long to find a team I could trust wholeheartedly in terms of their professionalism, abilities and talent, work ethic, and loyalty, I would say that it can take a long time involving a process of ongoing trial and error. The team I started with at my last employer is not the same one I ended up with. Rather, the team that I ultimately got to lead was a result of change over several years until each member of the team I got to work with and appreciate so much found their right place in what became a 'well-oiled machine.' Our knowledge, talents, and personality traits ended up complementing each other. Mind you, it took me 25 years to find such a 'dream team,' other excellent staff members and teammates from the past notwithstanding. Again, I must conclude that finding the 'perfect team' was possible only after so many years of learning and applying the lessons from so many past experiences.

In the end, my success as a leader in education can be mainly attributed to my ability to learn through ongoing reflection, as well as to apply the lessons derived from such learning. Certainly, one's education can also help enormously, especially if it is relevant to the work one does in language program administration. In my case, my studies in education and business have served me well as the ideal combination for my roles as academic coordinator, branch manager, project manager, and director of studies. But the real lessons come from life and the people we meet and interact with over the years. If we can learn to master the art of reflection as a powerful tool for lifelong learning, our chances of success as leaders in education are greatly increased. At this point in my career, I am looking forward to a whole new learning experience as an academic entrepreneur. Needless to say, I will continue to engage in reflective practice in my new roles and I look forward to exploring a whole new array of situations and challenges that await.

> **Reflective Break 47:** The politics of the workplace are mentioned by Leo, which all workplaces have, making such politics normal and natural—but they can become problematic. Have you experienced a workplace politics situation that led to problems? If so, how was that situation addressed by the leaders of that organization at that time?

Andy Curtis: Stepping and Stumbling (Back) into the River

According to the pre-Socratic Greek philosopher, Heraclitus of Ephesus (around 535–475 BCE): 'You cannot step twice into the same river,' and in spite of my aversion to the watery metaphors of RP (see Question One) I have always liked that saying, even before I fully understood its meaning. Perhaps we have to live such sayings before we can fully grasp their ontological undercurrents, and so it was for me in Hong Kong. My first time there was from 1995 to 2000, while wrapping up my doctoral dissertation, which I completed at the University of York in 1996.

My PhD was largely about doing PhDs—specifically how international graduate students at universities in England coped with the lack of support systems in place for them at that time. Some of the students whom I interviewed for the study came from Hong Kong, so that became one of the places that I set my sights on seeing/being part of, as soon as I was done with the dissertation. For those first five years in Hong Kong I bounced around, starting with a year at the country's main teacher training institute, followed by a couple of years at one of the polytechnics there, then two years at one of the top universities in Asia. In 2000, I left Hong Kong and went to Ontario, Canada, so we three (my future wife, my future step-son, and I) could work on being a multilingual, multicultural 'reconstituted family', officially defined in Canada as 'a family in which at least one of the partners is acting as a step-parent' (Talbot, 1981, p. 1803). Our 'reconstitution' included marrying languages and cultures from Mainland China, Hong Kong, England, India, Guyana, and elsewhere.

> **Reflective Break 48:** One of the ultimate linguistic and cultural challenges is to marry (or to live with, for a long time) someone from a markedly different language and culture to your own—as I did and as some of the other RTLs have done. Either from personal experience, or from a speculative perspective, what have you found, or what do you think you could find, are some of the difficulties and some of the rewards of taking on that ultimate relationship challenge?

Those first five years in Hong Kong (1995–2000) enabled me to clear the student debt I had run up during my master's and doctoral studies, and to establish a firm foundation of researching and writing, publishing and presenting, on which the next 20 years were built. So far, so good. But, when I decided to return to Hong Kong, seven years later—to the same ELT unit and the same university that I had left in 2000—the problems of trying to step back into the same river nearly sunk me. The main problem was related to the fact that most of the teaching staff from my first time were still there, seven years on, in 2007; still in the same place, still doing the same things. I initially thought that would be a bonus, as we had known each other before, liked and trusted each other, and worked well together. However, in addition to the Me-Myself-and-I triangle discussed earlier, a second triangle came into play; one that I have referred to as the three-part EAR model (Curtis, 2020), which I presented in Question Two. To briefly recap, the model represents the relationships between our Expectations, Assumptions, and the Reality of the situation, and with RP, we are able to explore how closely aligned or how far apart the three are, and to narrow the gap if necessary/possible.

What happened was that many of my former co-workers now reported to me as their supervisor, as I had left them when I was a Senior Instructor and returned as the Director, thereby going from 'a colleague' to 'the boss' (which is how the staff referred to me, in front of me, which they said was a mark of respect). Although I did not think about that situation in this way at the time, perhaps it was something like when Hong Kong, on 1 July 1997, reverted back to Chinese rule, after the 99-year lease negotiated with the British Empire, on 9 June 1898 (Vines, 1997), expired. I was there that day, and saw how, on the surface, everything appeared to be much the same as before, but in reality, underneath, everything was different. Everything had changed. Yes, these were the same people I had socialized with when I had been there before, at the end of the 1990s. The same people that I had known first as strangers, then as colleagues, then as friends. But they now 'reported to me,' and not just that, I was their supervisor in a system that was culturally far more hierarchical than anything I had known before.

As one of my colleagues put it: Hundreds of years of British Imperial Civil Service history meets thousands of years of Imperial China. What could possibly go wrong? As we saw in the 2019 riots in Hong Kong—and in 2020 and 2021 too—an awful lot can go wrong in such post-colonial and undemocratic systems (McDonell, 2019). For me, professionally and personally, what went wrong was that I assumed that the teachers would accept me as their new leader, because we had known each other before. However, some teachers assumed that, because we had worked together before, our history would entitle them to certain 'privileges.' I did not see that coming. Two completely different sets of assumptions, based on the same set of prior relationships.

As you can imagine, the situation escalated, with some of the long-standing local (Hong Kong-born, Cantonese-speaking) senior teachers wanting to know why a foreigner like me had been given the 'top job' over them, as Director. In some ways that was a valid grievance, especially as the year of my return, 2007, was the tenth anniversary of the end of 150 years of British Colonial Occupation, to be reunited with the Glorious Motherland (see Flowerdew, 1998 and *China Daily*, 2019, for examples of and notes on the use of such language). One answer to the justifiable gripe of the local teachers was that the university wanted leaders in language education who had an international profile, in terms of having lived and worked in different countries, which I had done by then, rather than someone who had lived all their life in the same place. Regardless of the pros and cons of having local vs non-local leaders, all of the universities in Hong Kong at the time were vigorously recruiting faculty members from around the world, including from Mainland China, to show how 'international' they could be when it came to worldwide university rankings and 'league tables.'

On the other side of the (negotiating) table were the teachers from England, who had come to Hong Kong when it was the jewel in the crown of the British colonial university system; the days when the sun never set on the Empire. Consequently, they had enjoyed a lifestyle and privileges that would have been beyond belief back home in Olde England; from live-in, 24-hour maids, to salaries and terms and conditions of employment that included free/fully-paid-for luxury housing, bonuses, business-class travel allowances, children's private-school fees paid for, and more. As a reporter for the *South China Morning Post* newspaper put it, two decades after the lease expired: 'Hong Kong cast off its colonial shackles and became one again with China almost 20 years ago ... Yet tens of thousands of civil servants still get the sort of perks that British expatriates [used to get] ... Spacious flats in prestigious locations, housing allowances and even overseas education for children' (Kammerer, 2017). Perhaps not surprisingly, then, the teachers in the unit who were from that British background hoped that someone like me, 'a fellow-Brit,' would help them hang on to some of the privileges that had been gradually chipped away over the ten years between 1997 and 2007.

Being stuck between that particular rock and a hard place, I tried to appease both parties, as a result of which I ended up being seen by the expatriate teachers as 'pandering to the local staff,' while the local staff saw me as being some kind of 'post-colonial agent of privilege.' I was eventually able to show that I was being consistent in rejecting some requests while accepting others—regardless of whether the request was being made by the ex-pats or the local teachers. But not before falling into the trap of thinking that maybe I could be all things to all people; keep my friendships from before I became the boss, make new friends, and still be seen to be an impartial leader—writing that line now makes me wince at my naïveté then! At some point, such roles and responsibilities became a set of mutually exclusive propositions, so that, if I wanted to be seen to be a fair, impartial, and consistent leader, I would have to say goodbye to some long-time friendships, which is what I ended up doing.

Perhaps the single biggest mistake you can make is to return to somewhere you once worked, to somewhere you once knew well, where you worked well and were well-liked, thinking that you *still* know the place and the people. You have changed, they have changed, and the place has changed—which has been especially true in a place like Hong Kong, transitioning from more than 150 years of British rule, reverting back to millennia of Chinese rule. I have since learned that I am not alone, and that many leaders have fallen into this same trap, assuming they are returning to the same river, only to discover that the tide and the times have changed irrevocably.

To sum up, with more than a decade's hindsight since leaving that position in Hong Kong, here are five lessons I learned from my (second) five years there. First, do not assume you know a place and a people, just because you spent time there before (even a lot of time). Second, let go of whatever it is you think you know about that place and those people—things change, people change, and memories fade, selectively. Third, research the place that you are returning to as though you had never been there before, especially in relation to language education policies, as well as the current languages, cultures, politics, etc. of the place—*as it is today*. Fourth, do not expect that a positive prior experience as a co-worker will automatically translate to you being willingly accepted as 'the boss'. Lastly, be willing to say goodbye to some friendships that you once thought might last a lifetime.

> **Reflective Break 49:** As my Question Four response shows, relationships change when we move from mostly classroom teaching into more of a leadership position, as a result of which some new friendships may be formed, but some old ones will often have to be left behind. Are there some friendships that you have had to leave behind because of making such a move? Are there some new friendships that you have made as a result of making such a move? Do the gains make up for (or even exceed) the losses?

Marjorie Rosenberg: Facing the Challenge of Leadership and the Transferal of Skills to Our Jobs as Teachers

Thinking back, I would have to say that my first year as IATEFL President presented the most complicated leadership challenges that I have faced. My entry into the position was somewhat unusual as IATEFL elects an incoming Vice President who serves for a year while having the chance to attend all Trustee meetings, chair a committee, and work closely with the outgoing President who is serving in their second term. The handover occurs at the Annual General Meeting at the annual conference, which is held in the UK, usually in April. However, as the elected incoming VP decided, for personal reasons, not to continue in the position, I came in as 'acting VP' in February 2015 and only had two months to prepare for and learn about the President's role. Having served as an Special Interest Group Coordinator for five years, which included running committee meetings and attending SIG Coordinator meetings chaired by the SIG Representative and attended by the President of IATEFL, as well as having served on the Membership Committee of IATEFL, I thought I had a fairly good picture of the way things worked. However, the Board of Trustees is quite different from SIG Committees, as all Trustees have an equal voice and are all briefed on the same information.

The President chairs meetings and looks over the agenda in advance but all of the Trustees (except for the Secretary) chair the Executive Committees or represent other parts of the IATEFL family such as the SIG Representative and the

Associates Representative. The other major difference is that IATEFL is both a UK charity as well as a trading company which deals with certain aspects of sponsorship and the conference, all based on UK law. As an SIG Coordinator or a member of an Executive Committee, one is rarely confronted with the implications of this arrangement. As a Trustee, however, one is responsible for keeping within the guidelines and steering the organization, with the invaluable help of Head Office staff, in the right direction.

There were many aspects of the job to get used to, such as realizing that the Trustees are actually the employers of the staff and responsible for certain aspects of employer-employee relationships. It was also necessary to learn about UK charity law and be responsible for the financial health of the organization. Balancing the different interests of the Trustees was also new, as this had not come up on the SIG committee I chaired. As an SIG Coordinator, I had been in some ways responsible for the SIG and 'in the know' about policies from Head Office, which was, as mentioned above, quite different from being one of eight Trustees. As Trustees, we also had to run risk assessment exercises, which were interesting but new to me, as well as being responsible for setting policies that affected the organization as a whole.

Once I got into the actual running of the Association, I had more and more questions and in looking for answers discovered that over the years some of the procedures in place had not been put into writing. This was something I felt important to work on, and one of the ways I approached this was to simply start codifying procedures and information, partially based on what I had learned from being an SIG Coordinator. This was quite a challenge as it was a learning experience for me and I found it important to stick to the facts. Now these documents are available to both members as well as current and future Trustees. It was an interesting exercise, as when we got started, we began to see the far-reaching implications of creating rules that may be challenged by members and other stakeholders. But we worked hard at being fair to all, while ensuring that the Board of Trustees provided a stable atmosphere for the Association through its leadership. Taking over from the President before me, the Board and I also continued to work on the job descriptions of each of the Trustees. This was a major task and, in hindsight, I now think we could have involved previous role-holders for advice in writing those descriptions. The job descriptions were extremely helpful, however, in looking at the workload and shifting some jobs from one Board position to another. The Advisory Council of IATEFL was very helpful in this particular exercise.

Perhaps the biggest challenge came towards the end of my first term when we had to find a new Chief Executive (CE) for Head Office. This job had been held by the same person for many years and this was the only person I had ever worked with in that capacity, since I had gone from being 'just a member' to working as a volunteer within the organization. It was clear that this needed to be done carefully, but also that we had a time limit and had therefore to begin as soon as possible. I was fully aware that this was an area of expertise I did not possess as I had never worked in an HR position and had not been on either side of the employer-employee relationship in the UK. Luckily, we had other Trustees with experience and it was clear to me that forming a committee and assigning different Trustees to different jobs would be the way forward. We looked at a number of other job descriptions and discussed what we wanted in a CE. One of the things I feel we did right was to be open to changing the job description from what we all had known it to be in the past.

> **Reflective Break 50:** Becoming a leader in language education often entails acquiring a whole new set of knowledge and skills, as Marjorie's response shows. What is the most challenging set of knowledge and skills that you have had to acquire? What were some of the challenges and some of the rewards of acquiring that new knowledge/skill set?

As the times were different than when our last CE had come on board, over a decade before, it was clear that we needed to look carefully at the job in terms of social media, internet presence, membership numbers, getting information out to members, the annual conference, knowledge of the ELT world, etc. There were a number of new initiatives coming up, such as a 'greener' conference, having different opening hours for the exhibition, new formats for presentations, etc. Another major discussion point was the website, which everyone agreed needed updating, but presented certain challenges and needed to be dealt with carefully. The danger with the recruitment process was that only a few of us were involved, but in a way, we were lucky as we were questioned about it by the IATEFL Advisory Council fairly early on, so I sat down and wrote out the steps we took. That then became a document that can be used and adapted in future when the situation arises again. In general, writing up a process during and after it is being carried out can be a form of reflective practice and is something that I would highly recommend to anyone in such a position.

Looking back, what I feel I could have done better also involves reflection. I think that I may have rushed in too quickly when I started my first term as President, thinking that because I had worked in the Association for six years, and had been a member for 20, I knew a lot more about it than I actually did. I had a brief orientation, to which I suggested changes when I was in the position to do so. I felt it was important to discuss different aspects of the Association with a new Trustee and explain the basics such as the Memorandum and the Articles of Association as well as the documents that describe roles, procedures, etc. I also thought that training in charity law should be held every few years for new Trustees, as I felt we had all benefited from it. Due to my experience of a short lead-in time and the incredible help and support I got from the President before me, new requirements for the job were put into place, including having a chat with the current office holder—which had been recommended before, but was now required. It is vital that the incoming Vice President and the current President are on the same page regarding the vision and the practicalities of running the Association.

Although it is primarily a teacher association, IATEFL is also a registered charity and a trading company and employs around ten people in the UK. These are all considerations that need to be taken into account and not taken lightly. Looking back, it would have been helpful to have had training on different working styles. Having investigated these in my role as a business English teacher and trainer, I see now where the conflicts can arise. We may fall into the trap of assuming that, as we all come from the world of English Language Teaching, we will think and work alike, forgetting that we may have very different linguistic and cultural backgrounds and experiences, and teach in widely different contexts. It is also important not to compare ourselves with those who came before us and feel that we have to work in the same way. It is necessary to find our own strengths and weaknesses, and to find someone we can turn to as a mentor who will build us up when we need it, and also let us know when we need to improve in an area or take a step back. Being a leader also involves keeping our personal emotions out of the business of leading—and this may be one of the most difficult things to learn to do.

For me, the main things I learned from the experience of leading an organization were those skills my corporate students use every day. When we discuss setting agendas, approving minutes, running meetings, holding conference calls, recording speeches to give virtually, making decisions, and dealing with people from diverse cultures, they see me as one of them as they know I too have done these things. One of them told me that they appreciate that I not only teach them English but that I truly understand these aspects of their jobs. The skills we discover while working in leadership positions in ELT are therefore transferable to the job we have, mainly helping others to become proficient and effective communicators in English in order to get things done.

Rosemary Orlando: The Road Taken to Vietnam

My first visit to Vietnam was in the Fall of 2006. Southern New Hampshire University in Manchester, New Hampshire was still in talks with Vietnam National University—Hanoi (VNU) to develop a partnership for a Master of Science in Teaching English as a Foreign Language (MS TEFL) degree program that already existed on our Manchester campus. A connection was made at the higher levels of leadership between the two universities and the details were being worked out within my department. I was on the team that was shaping the program and choosing the courses and framework for the partnership. I traveled to Vietnam to have a look at the campus and meet some of the people who were to be a part of the new program.

As soon as I arrived, I discovered that some of the people I had been emailing with back and forth about details and concerns were not the ones I met once on the ground in Vietnam. In my opinion, we were rather naïve in our initial dealings with the Vietnamese university personnel and in hindsight should have asked more questions at every step. A number of things we had been told about where we would teach, where we would live, who would help administer the program, and so on were completely different from what I observed upon landing in the country. Right from the beginning during that initial trip in 2006, I was learning that although we had been told how the program would operate from their end, it was best to be prepared for something quite different.

A little over a year later, in January 2008, I arrived in Vietnam to begin teaching the first group of students. I also served as the administrator of this program while another colleague in New Hampshire coordinated the schedule. The students were all Vietnamese teachers of English from different provinces of Vietnam. Some had years of experience teaching while others were novices. We were all excited that the program was finally underway. I was proud and happy to be a part of this and optimistic that we could figure things out along the way. For the majority of the students, I was the first Westerner that they had ever met, and they were very curious about me, my life, and my way of teaching, which recalled Parker Palmer's maxim: 'We teach who we are' (Palmer, 1998/2007, p. 1). I was comfortable in that role and happy to answer any and all questions they had. In turn, they began to trust me and quietly let me know what life was like for a teacher of English in Vietnam and some of the challenges that went along with that.

Although I had done a fair amount of reading and research on schools in Vietnam, I was unprepared for just how tightly the educational system was controlled and monitored by the Ministry of Education and Training (MOET), from primary school all the way up to the university level. I had wanted my students to try new ways and methods in their classrooms regarding teaching listening and speaking, reading and writing, but they were not allowed to make many changes. Had they dared tried something new or more 'Western,' they risked reprimand and even lowered salaries. Their day-to-day reality was teaching classes of 40, 50, or even 60–75 students in a class, which was why they relied so heavily on grammar-translation methods of teaching.

Looking back, perhaps it was better that I had not known how limited and restricted the teaching atmosphere was in Vietnam at all levels. I might have felt defeated from the start and might not have been so confident that our program could make a difference in their teaching and learning. I learned a great deal by asking questions about their classrooms and their individual teaching contexts. I did not come onto the scene as an 'expert' in Vietnamese education and I think they appreciated that. I knew my course content but remained flexible to make it more in line with what they could manage to integrate in their classrooms. Along with the teaching, I interacted with various department heads from our campus in the US. This program was new to them so there were many details to sort out regarding paying tuition, transfering credits, receiving grades, and so on. At times there was much uncertainty and some trepidation about how to proceed in certain matters. As the liaison between my university and VNU, I was responsible for smoothing over the many bumps and miscommunications.

> **Reflective Break 52:** Rosemary refers to Parker Palmer's statement: 'We teach who we are.' Who would you say you are? That is, of course, too big a question for a short answer to be given! So, to make it more manageable, if you were writing a profile for, say, the social media site for professionals, LinkedIn, what would you write? What would you want other language educators, around the world, to know about you, and why?

Upon reflection I realized something that I knew all along to be true, as the importance of treating others in a kind and civil manner had been instilled in me by my parents from a young age. In dealing with an international partnership between two universities, you must work hard to keep your own superiors/bosses as well as the leaders of the other university happy, but, more importantly, you need to win local support and approval from the students and staff in order to be successful. The way you treat people makes all the difference in what they are willing to do in terms of being helpful and being willing to work hard for you, personally, as the leader, when they know you respect and support them. It makes for a pleasant environment when you allow people to do their jobs if they have the knowledge, dedication, and motivation to do well. It is not necessary to micro-manage every little detail. I had to interact and communicate with employees from various departments within the university and I treated them with respect and politeness. Within my own department, the faculty and staff were willing to put in extra time and go the extra mile to help administer this program, since they knew I trusted and respected them. Allowing others to do their jobs when they are capable and trustworthy goes a long way. When employees are engaged, they feel appreciated and valued. They are committed to the program's success because they believe their leaders are also committed to their success.

It is also necessary to treat students with respect. In Vietnam I always made time if a student appeared before me and wanted to talk. I know it is okay to say that you are busy or ask them to make an appointment, but sometimes someone just needs a few minutes of your time. Trying to be a good listener and being compassionate can go a long way in a professional setting. Studies have shown that when employees (or in this case, students) do not feel respected, their performance suffers. It only takes a few extra minutes at times to speak with someone face to face who might really need to feel that their opinion has been heard. A growing number of research studies '... suggest that rudeness can harm an employee's well-being and job performance. ... it occupies cognitive resources and focuses our attention on processing the unpleasant interaction' (Wallace, 2017, p. C3).

Over the years, the VNU program has grown and flourished. Several years ago, changes were made in the leadership of the program in Vietnam as VNU personnel retired or moved on. It is now in the 12th year of operation and I continue to serve as the main point person and leader of the program. When I am in Vietnam, I occasionally run into some of the original administrators of the program and they greet me warmly. One of the VNU Deans who I worked with years ago is proud to point out that our degree program is the longest running partnership that VNU has had with an international university.

I think one of the reasons for our success was the fact that we adapted to the culture of the university in Vietnam as opposed to forcing our university culture upon them. I was determined to bring together the two cultures and allow for differences as I learned from my mistakes. As Lublin (2020) points out, 'An inadequate assessment (of a workplace culture) can lead to a misfit, ... and you are less likely to thrive in an incompatible culture' (p. B5). After overcoming a series of hurdles, this program has given me many opportunities to pause and reflect. It forces me to think and rethink how we do things, why we do them in a certain way, and what we might consider changing as times goes on. As I look back in order to lead forward, I reflect upon the positive aspects within myself as a leader that keep me energized and improving, to maintain a strong program to leave for those who may follow in my footsteps.

Reflective Break 53: Rosemary emphasizes the importance of respect in building professional relations. Do you believe that being respected is a right for those in leadership roles, or do you believe that such respect is earned? If the latter, how can respect be earned? And what kinds of behaviors and language do you believe are 'disrespectful'?

Rosa Aronson: TESOL as a Business

Like many professional associations established first in the United States, TESOL operates under US government tax laws. The 'not-for-profit' status of an association refers to a special classification which allows the organization to be exempt from paying federal, state, and local taxes, provided it follows a certain number of rules. Unfortunately, the term 'not-for-profit' is often interpreted narrowly to mean that the organization in question should not make a profit at all. In reality, a not-for-profit organization is a mission-driven business, but a business nonetheless. This means that, to advance its mission, it needs to realize greater revenues than expenses in order to reinvest the profit (the difference between revenues and expenses) back into the organization.

When I began my tenure as Executive Director of the TESOL Association, I was confronted with the cultural belief that an association like TESOL should not be making a profit and should not operate as a business. In this mindset, a business is a corporate entity, which realizes profits and does not necessarily reinvest the profits in the organization. In part, this idea came from watching numerous profit-driven businesses emerge as the field of TESOL expanded. The quality of their offerings was unregulated and varied tremendously. Language schools with or without credentialed faculty could open without any obligation to demonstrate necessary competencies or results. While some were quality businesses, others were simply driven by profit. On a weekly basis, we received messages from individuals, students, or teachers who had been disappointed by these companies, and who were under the impression that the TESOL Association was either operating or endorsing these businesses. We had to let them know that the TESOL Association had nothing to do with these shady operations, even though the 'TESOL' acronym appeared in their names. A few of these companies even went as far as 'borrowing' our logo, which was easier to address, since our logo was a legally protected trademark. But even then, by the time our attorneys intervened, the damage to our name had already been done.

This ongoing challenge certainly shaped members' belief that all businesses were driven by greed and profit. But when the idea became dominant among members who were the most engaged in the TESOL Association, it became part of the culture of the organization. I still remember the first time I met the Interest Sections' leaders, accompanied by the Executive Committee. I was surprised by the level of animosity and discontent that prevailed among such dedicated members. My interpretation of their criticism was that the Board of Directors and the leadership team of staff members were deliberately making decisions that ran against the interest of the members of the Association, for example by refusing to allocate more resources to the operations of their Interest Sections, or by imposing unfair rules to their groups. One member was very vocal in accusing the TESOL Association of becoming too corporate. Another criticized the TESOL Association for hiring a professional staff and renting offices. This person felt that the TESOL Association should be able to operate completely with volunteers and could rent a much cheaper office at a university. The reality, though, was that the TESOL Association had grown from the early days of its existence to a new phase, where a professional staff was necessary in order to carry out its mission through research, programs, policy and advocacy, publications, and other strategies. I believe this was a difficult transition for volunteer leaders, as they saw their decision-making power diminishing and clashing with the culture of inclusivity that had dominated the early years of the organization.

The unfortunate result was a growing divide fed by a lack of trust between a number of volunteer leaders on one side, and the Board, Executive Committee, and leadership staff on the other side. This particular challenge may not be unique to language organizations but I had never experienced it in my previous organization. Also, in speaking with other educational organizations' executive directors, I didn't get the sense that this was a particular issue for them. As a result of this situation, any change that was initiated by the governing body of the Association was seen with suspicion and resistance. This challenge only grew as the Association needed to make some changes to the way it was organized in order to adjust to the shifting environment of international language education. A proposed change to the internal structure of the organization, including interest sections and committees, was initially met with the same resistance.

Reflective Break 54: Like many of the responses in the previous parts (for example, Chapter 3, Reflective Break 33), trust turns out to be an essential factor. What are some of the ways that you enable people to trust you, and what is it about your colleagues that makes you have trust in them, or makes you not trust them?

In summary, the challenge I was faced with was a clash between the dominant culture of the organization and the strategy needed to move the organization forward. The Board of Directors and I decided to proceed slowly. The entire process lasted five years. A special task force on governance restructuring was entrusted with the charge of researching best practices in association governance, surveying members, and offering recommendations to the Board. Two years later, the findings of the task force confirmed that there was a lack of alignment among different groups within the TESOL Association and no clear direction given to committees and interest sections. In addition, the task force report mentioned that 'the strong culture of inclusiveness and equality in the [A]association and the field often serves as the primary criterion for governance decisions' (TESOL International Association, 2014, p. 4). The task force did not make recommendations, however. Instead, it outlined possible next steps, which included different approaches, from doing nothing to dramatically changing the governance structure of the organization. Each potential step included a list of advantages and disadvantages for the Board to consider. It took three more years for us to select and implement the pathway that seemed both appropriate and effective; a compromise between the two extreme 'solutions.' Along the way, members and volunteer leaders were informed and invited to share their feedback. It was important to dispel the notion that changes were being imposed from above. When I retired in 2017, most of the changes had been implemented, with mixed results. Volunteer leaders now had job descriptions, committees and councils had specific charges and tools to communicate. But fundamentally, I do not think we were able to change the culture of the organization.

Looking back, on the positive side, there is more clarity in roles and responsibilities for members interested in leadership positions at the Association. There is also, I believe, better communication among the different governance structures. However, when I left, there was still a culture of distrust for the 'business' side of the organization. I don't necessarily consider this experience a failure but, in retrospect, I believe I missed some opportunities to be more effective as a leader. This is my advice to leaders of language institutions and organizations interested in implementing change in their leadership and governance structure:

- Do not underestimate the power of tradition and established culture before undertaking changes. Understanding cultural issues is what we do well in language education. Yet, as leaders, we sometimes dismiss the impact these cultural norms have on the management of an organization. Show respect for the dominant culture but consider it with a critical mind. Ask yourself, not only how these cultural beliefs support the organization, but also how they can/may undermine progress. Your responsibility is to the future of the organization or institution you lead.

- Do take the time to take the pulse of your organization but don't linger too long in that phase. Although it is important to be transparent and build trust, taking an inordinate amount of time in that phase of the work will not change minds and may inadvertently give the impression that you are vacillating. Taking your time to be reflective is beneficial but decisions need to be made and implemented lest your reflective practice turns into indecisiveness. As a leader, you are often judged for your character but also for your effectiveness. As Henry Cloud writes in *Necessary Endings: The Employees, Businesses, and Relationships That All of Us Have to Give Up in Order to Move Forward*, 'Everything has seasons, and we have to be able to recognize when something's time has passed and be able to move into the next season. Everything that is alive requires pruning as well, which is a great metaphor for endings' (2011, p. 20).

- When undertaking a change process in an organization or institution, expand your thinking beyond the relatively small circle of those who have a stake in the status quo. Extend your message to as large a group as you can reach. Why? Because new ways of thinking are not necessarily going to come from your inside group. Also, by addressing communications to those who have not been closely involved in your organization, you open up a pathway to new and future leaders. These individuals often hold a different perspective on what you are trying to accomplish.

- Expect to be criticized. Be open to it. Listen to the charges brought against you but don't take them personally. Through your reflective practice, you are undertaking difficult strategies for the benefit of the organization and its stakeholders. Ethical leadership is also about following your pathway amidst praise or criticism without letting either affect your practice and your state of mind.

- Know that the lessons you will learn from your mistakes will be more powerful than the lessons you learn from your successes.

Reflective Break 55: 'Expect to be criticized,' writes Rosa. Nobody likes to be criticized, and we all have our different strategies for coping with being criticized. And it is important to note that offering constructive criticism and thinking critically are not the same as being criticized. How would you describe the differences between constructive criticism, thinking critically, and being criticized? How do you respond to and cope with being criticized? How do you give critical feedback?

Deborah Healey: Office Politics and Geopolitics—It's All About People

A systems view helps see the roles of a variety of factors in the success of an institution. Most Intensive English Programs (IEPs), especially within the US, are self-supporting and need to generate revenue. Large-scale factors that influence institute revenue streams include global student mobility, which is affected by geopolitics, financial markets, news media, and international events. More locally, factors include the institute's position within an institution, such as a university; the support of whatever kind that institution offers, such as housing and recruitment help; conditional admission and the ability of the institute to recommend students into the institution without standardized test scores; and the overall attractiveness of the institution, the location, and the community. Institute finances and financial decisions affect the number and type of faculty and staff and the resources available for administration, teaching, and learning. The climate within the institute can be collegial or competitive.

Self-supporting language institutes are primarily dependent on student enrollment for their revenue. As a result, institutes are highly vulnerable to changes in enrollment and very much in need of multiple sources of revenue. At the institute where I worked, we offered short-term English language programs in our 'Special Programs' arm, drawing students from different countries. The advent of the world wide web dramatically increased global interest in technology in teaching, and we started offering a multi-week Technology Seminar in the late 1990s as a different kind of special program. One of the wiser moves we made was to create a Council of Advisors for the institute made up of high-level faculty members from colleges with large numbers of international students, such as Business, Engineering, and Education. These professors were our sounding board for new ideas and ways to generate revenue, giving us expert advice for marketing and promotion. They were advocates familiar with our mission and our operations. The Council also served to enmesh us more broadly in the university, improving our strategic position. Sadly, the Council of Advisors gradually diminished over time with job changes and retirements. We would have been well-served to continue to draw upon their expertise and support.

As a teacher and at every level of administration from about 1993 to 2008, I was acutely aware of the effects of international events on enrollment and revenue. Our Kuwaiti numbers were very large after the 1990–1991 Gulf War, when most Kuwaiti universities were closed for repairs. The students coming from post-war Kuwait had clearly been deeply affected by the war. We would later identify the issue for many of them as post-traumatic stress disorder (PTSD). In retrospect, all of us at the university should have been better prepared and able to help them. We were doing fine at the institute until the Asian economic crisis in 1998, when we had a 30 percent drop in enrollment within about three months. We no longer had large grants and our special programs groups were largely Asian, so this was another major downturn for the institute and the university. We shifted to trying to recruit in Latin America, without a great deal of success. We were told repeatedly by our recruiters that the rainy climate of our relatively unknown state in the US was not helpful.

I became Director of the institute in 1999 and put grant-writing at the top of my list of ways to broaden the revenue stream. We looked at state and federal grants and partnerships with other units on campus. We worked with the School of Education, College of Engineering, English, Chemistry, and the university library on some grants, and used faculty from Philosophy and Education in our World Bank grant. This again seemed to be a strategic way to use external resources to improve our position at the university, to add another source of revenue, and to provide professional development for our faculty and staff who were part of the grants. Having skilled faculty and staff allowed us to be flexible.

The climate within the institute was largely collegial. Many of the faculty and staff had been there for a decade or more, collaborating on projects and watching each other's children grow up. The drop in enrollment meant that we could not support everyone in full-time teaching positions. We lost almost all of our adjunct faculty and three of our year-long faculty. We would have lost more, but the remaining faculty agreed to 'share the pain' by taking a cut in hours and pay. This included the director and all faculty administrators, most of whom still worked full time but at reduced pay. Collegiality helped everyone get through a very difficult financial time.

We were starting to recover from the Asian economic crisis when we had the World Trade Center attack in 2001. Most of our Asian students immediately disappeared due to safety concerns, even though we were 3,000 miles away on the opposite side of the US. We were very grateful to our Korean students, who came despite concerns. We also ended up with more Saudi students in the years following the attack, as the Saudi government pledged to build bridges by sending its young people to the US. We increased our large Middle Eastern numbers as the Arab Spring began, in 2011. We adjusted the curriculum and added more orientation for students and faculty—including university faculty—as our demographic shifted from largely Asian to largely Middle Eastern.

Reflective Break 56: Do you work in a self-funded or self-financed language teaching unit or organization, as Deborah has done? If so, what are some of the challenges and some of the benefits of working in such an organization? If you work in an organization that is centrally funded, how does that affect the language teaching and learning that takes place in your context?

A more recent example of geopolitical effects is the surge in undergraduate students from China. There were always graduate students from China on student visas in US universities. As the Chinese economy strengthened, more families moved into the middle class. Many parents saw their one and only child as a potential key to improving the family business and wanted to send them for further studies abroad. The improved Chinese economy and family structure meant that US embassy officials could now reasonably believe that Chinese undergraduate students would return home. When US consulates in China started giving student visas to undergraduates, the floodgates opened, and in 2010 very large numbers of Chinese students appeared in IEPs and on university and college campuses. University administrators were delighted. Graduate students usually receive assistantships or other financial support. Undergraduates pay full non-resident tuition at state schools. As many state governments have reduced their support for public universities and colleges, these institutions look to non-resident students to subsidize in-state students. The institute was again called upon to provide additional cultural orientation for university faculty, as well as to help those faculty adapt to classes that were often filled with Chinese-speaking international students. Skilled faculty and robust student-support services were essential.

National trends and events can affect an institute, and leaders need to be prepared. US foreign policy was a benefit in the early 1990s with Kuwaiti students. At any time, anti-immigrant, anti-foreign rhetoric and newsworthy actions against nationals of other countries, such as high-profile arrests, can send ripple effects through global student mobility. School shootings generate global news. At the institute, we had to proactively counter the narrative of the US as an unsafe place with targeted marketing and media highlighting the positive experiences of individual international students studying with us.

After nearly 30 years at one university-based IEP and numerous administrative positions, including nine years as Director, I moved out of administration and back to teaching at a different university-based IEP. The two universities and institutes serve as an interesting contrast, with different contexts and trajectories. Institute A was the only teaching unit within an administrative program for international students and those going on study abroad programs. Institute B was within an academic department with more sympathy for taking term breaks away from the office. Institute A was at a technology/engineering/education/agriculture university with a long tradition of international grant-funded projects and a very strong online learning arm. It was relatively easy to work with the university to negotiate budgets with sponsor-related and international quirks. Institute B was at a liberal arts university, where negotiating international grants was more difficult. That institute's massive open online course (MOOC) was the first for the university, so getting it through the university approval process was challenging. Still, through the work of dedicated faculty grant-writers and administrators, Institute B developed a very strong and extensive online English language teacher-training program, largely federally funded.

In 2008, University A's provost saw a new public-private partnership that would take over the IEP as a quick way to increase student enrollment. With the focused support of the provost and university financial resources, the change was implemented. A new living-learning center was built with housing and classroom space. The change was good for the more junior institute faculty as many of the senior faculty and administrators retired or left, and others could move up to take their place. Earlier ally-building with the Faculty Senate at the university paid off when the Senate affirmed that those who taught for the new partnership were still full university faculty and could keep full university benefits. The highly skilled staff of the institute remained in place. The new partnership was very good for me as an impetus for change. I shifted to teaching in an IEP where I had a five-minute bike ride to work rather than an hour's commute each way by car. University B made a strong commitment to retain its IEP. Large numbers of Chinese students appeared, starting in 2010, increasing enrollment at no cost to the university. The institute expanded very rapidly. It was generating enough revenue to get dedicated office and classroom space in a building. Teachers were hired directly from master's programs in TESOL into full-time jobs with benefits. The changes happening at this university, though, included unionization of tenure-track and non-tenure track faculty. The self-supporting institute was financially affected, requiring curriculum and contract changes.

The current downturn in international student enrollment has affected institutes and universities. IEPs can view this as cyclical, reducing faculty and staff once again to weather the storm. The challenge to universities that took student migration for granted, not viewing it as part of an international system, is much larger. The ultimate effect is as yet unknown.

When I look back at my administrative work over the years, not just as a Director, it is clear to me that reflecting with a longer, more strategic view was a good approach. My first institute had already decided that it was better to give faculty full-time work with full benefits, even though it was more expensive for the institute, than to keep everyone at lower pay with no benefits. This was our collegial basis. Working with the faculty, we generated a new pay scale that brought people's salaries from very low to not-so-low, and then up from that level. Administrators would come internally, and the first step would be a vote by all faculty for their top three choices—chosen from the list of all faculty. This process encouraged women to take on the role more freely because they knew from the beginning that they had the support of the faculty. Working together, we devised a way to 'share the pain' in the inevitable downturns in enrollment: everyone, including administrators, would take a drop in hours for a cut in pay and allow more people to continue working. We also expanded our revenue basis by consistently seeking state, federal, and international grants. Most of these were in partnership with other university departments and colleges, building connections and bridges. I did my best to encourage faculty and staff to expand their expertise and to build leadership pathways.

Being Director during downturns and takeovers is very stressful, and real vacations are few and far between. I was able to take a long-term view of the system as a whole, find the right niche for people, encourage individual and institute growth, and build community within and outside the institute. I learned a great deal about leadership and about myself. Similarly, being on the TESOL Board of Directors and part of the ExCom has been an opportunity to think about the Association as a complex system. I have tried to consider each element—including members; stakeholders such as affiliates, publishers, and government entities; volunteer leaders; TESOL's Executive Director and staff; and the Board—within their relationships to other elements. As President, I sought ways for the individuals I worked with to feel empowered and part of our community, thus strengthening the Association. This was constant work and not easy. Nonetheless, despite the stress and struggles, being a thoughtful leader and feeling that I have made a difference has been enormously rewarding.

Overall, I have found reflective practice, using strategic and systems thinking, to be especially useful in leadership positions. It encourages considering a range of what-ifs, understanding strengths and weaknesses, and striving to be prepared for a variety of situations. A good sense of humor in the face of adversity has also been essential.

Reflective Break 57: Deborah describes two language teaching-learning institutes, which she refers to as 'Institute A' and 'Institute B'. Given the choice, which one would you choose to work at, and why? And why would you not want to work at the other institute?

Neil Anderson: Facing Challenges

When we think of the word *challenge*, perhaps we often assume a negative connotation. A challenge seems to imply that something negative or bad is happening and that we need to make changes in order to overcome the challenge. I also believe that a challenge can be positive. Allow me to provide two examples of 'leadership challenges' that I have faced: one negative and one positive.

Example 1, Part 1. As I indicated in Chapter 1, early in my full-time employment as a TESOL professional, I recognized that I wanted to be a teacher educator and that I would need to earn a PhD degree. As I was employed at the English Language Center at Brigham Young University (BYU), I had two colleagues who went to the University of California at Los Angeles (UCLA) to earn their PhD degrees. I decided that I wanted to follow their example. I knew the date that my non-renewable contract would end at BYU and so I set my sights on starting the PhD program at UCLA in the Fall semester of 1984. I submitted my application for the program in early 1984. I looked forward with great anticipation to receiving my acceptance letter. In approximately May of 1984, I received the much-anticipated letter. Unfortunately for me, it was a letter of rejection, not acceptance. It had never occurred to me that I would not be accepted. I had made an assumption that my excellent work as an emerging TESOL professional and my clear desire to focus on teacher education at one of the finest universities in the US was all I needed.

I was completely overwhelmed by this challenge. It immobilized me for several days. Not long after receiving the devastating news, I received a call from one of my former faculty advisors at BYU, inviting me to meet with him. He asked some very probing questions about my assumptions. He asked what I was going to do. I had no plan. He asked why I had not applied to other universities. Certainly, I knew that there were other PhD programs that would allow me to achieve my goals. He asked what I knew about the University of Texas at Austin. All I knew was that he had graduated from UT Austin. He placed a phone call while I was meeting with him and alerted the Director of the PhD program that I would be applying and that he hoped the Director would give my application a fair evaluation. Within a few short weeks I received an acceptance letter to begin PhD studies in Teaching English to Speakers of Other Languages at the University of Texas at Austin.

Example 1, Part 2. Simultaneously to submitting my application to UT Austin, I received another phone call from the Administrative Assistant to the Linguistics Department Chair at BYU, who had learned of my situation. She had just received a phone call from the Center for Applied Linguistics (CAL) in Washington DC. They were looking for a young TESOL professional with experience in language testing and assessment. At that time, I was the language testing coordinator at the

English Language Center at BYU. She gave me the name and telephone number of the individual I needed to contact at CAL. I placed the phone call and was invited to fly to Washington DC for an interview.

Within a short period of time, I received an offer to be the Program Associate for Measurement and Evaluation at the Refugee Service Center in Manila, the Philippines. This job provided an opportunity to direct the testing of refugees from Southeast Asia resettling in the US. I would be working with professionals in refugee camps in the Philippines, Indonesia, and Thailand. Now, I had been accepted to the PhD program at UT Austin and I had an incredible job offer from CAL. At this point I had options, an opportunity to make a choice. I was much more empowered because there was a choice. I was able to examine the assumptions about my future and what I ultimately wanted to accomplish. I decided that the position with CAL was a once-in-a-lifetime opportunity for me and my family to live and work outside of the US and to be employed by a highly respected, non-profit organization involved in language education issues. At the same time, I did not want to miss out on the opportunity to earn a PhD and attend the program at UT Austin. I contacted the Program Director in Austin and asked for an extension to my admission. It was granted. I was then able to accept the job with CAL, and two years later enter the PhD program at UT Austin. In this situation *questioning all assumptions* ultimately led from a very negative experience to a very positive one.

Reflective Break 58: The normal, natural need to make assumptions—that may or may not turn out to be correct—has been one of the recurring themes throughout this book (for example, Chapter 2, Reflective Break 18, and Chapter 3, Reflective Break 22). Neil's Question Four response is based on the idea of 'questioning all assumptions.' What are some of the biggest assumptions in your work/life that you have challenged? What are some of the assumptions you still need to make regularly, and how do you assess how correct or incorrect those assumptions are?

Example 2. After completing my PhD studies, I accepted a faculty position at Ohio University (OU) in Athens, Ohio. It was a perfect position for me because I had the opportunity to teach in the TESOL MA program and at the same time to teach language learners in the Ohio Program of Intensive English (OPIE). The position provided a perfect blend of language teaching and teacher education. I had made an assumption that I would remain at OU for many years. After achieving the rank of Associate Professor, I had an opportunity to evaluate my situation and decide if I would remain at OU. My family encouraged me to seek new opportunities. I applied for two open faculty positions: one at Indiana University—Purdue University Indianapolis (IUPUI) and the other at BYU. I had successful interviews at each campus and received offers from both universities. I ultimately accepted the position at BYU. After 16 years at BYU, I received a telephone call from a search firm in Hong Kong asking if I would be interested in a position as the Head of Department at a respected TESOL program there. I had assumed that I would remain at BYU until my retirement. After reviewing all of the input, I agreed to a telephone interview. The telephone interview went well and also got me thinking about other possibilities. A position at another university in the US came to my attention. I was invited for an interview.

In the Spring of 2014, I attended the annual convention of the TESOL International Association. While at the convention I spent time with one of my trusted colleagues, Mark Wolfersberger, who was a former graduate student of mine at BYU and who was then employed at Brigham Young University—Hawaii (BYUH). I verbalized to him my assumptions and my pursuits in applying for positions in Hong Kong and at another institution in the US. He asked if I would consider applying to BYUH. I knew that BYUH had an opening, but I also knew that I was highly overqualified for the position. They were looking for someone who had recently graduated with an MA in TESOL with three years of teaching experience. I had a PhD and 34 years of teaching experience. It did not seem like an appropriate match. Mark asked me to *question my assumptions*, put them aside, and consider the possibility of what I could contribute to the programs at BYUH. That discussion led to an interview and an offer from BYUH. At the same time, I received an offer from the other US-based institution. Again, I was in the positive position of having options. I was able to make a choice for my future. I accepted the position at BYUH.

Currently I am a teacher educator at Brigham Young University—Hawaii and an Associate Director at the Edward D. Smith Center for Learning and Teaching (CLT). BYUH currently consists of 45 percent international students from 70 different countries who speak English as an international language. The university is consistently ranked as having one of the highest percentages of international students among BA-granting institutions in the US. The linguistic and ethnic diversity here among faculty, staff, and students is absolutely amazing. In my role at the CLT, I have the opportunity to interact with faculty members in all disciplines on campus. Along with my colleagues at the CLT (Mark Wolfersberger being one of them), we observe faculty, meet regularly to discuss teaching on our campus, and identify ways to increase engagement in the classroom. This is the best situation for me in the final years of my career as a TESOL professional.

What have I learned? There are four key lessons I have learned from my leadership experiences over the past 40 years. First, examine the assumptions that influence your thinking. What we think may be the outcome for us is influenced by the assumptions that we make. By *questioning the assumptions*, we open up our view to many more possibilities. Second, consistent engagement in RP is powerful for me as an individual and a professional. Through my heightened awareness through metacognitive engagement, I have gained new insights about how I can continue to grow and develop. Next, make sure that you have options available to you. When I applied to the PhD program at UCLA, I did not consider applying to any additional schools. I have learned that we want options. When we have options, we are empowered to make better informed choices. Finally, along our leadership path, we are going to have encounters with colleagues, family members, and friends who can provide inputs and perhaps new perspectives on our assumptions. Maybe there are options available to us that we have not yet considered.

I am so fortunate to have worked with the students and colleagues I have had since I decided to become a TESOL professional. Through 40 years of consistent engagement with RP, I think I am the one who has benefited the most.

> **Reflective Break 59:** Which of the two examples presented by Neil resonated more with you, and why? What did you learn about LiLE from your preferred example?

Kathleen M. Bailey: Learning to Let Go—Ruminating on Delegating

Some time ago, as noted in Chapter 1, I had a job in which I supervised a large group of teaching assistants in a university ESL program. My responsibilities involved being the instructor of record for the courses taught by the TAs, which included signing off on the final grades the TAs assigned for all the ESL students in the program. In summarizing this particular dilemma, I am focusing on only the upper-intermediate level of that ESL program. At the time this incident occurred, there were 12 different TAs teaching at that ESL level. There were 24 students in each class, for a total of 288 students in that level at the time.

I had been working with four of the TAs to develop a scoring rubric to use in evaluating the students' compositions on the final exam. The other TAs had numerous chances to review the drafts of the rubric, both in staff meetings and in discussions with me and with other TAs. We were on the quarter system, which meant that each term lasted ten weeks. The ESL students wrote five composition assignments during the term. Throughout this period, all the TAs pilot-tested the new scoring rubric while they were marking their own students' essays. As the final exam date approached, I was quite confident that all the TAs understood the new scoring rubric and were comfortable using it to evaluate their students' writing.

It was the policy that the TAs would not score the final exam compositions of their own students. Instead, each of those essays was rated independently by two different TAs. As a result, each TA was responsible for scoring 48 compositions, all of which had been written by students he/she had not taught. Each essay received the average of the scores assigned by the two raters. When there was a large difference between the two scores, a third rater evaluated the composition (and I was often the third rater). A score which was quite high or very low would be deleted and replaced by the score assigned by the third rater. The teaching assistants were all aware of these policies and procedures and had agreed to abide by them.

When the final exams had been administered, each TA picked up 48 essays. There was a very tight deadline for filing the students' grades, so it was important that all the ratings be done in a timely fashion. All the TAs needed to rate the 48 compositions they had been assigned in two days. They had known about this responsibility since the beginning of the term. As the scoring results were submitted, I saw that one TA had consistently given very low marks to all the compositions he had read, even though he had participated in the rater training and norming processes. He had not raised any concerns about our new rubric during the training. But now—when the ratings really mattered—many of his marks were extremely low, even punitive. As I compared his scores to those of his two reading partners, it was clear that, to be fair to the students, all the essays he had scored would have to be re-evaluated. Unfortunately, that job had to be done by the next day in order for me to meet the university's grade submission deadline.

Reflective Break 60: What advice would you have given Kathleen if she had come to you as a colleague and asked for guidance on how to proceed? Have you been in a similar situation yourself, and if so, how was it resolved?

What would you have done? What could I do? It seems I had three choices. I could have contacted that particular TA, counselled him about his scoring, and required him to re-evaluate his assigned essays that night. I could have contacted one or two other TAs who had not read these particular essays and who had not been the teachers of these 48 students. But was it fair to ask them to score these papers? They had already completed their own grading responsibilities. Should I request their help, especially under such oppressive time pressure? Either of these two options would probably also have meant missing the university's deadline for filing course final grades for these 48 students. One other possible course of action remained: I could score these 48 essays myself.

So, the issue boiled down to three options: (1) holding the individual TA responsible and forcing him to rescore all 48 essays that night (or as soon as possible); (2) delegating his work (and my associated responsibility for submitting final grades) to other TAs that night; or (3) scoring the papers myself that night. Each possibility presented advantages and disadvantages. The first option meant I had to contact the TA, try to understand why he had assigned such low scores, and get him to re-read and re-rate all 48 papers. How long would that take? Would he do it? More importantly, would he do it well?

There were also pros and cons of asking other TAs to evaluate these 48 essays, especially under these severe time constraints. Were other TAs available? How long would it take? Was it appropriate to ask them? And if I were to require either the original TA or any of his colleagues to evaluate these essays that night, would they be able to rate the compositions fairly? The ESL students' final exam grades were important: for some of them, those grades would determine whether they had to repeat the course, which would have potentially had serious financial implications, as well as implications for the time required to complete their degrees. As you might have guessed from reading this angst-ridden analysis, I caved in and rated all 48 compositions myself that night. Fortunately, my scores were quite close to those of the two original raters. I was able to discard the harsh scores and submit the grades on time. But was this choice really the best course of action?

Christison & Stoller (1997) identify delegating as a strategy for managing time reflectively: 'Learning how to delegate is important for one's health, sanity, and language program' (p. 244). Indeed, delegation is viewed as an important leadership strategy, as shown in this quote from White et al. (2008):

> An effective manager is one who can delegate tasks successfully. We know this intuitively, and yet it often seems to be one of the most difficult elements of a manager's job, often to the point where the manager actively avoids delegating and does things personally. Typical reasons that managers might give for this are:
> - 'It's easier to do it myself.'
> - 'By the time I've explained what I want to be done, I could have done it myself.'
> - 'I still have to keep track of what people are doing, and that takes up time too.'
> - 'It's not fair to ask my staff to do some of these tasks.'
> - 'I can do it better.' (p. 70)

These bulleted points are legitimate, but there are at least five reasons to delegate. First, delegating tasks that can be done by others can save time and energy for the leader. Second, the followers who carry out the delegated tasks will ideally develop their own skills in the process. Third, delegating—as a form of sharing—distributes the work to be done throughout the team. Fourth, the followers who carry out the tasks may actually have better ways of doing them than does the leader. Finally, collaborative delegations of tasks, in which the leader and followers communicate, can be synergistic.

In the development of the new composition scoring rubric, a team of four TAs worked with me to design the tool. These four TAs were particularly interested in the teaching of writing. I could have designed the rubric myself, but working with the team of four TAs generated a better result and may have contributed to the greater likelihood of buy-in by the other teaching assistants. We might consider this situation (i.e., a faculty member supervising TAs who teach many sections of the same course) to be *programmatic delegation*, since it involved a particular program-based initiative. That can be contrasted with what might be called *institutional delegation*, as the teaching and grading of the ESL students' work was the responsibility of the TAs. However, I had not planned for the dilemma that arose when 48 essays had to be re-rated in a very short period of time. To require the original TA to re-score his assigned compositions would not have been delegation: It would have been requiring him to complete his own responsibility correctly. Asking other TAs to redo his work would have been delegating, but would it have been appropriate and fair? So, the crux of the issue for me as a reflective leader boils down to this: Was rating those 48 essays that night myself the right thing to do? Should I have made a different decision?

The time factor cannot be ignored. If the final grades had not been due the next day, there might have been an opportunity to work with that TA, to understand what factors might have led to his low scores. What I chose to do did allow me to submit the grades on time, and it didn't result in an unfair workload being assigned to other TAs. It created an unnecessary hassle for me, but solving unanticipated problems is an essential aspect of leadership. Not forcing the original TA to re-rate the papers avoided a potentially bitter encounter. Also, I was afraid that if I forced him to revise his ratings, some of the students might still have been penalized. Making sure the scoring was fair would have involved me sitting with the TA and working with him on several of those essays, so I chose the most expedient course: doing the job myself.

Let's acknowledge my own context as well: I was a very junior faculty member in a leadership role that stretched me to the limits. I desperately wanted to do a good job—including submitting the final grades on time. If I were faced with this same dilemma today, I would have submitted the grades for everyone except the 48 students affected by the unacceptably low scores. I would have contacted the registrar's office and told the staff that those grades were forthcoming. I would have met with the TA and worked through the rating process with him, while trying to understand what had led to the abysmally low ratings. (Was he rushed? Was he frustrated? Was he facing a severe deadline on one of his own projects?)

Clearly, I am still ruminating over this vexing situation, even though the event occurred many years ago. My choice to score those 48 essays myself got the job done in a timely fashion. The other teaching assistants were not inconvenienced, but the TA involved did not learn anything in the process. My solution was not optimal for me, but it worked (i.e., it got the main administrative job done) as part of a complex system of roles and responsibilities.

In closing, I want to share a quote from Stephen Kemmis, one of the leaders of the action research movement:

> Reflection is not just an individual, psychological process. It is an action oriented, historically embedded, social and political frame, to locate oneself in the history of a situation, to participate in a social activity, and to take sides on issues. Moreover, the material on which reflection works is given to us socially and historically; through reflection and the action which it informs, we may transform the social relations which characterize our work and our working situation. (1986, p. 5; see also Kemmis, 1985, p. 140)

Reflective Break 61: As Kathleen's Question Four response show, she has struggled with delegation—whether or not to delegate; to whom to delegate; when to delegate, etc. What are some of the challenges you face when you need to delegate and how do you meet those challenges?

Reflective Break 62: Having read the ten RTL responses to Question Four, choose one or two that were of most interest to you. What was it about those particular responses that stood out for you? What did you learn about RP and LiLE from reading those responses?

REFERENCES

Arnau-Sabatés, L., & Gilligan, R. (2020). Support in the workplace: How relationships with bosses and co-workers may benefit care leavers and young people in care. *Children and Youth Services Review*, *111*, 1–7.
https://doi.org/10.1016/j.childyouth.2020.104833

Ashbaugh, C. R., & Kasten, K. L. (1991). *Educational Leadership: Case Studies for Reflective Practice*. White Plains, NY: Longman.

Avolio, B. J., Howell, J. M., & Sosik, J. J. (1999). A funny thing happened on the way to the bottom line: Humor as a moderator of leadership style effects. *Academy of Management Journal*, *42*(2), 219–227. https://doi.org/10.2307/257094

Bailey, K. M., Curtis, A., & Nunan, D. (2001). *Pursuing Professional Development: The Self as Source*. Boston, MA: Heinle & Heinle.

Baldoni, J. (2020). Leading with humor: Laughter is an affirmation of humanity. *SmartBrief.* Retrieved from: https://www.smartbrief.com/original/2020/07/leading-humor-laughter-affirmation-humanity

Bien-Gund, S., & Elrowmeim, S. (2019). Building trust and cultivating connection, leadership, and empowerment in a community-based program. *New Directions for Adult and Continuing Education*, *164*, 59–69. https://doi.org/10.1002/ace.20356

Bright, D. (2014). *The Truth Doesn't Have to Hurt: How to Use Criticism to Strengthen Relationships, Improve Performance, and Promote Change*. New York: American Management Association.

Brookfield, S. (1995). *Becoming a Critically Reflective Teacher*. San Francisco, CA: Jossey-Bass.

Caldwell, C., & Jeane, L. (2007). Ethical leadership and building trust—Raising the bar for business. *Journal of Academic Ethics*, *5*(1), 1–4.
https://doi.org/10.1007/s10805-007-9044-6

Carnevale, D. G. (1995). *Trustworthy Government: Leadership and Management Strategies for Building Trust and High Performance*. San Francisco, CA: Jossey Bass.

China Daily Global News. (July 8, 2019). Former HK colonial governor blasted for remarks. Retrieved from: http://www.chinadaily.com.cn/global/2019-07/08/content_37489049.htm

Christison, M. A., & Murray, D. M. (2009). *Leadership in English Language Education: Theoretical Foundations and Practical Skills for Changing Times*. New York: Routledge.
https://doi.org/10.1007/BF00380336

Christison, M., & Stoller, F. L. (1997). Time management principles for language program administrators. In M. Christison & F. L. Stoller (Eds.), *A Handbook for Language Program Administrators* (pp. 235–250). Palm Springs, CA: Alta Books.

Cloud, H. (2011). *Necessary Endings: The Employees, Businesses and Relationships That All of Us Have to Give up in Order to Move Forward*. New York, NY: HarperBusiness.

Conn, M. (1990). No bosses here: Management in worker co-operatives. *Journal of Business Ethics*, 9 (4/5), 373–376.

Coombe, C., McCloskey, M. L., Stephenson, L., & Anderson, N. J. (Eds.). (2008). *Leadership in English Language Teaching and Learning.* Ann Arbor, MI: The University of Michigan Press. https://doi.org/10.3998/mpub.231735

Craig, W. (October 16, 2018). 10 things transparency can do for your company. *Forbes.* Retrieved from: https://www.forbes.com/sites/williamcraig/2018/10/16/10-things-transparency-can-do-for-your-company/#213e3f4e25d0

Crandall, D., & Kincaid, M. (2017). *Permission to Speak Freely: How the Best Leaders Cultivate a Culture of Candor.* Oakland, CA: Berrett-Koehler Publishers.

Cunningham, C. L. (2012). Critically reflective leadership. *Australian Journal of Teacher Education, 37*(4), 49–61. https://doi.org/10.14221/ajte.2012v37n4.5

Curtis, A. (2009). On the edge: Leading from the periphery. In M. Christison & D. E. Murray (Eds.), *Leadership in English Language Education: Theoretical Foundations and Practical Skills for Changing Times* (pp. 98–109). New York, NY: Routledge.

Curtis, A. (2013). A gap in our field: Leadership in language education. *TESOL International Association.* Retrieved from: http://exclusive.multibriefs.com/content/a-gap-in-our-field-leadership-in-language-education

Curtis, A. (2015). Series editor's preface. In C. Hastings, *Perspectives on Teaching English for Specific Purposes in Saudi Arabia* (pp. v–vii). TESOL Press.

Curtis, A. (2017). *Methods and Methodologies for Language Teaching: The Centrality of Context.* London, UK: Palgrave Macmillan. https://doi.org/10.1057/978-1-137-40737-5_2

Curtis, A. (2018). Race, ethnicity, and NNESTs. In *The TESOL Encyclopedia of English Language Teaching* (Eds. J. Liontas & M. DelliCarpini). Wiley Online Library. https://doi.org/10.1002/9781118784235.eelt0043

Curtis, A. (2020). Featured presentation: Living and Learning Online IN A Post-Pandemic World. *Qatar University 5th Annual International (Online) ELT Conference: English Language Teaching and 21st Century Skills—Communicate, Collaborate, Create.* November 7 and 8, 2020. http://www.qu.edu.qa/foundation/Conference/Conference-2020/Program

Curtis, A., & Romney, R. (Eds.). (2006). *Colour, Race and English Language Teaching: Shades of Meaning.* Mahwah, NJ: Lawrence Erlbaum.

Farrell, T. S. C. (2001). Critical friendships: Colleagues helping each other develop. *ELT Journal, 55*(4), 368–374. https://doi.org/10.1093/elt/55.4.368

Flowerdew, J. (1998). *The Final Years of British Hong Kong: The Discourse of Colonial Withdrawal.* Hampshire, UK: Palgrave Macmillan. https://doi.org/10.1007/978-1-349-26135-2

Gardner, N., & Davis, J. N. (1965). *The Art of Delegating.* Ann Arbor: The University of Michigan Press.

Gordon, J. (2017). *The Power of Positive Leadership: How and Why Positive Leaders Transform Teams and Organizations and Change the World.* Hoboken, NJ: Wiley & Sons.

Gray, J. A. (2018). Leadership coaching and mentoring: A research-based model for stronger partnerships. *International Journal of Education Policy and Leadership*, *13*(12), 1–18. https://doi.org/10.22230/ijepl.2018v13n12a844

Hofstede, G. (1980). Culture and organizations. *International Studies of Management & Organization*, *10*(4), 15–41.

Hofstede, G. (1991). *Cultures and Organizations: Software of the mind*. New York, NY: McGraw-Hill.

House, R. J., Dorfman, P. W., Javidan, M., Hanges, P. J., & de Luque, M. F. S. (2014). *Strategic Leadership across Cultures: The GLOBE Study of CEO Leadership Behavior and Effectiveness in 24 Countries*. Los Angeles, CA: Sage. https://doi.org/10.4135/9781506374581

Jasper, M. (2010). Reflective leadership: Editorial. *Journal of Nursing Management*, *18*(4), 351–354. https://doi.org/10.1111/j.1365-2834.2010.01111.x

Jeffers, S. J. (2007). *Feel the Fear and Do It Anyway: Dynamic Techniques for Turning Fear, Indecision and Anger into Power, Action and Love*. Santa Monica, CA: Jeffers Press.

Joyce, P. (2010). Leading and leadership: Reflections on a case study. *Journal of Nursing Management*, *18*(4), 418–424. https://doi.org/10.1111/j.1365-2834.2010.01090.x

Kammerer, P. (March 27, 2017). Why is Hong Kong still giving out colonial-era perks to its civil servants? *The South China Morning Post*. Retrieved from: https://www.scmp.com/comment/insight-opinion/article/2082404/ why hong kong still giving-out-colonial-era-perks-its-civil

Kaufman, C. (2016). Overcoming faculty fears about civic work: Reclaiming higher education's civic purpose. *New Directions for Community Colleges*, *173*, 69–76. https://doi.org/10.1002/cc.20191

Kemmis, S. (1985). Action research and the politics of reflection. In D. Boud, R. Keogh, & D. Walker (Eds.), *Reflection: Turning Experience into Learning* (pp. 139–164). London, UK: Croom Helm.

Kemmis, S. (1986). *Critical Reflection*. Unpublished manuscript. Deakin University, Geelong, Australia.

Lublin, J. S. (January 16, 2020). Check out the culture before a new job. *Wall Street Journal*, p. B5.

McDonell, S. (August 17, 2019). Hong Kong: 'The riot police are running in'. *BBC World News*. Retrieved from: https://www.bbc.com/news/av/world-asia-49381633/ hong-kong-the-riot-police-are-running-in

Mendoza, M. (2015). The evolution of storytelling. *Reporter Magazine*. Retrieved from: https://reporter.rit.edu/tech/evolution-storytelling

Nicholas, T. (1993). *Secrets of Entrepreneurial Leadership: Building Top Performance through Trust & Teamwork*. Chicago, IL: Dearborn.

Palmer, P. J. (1998/2017). *The Courage to Teach: Exploring the Inner Landscape of a Teacher's Life*. San Francisco, CA: Jossey-Bass.

Pellicer, L. O. (2008). *Caring Enough to Lead: How Reflective Practice Leads to Moral Leadership*. Thousand Oaks: Corwin Press.

Pereira, L. J. (2008). *Between the 'Real' and the 'Imagined': Professional Learning, Reflective Practice and Transformational Leadership*. Rotterdam: Sense Publishers. https://doi.org/10.1163/9789460911385

Perkins, I. P. (2020). *Recognizing Lexical Patterns That Arise in the Wake of White Nationalist Unrest*. ODU Digital Commons. Retrieved from: https://digitalcommons.odu.edu/undergradsymposium/2020/artsletters/2/

Rakowich, W. (2020). *Transfluence: How to Lead with Transformative Influence in Today's Climates of Change*. New York: Post Hill Press.

Reynolds, M. (2020). *Coach the Person, Not the Problem: A Guide to Using Reflective Inquiry*. Oakland, CA: Berrett-Koehler Publishers.

Rubenstein, D. M. (2020). *How to Lead: Wisdom from the World's Greatest CEOs, Founders, and Game Changers*. New York: Simon & Schuster.

Safferstone, M. J. (1999). Did you hear the one about...? Leading with humor pays dividends. *Academy of Management Perspectives, 13*(4), 103–104. https://doi.org/10.5465/ame.1999.2570560

Smith, S., & Ashby, M. (2020). *How to Future: Leading and Sense-Making in an Age of Hyperchange*. London: Kogan Page.

Soukup. R. (2019). *Do It Scared: Finding the Courage to Face Your Fears, Overcome Adversity and Create a Life You Love*. Grand Rapids, MI: Zondervan.

Talbot, Y. (1981). The reconstituted family. *Canadian Family Physician, 27*, 1803–1807.

TESOL International Association. (March 2014). *Governance Review Task Force Report to the Board of Directors*. Retrieved from: https://www.tesol.org/docs/default-source/governance/grtfboardreportmarch2014-final-public.pdf?sfvrsn=4&sfvrsn=4

Vines, S. (January 3, 1997). A lease no one thought would run out: Hong Kong handover. *The Independent*. Retrieved from: https://www.independent.co.uk/news/world/a-lease-no-one-thought-would-run-out-1281384.html

Wallace, J. B. (August 19–20, 2017). The high costs of workplace rudeness. *Wall Street Journal*, p. C3.

Waters, A., & Vilches, M. L. C. (2005). Managing innovation in language education: A course for ELT change agents. *Regional Language Centre Journal, 36*(2), 117–136. https://doi.org/10.1177/0033688205055566

Welch, D. V. (1998). *Reflective Leadership: The Stories of Five Leaders Successfully Building Generative Organizational Culture*. Cincinnati: Union Institute.

White, R., Hockley, A., van der Horst Jansen, J., & Laughner, M. S. (2008). *From Teacher to Manager: Managing Language Teaching Organizations*. Cambridge, UK: Cambridge University Press.

Zan, B., & Donegan-Ritter, M. (2013). Reflecting, coaching and mentoring to enhance teacher–child interactions in head start classrooms. *Early Childhood Education Journal, 42*(2), 93–104. https://doi.org/10.1007/s10643-013-0592-7

ABOUT THE AUTHORS

Dr Okon Effiong is a lecturer in the Foundation Programme, Qatar University. He is a member of the TESOL Board of Directors and served on its Nominating Committee, Diversity & Inclusion Committee, as Chair-elect of the EFL-Interest Section. He is founder and Past President of Africa TESOL. He was the President of Qatar TESOL.

Dr Christel Broady is Chair of graduate programs, as well as Director of the ESL Program at Georgetown College, Kentucky, USA. An international leader, Christel has served in many leadership roles with TESOL International and affiliates. Her list of domestic and international publications, keynotes, presentations, and awards is extensive.

Leo Mercado has been in the field for more than 25 years, making contributions as a director of studies, e-learning and proficiency testing specialist, project leader, author, and academic entrepreneur. Based in Atlanta, Georgia, USA, he has also successfully led two international accreditation processes, as well as large-scale, nationwide projects at the Ministry of Education level.

Andy Curtis (PhD) is a Professor in the Graduate School of Education at Anaheim University. From 2015 to 2016, he served as the 50th President of the TESOL International Association. He has (co)authored and (co)edited 200 articles, book chapters and books, he has presented to 50,000 language educators in 100 countries, and his work has been read by 100,000 language educators in 150 countries. He is based in Ontario, Canada, from where he works with learning organizations worldwide.

Marjorie Rosenberg has been involved in tertiary and adult education in Austria since 1981. She is an active teacher trainer, conference presenter, and ELT author. Marjorie served as IATEFL President from 2015 to 2017. Her latest project is working as a mentor through a program designed by EVE and Africa TESOL.

Dr Rosemary DePetro Orlando is a Professor at Southern New Hampshire University, USA. She regularly travels to Vietnam National University in Hanoi to teach MS TEFL courses in a university partnership degree program. As a language teacher educator, Rosemary regularly presents at national and international English Language Teaching conferences worldwide.

Dr Rosa Aronson is the Interim Executive Director of the TESOL International Association in Alexandria, Virginia, USA. Her career in Education began as an EFL teacher in France and continued in the USA in professional educational organizations. She has served as an English Language Specialist focusing on organizational leadership. She holds a PhD in Social Foundations of Education from the University of Virginia.

Dr Deborah Healey was the 2020–2021 President of the Board of Directors of the TESOL International Association. An online and face-to-face teacher educator, she writes and presents extensively internationally (Africa, Asia, Latin America, Europe, US) on appropriate use of technology in language teaching. Her doctorate is in Computers in Education.

Dr Neil J. Anderson has been actively involved in leadership roles and reflective practice for over 40 years. He currently teaches at Brigham Young University–Hawaii, USA. Neil served as President of the TESOL International Association for 2001–2002. He received the prestigious James Alatis Award from TESOL in 2014.

Dr Kathleen M. Bailey is a Professor of Applied Linguistics at the Middlebury Institute of International Studies at Monterey (MIIS), California, USA. She completed her MA and her doctorate at the University of California at Los Angeles. Her research interests include teacher education, language assessment, and the teaching of listening and speaking.

Chapter 5

Recapping and Reflecting Forward

Andy Curtis

In the first issue of the first volume of the journal *Reflective Practice*, Alan Bleakley (2000) wrote about 'narrative, confessionalism and reflective practice' (p. 11). Bleakley is critical of that kind of RP, but in a section of his paper titled 'The erotics of narratives of "practice"' (pp. 20–21), he asks: 'If secular humanistic, personal-confessional narratives, offered as therapeutic, repress, or marginalise, other genres for writing "practices", what will happen to those repressed genres?' (p. 21). As we noted at the beginning of this book, a common problem in educational publishing is professional academics writing for each other, often using exclusionary language that can only be understood by others in their 'in-group,' which does not usually include busy classroom language teachers. Therefore, in spite of Bleakley's claimed concerns about the evils of 'personal-confessional narratives,' that is what we have in the notes below, which reiterate the main RP and LiLE learning points of the previous chapters, using 'personal-confessional' examples from my own life.

In Chapter 4, we referred to the early work of Stephen Brookfield (1995) on Critical Reflective Practice, which was adapted and expanded on by Christine Cunningham (2012) to create Critically Reflective Leadership. Brookfield (1995) described the 'examples from my life that illustrate points I'm making' (p. 2) as 'narrative disclosure' (p. 3). Though he was aware of the risk of his disclosures being seen as arrogant, self-important, and/or self-indulgent, he disclosed anyway, because 'students across the years have told me that this captures their attention and helps them understand a new concept' (p. 2). In Reflective Break 37, I wrote that 'narrative disclosure … is really just a fancy way of referring to story-telling.' By this point, having read the 40 accounts of the ten RTLs, from their compacted bios to their LiLE challenges, we can see the importance of the 'disclosure' part of 'narrative disclosure,' as some of the RTLs in this book shared 'personal-professional, sometimes-confessional' narratives that I heard and read here for the first time—even after knowing them for decades!

As we have noted in earlier chapters, language teachers appreciate the value of carefully thought out, deliberate 'strategic repetition' to help with understanding and with remembering. So, in the sections below, we will re-present the main RP and LiLE learning points from the Question One, Question Two, and Question Three responses (we have just seen the Question Four response summaries). But, in the spirit of 'repetition with a twist', I will add a brief paragraph to each of the learning points, using some of my own 'personal-professional, sometimes-confessional' narratives, in some cases being shared here for the very first time publicly and in print.

RECAPPING, REITERATING, AND EXPANDING ON THE QUESTION ONE RESPONSES

(i) It is never too early for a teacher to start thinking about and preparing for an educational leadership role—even if they are not expecting to be in such a role.

(ii) It is never too late to start your leadership journey.

(iii) Coming from humble beginnings, with few, if any, of the privileges enjoyed by the majority of those around you, you can build resilience, determination, and perseverance—all essential leadership qualities.

(iv) Accelerated Language Learning may be more myth than method, but Accelerated Leadership Learning in language education is possible—just beware of burnout.

(v) Leaders in language education often follow different paths to those of their peers, and different paths from the ones laid out for them, which can make the journey difficult but all the more rewarding for that.

(vi) Diversity is a strength, but with diversity also comes the challenges of (very) different ways of understanding ourselves and the world around us, and the connections between the two.

It is never too early for a teacher to start thinking about and preparing for an educational leadership role—even if they are not expecting to be in such a role. As part of my mis-spent youth, growing up in England in the 1970s, I joined the local chapter of the Boy Scouts Association of Great Britain, whose famous motto is 'Be Prepared,' more specifically, 'Be Prepared in Mind' and 'Be Prepared in Spirit.' Not surprisingly, to those who know me, my time in the Scouts did not end well, as it did not take long for me to break all ten of the Scout's Commandments (and then some). But, more than 40 years later, here I am reflecting on my time as a Boy Scout, and on the idea of being prepared, in this case, to become a leader in language education. Perhaps the simplest ways to be prepared for a LiLE role are: (i) never rule out the possibility of taking on such a role; (ii) know that you may find yourself in such a role when you least expect it; (iii) be aware of the leaders around you, looking closely and carefully at those whom you believe to be examples of 'good' and 'bad' leadership; (iv) read the occasional online article about LiLE and, if you find those helpful, read more, take notes, and be ready.

It is never too late to start your leadership journey. This is, of course, the flipside of the first point above. But it is still worth mentioning, because of the many teachers I have met in classrooms around the world, who have told me that they feel ready to take on the challenges of LiLE but they also feel that they may be 'too old to start now.' As language educators, many of us may have seen some inspiring teaching from new teachers, and some dishearteningly dull teaching from teachers with decades of experience. So it is with LiLE, i.e., some long-time leaders can be great and some poor, with the same applying to new leaders. It is, then, not the number of years that counts, but more what we have done in and with those years. Although I reject the idea that 'age is just a number,' there are some benefits to starting the leadership journey later, such as bringing to bear all of the accumulated knowledge, skills, and understanding from everything we did before. For example, in my experience, the board member who keeps engaging in attention-seeking, distracting behaviors during meetings can be managed in much the same way as a teacher manages a student who behaves that way.

Coming from humble beginnings, with few, if any, of the privileges enjoyed by the majority of those around you, you can build resilience, determination and perseverance—all essential leadership qualities. As various so-called world leaders, such as Donald Trump and Boris Johnson, have shown with painfully embarrassing clarity in recent years—especially during a global pandemic—having had a privileged upbringing can turn out to be a hindrance when it comes to leading. There may be nothing inherently wrong with privileges—as a man, I have enjoyed some of those, but as a person of color and a life-long 'visible minority,' there are many that I have not enjoyed. The problem comes when people-of-privilege are wilfully and blissfully unaware of how much they have benefited simply by being, for example, a white, male, native user of English born in a place like the US, the UK, Canada, or Australia. That spectacular cluelessness renders them (very) poor leaders, because they have little or no knowledge of the day-to-day lives of the vast majority of the people they claim to lead. Having experienced, directly and indirectly, significant poverty during my lifetime, I would not wish that on anyone.

But if you have lived that experience, then make use of it, tap into it, and channel it into your work as a sympathetic, empathetic leader.

Accelerated Language Learning may be more myth than method, but Accelerated Leadership Learning in language education is possible—just beware of burnout. Perhaps ironically, perhaps appropriately, as I write these personal-professional, RTL concluding notes, I am suffering from 'board member burnout.' In recent years, I have been a member of a board of trustees which has, for 25 years, been helping doctoral candidates complete their PhDs—that is a whole generation of scholars who have been helped, financially, when they needed it most. I am honored and humbled to have been able to work with a team of world-renowned educators, to support the next generation of scholars. But I can no longer continue, because I have allowed myself to become burned out, by taking on too much, not saying 'no' often enough, and saying 'yes' far too often. Two of the many other lessons I have learned over the last three years on this board of trustees are: Pace Yourself and Prioritize. Like 'Be Prepared,' such advice is easy to give, but can be difficult to take on board. Sure, everything is important, but everything cannot be *equally* important. And as we all know (though we seem to constantly forget), the work will always be there—but family, close friends, and other loved ones will not.

Leaders in language education often follow different paths to those of their peers, and different paths from the ones laid out for them, which can make the journey difficult but all the more rewarding for that. Sometimes, while working on this book, I have banged my head against the wall—and I do not mean in the metaphorical sense. From where I stand now, here at my faithful, old, breaking-down MacBook, I can see quite clearly (in the daylight, at least) the two indentations on the wall of my office, a few metres away from me. Notwithstanding the head-banging (which on occasion led to some helpful 'aha' moments about this book) one of the things that I have most enjoyed about working on this project—with people I have known and cared about, and who have kindly cared about me, for a combined total of many decades—is learning more about the details of their journeys. I realize how over-used the metaphor of the journey may be, as I allude to in Chapter 1. But the fact that that particular metaphor is still being used, after thousands of years, says something about how deeply ingrained in the human psyche is the notion of the journey. Another, more modern cliché says 'It's not the destination, it's the journey.' It is, of course, both. So, buckle-up and enjoy the ride!

Diversity is a strength, but with diversity also comes the challenges of (very) different ways of understanding ourselves and the world around us, and the connections between the two. Having many different ways of seeing, hearing, and knowing ourselves, each other, and the world around us is not just important. On an evolutionary level—and sorry if this sounds over-dramatic—the future of human civilization may depend on us being able to welcome those who are different from us. The more different, the better—but also, the more different, the harder. *Diversity is a mixed blessing.* You may, by now, have spotted the recurring theme of 'easier said than done' regarding these ideas, but we can and should still work towards achieving some of these goals. For me, the diversity high points have come when, in the middle of wrestling with the rightness of each other's worldview, we unexpectedly find a small piece of common ground, on which we can build beyond tolerance—and together create something deeper and longer-lasting. My diversity low points have been when I have witnessed dictators masquerading as guardians of democracy, sowing deep, painful divisions, for their own personal and political gain. They use ancient divide-and-conquer approaches, designed to force us to forget all that we have in common. But we must remember the unbreakable strength that there can be when we unite in our myriad differences.

RECAPPING, REITERATING, AND EXPANDING ON THE QUESTION TWO RESPONSES

(i)   RP means different things to different people. Therefore, before engaging in RP, it is essential for teachers to be clear on what they mean and what they understand by 'RP.'

(ii) RP requires the conscious, deliberate setting aside of time for more meaningful RP to be possible.

(iii) RP should not be seen as being a quick or easy solution.

(iv) RP can be thought of in relation to metacognition and to mindfulness, as RP can help us become more conscious and self-aware teachers, learners, and leaders.

(v)   Data-gathering of all kinds can help us with our RP.

(vi) It can be helpful to think of RP as a kind of deliberate stepping back, to get a better view, or even as a kind of stepping outside of ourselves, so we can see both the big picture and the close-up detail.

RP means different things to different people. Therefore, before engaging in RP, it is essential for teachers to be clear on what they mean and what they understand by 'RP.' At the end of the 1990s, I was invited to fly from Hong Kong to Canada, to give a workshop on RP for language educators at the University of Alberta. I was introduced by the person who had invited me, our far-too-soon dearly departed friend and colleague, Professor Robert Berman. It was the first time he and I had met, so I did not know about his sense of humor, but after my short talk, before the Q-and-A, Robert asked, playfully: 'Isn't all this reflective practice business just a whole lot of navel-gazing?!' (see introductory overview). After that, instead of talking about the pros and cons of the different ways of engaging in RP, the attendees and I spent the following hour talking about what RP meant to us. I look back on that talk, and on the moment that Robert asked his provocative question, as a lasting reminder of the importance of defining our terms, at least for ourselves, even if for nobody else. And if we choose to engage in RP with others, sharing our meanings does not require coming to any kind of consensus, as it is about hearing one another, not necessarily agreeing with each other.

RP requires the conscious, deliberate setting aside of time for more meaningful RP to be possible. Time is, in many ways, the great equalizer, as nobody (in the Gregorian calendar, anyway) gets more than 24 hours each day, or seven days a week, or 365 (occasionally 366) days a year. For most of the language teachers I have known, pretty much every waking hour seemed to be fully occupied with the preparing, teaching, marking, etc. of their work lives, and the family, friends, and others in their home lives. 'Then, how on earth do you expect us to find the time to do RP in the midst of all this chaos?!' asked an incredulous teacher at a Brazil TESOL conference in São Paulo some years ago. For the rest of the workshop, we looked at their schedules to find small amounts of time during their self-described 'crazy days,' which for them turned out to be early in the day or late at night. The key for these teachers was to engage in RP little and often, rather than occasionally for longer stretches. And in the same way as they exercised with their 'gym buddies,' some of them had great success sharing with their 'RP buddies.'

RP should not be seen as being a quick or easy solution. After another workshop on RP, a language teacher said to me, with a heavy sigh and radiating sadness: 'I tried RP but it didn't work.' From my days working with the parents of terminally ill children in hospitals in England, I drew on my grief counselling training which, to be honest, mostly involved a version of what language educators call 'active listening,' although I had known nothing of language teaching or learning at that point. As it turned out, there was so much tough stuff going on in that teacher's personal life, that she was bringing it with her into the classroom, which made it a struggle for her to teach well. She and I kept in touch in the years that followed, until she passed away recently. By the end, our roles had been reversed, and she was teaching me about RP. One of the many things she taught me was that RP is not the answer to the question, nor is it the solution to the problem. But RP can help you figure out what the questions and the problems are, and what you may be able to do about them, as well as how to celebrate the successes.

RP can be thought of in relation to metacognition and to mindfulness, as RP can help us become more conscious and self-aware teachers, learners, and leaders.

Many people—from Ancient Greek philosopher Homer to cartoon dad Homer Simpson—have written or said: 'What is matter? Never mind. What is mind? It doesn't matter.' These lines are a witty attempt to represent the complex relationship between our thoughts (mind) and the things that we are thinking about (matter), which relates to metacognition and mindfulness, the meanings of which overlap. Metacognition can be conceptualized as a conscious awareness of, while critically reflecting on, our thoughts. Mindfulness is more to do with slowing down the constant cascade of thoughts and feelings, so that the individual can squeeze, as it were, in between those thoughts and feelings, to find an internal stillness, even in the midst of chaos. For me, the metacognitive part of my process often comes during lesson planning, when I can hear myself asking rhetorical questions that are more why-questions than the other wh-questions. However, the mindfulness part for me usually happens in the midst of a lesson that is not going well, and I start to get anxious. At those times, my mindfulness helps me stay calm, stay focused, and slow down.

Data-gathering of all kinds can help us with our RP. This point is the counter-weight to the point immediately above, balancing the intrapersonal communication of metacognition and mindfulness with the gathering of external input, from outside sources. As part of my biomedical sciences education, I had to pass a number of courses on statistics. As a result, by the time I had found my true calling—teaching and learning languages and cultures—I was comfortable with numbers. However, I soon learned that my fondness for numbers was not shared by my language teaching colleagues. Our bosses seemed to have figured out that, if they wanted their language teaching staff to go glassy-eyed and agree with whatever they were proposing, then stacks of statistics would do the trick. My challenge was to learn that numbers and numerical data can only tell part of the story of what is happening in our classroom. For the complete picture you need words as well. So, I encourage teachers who want to engage in RP to become familiar both with numerical data, like simple frequency counts (e.g., how often something happened), and with the words and phrases of the teachers and the students, combining quantitative and qualitative data to be able to see the big picture.

It can be helpful to think of RP as a kind of deliberate stepping back, to get a better view, or even as a kind of stepping outside of ourselves, so we can see both the big picture and the close-up detail. In addition to data-gathering, another way of seeing what is (and is not) happening in our classroom is to physically, literally change our position. For example, after decades of teaching English, I went to South China (Guangzhou) to learn Mandarin Chinese. I was, by far, the oldest person in the crowded classroom, including our teacher, Ms Lee. I did learn some Mandarin

Chinese, but re-reading my notebooks from those classes, I can see that about half of the pages were language learning notes, while the other half were about language teaching. Although being so aware of what Ms Lee was doing distracted me from my language learning (with which I was already struggling) it was a real eye-opener to be sat at a desk, like everyone else, instead of being at the front of the classroom. I also became the kind of language learning student that I myself find challenging, as I was constantly asking questions, some of which were convoluted and some-what off-topic. Ms Less managed my interruptions gently but firmly, being patient with me, while also being respectful of my 'advanced years,' as she put it!

RECAPPING, REITERATING, AND EXPANDING ON THE QUESTION THREE RESPONSES

(i)   Set 'dedicated' time aside for RP, with no distractions, so your RP can be focused.

(ii) Read the published RP accounts of other teachers, but also read RP accounts from outside of education and language education, in other help-ing professions.

(iii) Gather data/feedback on what is happening in your classrooms and les-sons, for example, audio/video recordings, journal entries, teaching port-folios, etc.

(iv) Look for RP mentors whom you trust and who can help you figure out how, where, and when to engage in the kind of RP that works best for you.

(v)   Learn to set RP goals and to ask RP questions, in the same way as you do in your regular lesson and course planning and preparation.

(vi) In your RP, balance seeing the moment-to-moment interactions in your classroom with seeing the big picture and thinking long term.

Set 'dedicated' time aside for RP, with no distractions, so your RP can be focused. Successful language teachers are extremely skilled in using repetition judiciously, and this may be overdoing it just a little, but as one of the most commonly recur-ring themes in this book, we are going to repeat this one more time (tautology intended). Even though, when we are engaged in RP, our minds are very active, I sometimes draw on the sleep analogy when thinking about time and whether it is well spent or not. In my case, I function far better when I have had, for example, six or seven hours of refreshing, restorative sleep, than when I have been tossing and turning for eight or more hours. 'Less is more' can have helpful meanings, but I have heard too many education administrators say this when they are cut-ting budgets and asking teachers and learners do more with less. In the case of RP, the more I do it, the better I get at it, and by 'better' I mean I can learn about my teaching and my learners with a shorter amount of more focused time, rather than being distracted by the myriad personal, professional issues tugging at my cognitive sleeve, demanding my attention.

Read the published RP accounts of other teachers, but also read RP accounts from outside of education and language education, in other helping professions. If you have reached this last chapter, then I may be, as they say, singing to the choir. First, thank you for getting to this point in the book, which we hope will be not an ending, but a beginning. Second, the value of reading outside our language education field—even if just a little outside—is worth reiterating. For one thing, that kind of reading can be comforting, when we see that we in language education are not the only ones facing some of these challenges and struggles. I worked in hospitals in England for many years before becoming a language educator, and I still tap into those healthcare writings which I find helpful even after all these years. I left universities long ago because of their insistence on specialization, as a result of which professors know a great deal about a small area, but little or nothing about the big, wide world around them. That is not the professors' fault, but that of the universities and their funding agencies, who talk a lot about the importance of interdisciplinary work—but who then reward specialization. As one old fast-food advertising tagline goes: Think Outside the Box!

Gather data/feedback on what is happening in your classrooms and lessons, for example, audio/video recordings, journal entries, teaching portfolios, etc. Data-gathering has been discussed previously, but 'Data' can be a bit of a 'D-word,' similar to 'Diversity'; i.e., it is, in theory, welcomed—but in practice, it is more difficult. Two of the commonest problems I have seen in RP over the last 20-plus years is collecting more data than is needed, and/or collecting the wrong kind of data. Having made the claim that 'data-gathering of all kinds can help us with our RP,' I should stress the 'can' part. More data does not necessarily make our RP more enriching. But the 'best' data can make a big difference, and by 'best' I mean the most appropriate data—depending on what aspects of your teaching and learning you want to deepen your understanding of. For example, if you want to learn more about which students you do (and do not) call on in class, then video recordings can be very helpful for that, whereas surveys would be of little use. So, if you have a question within your RP, then use that to decide which data you want to gather. And if it is high-quality, reliable, and valid, a little data can go a long way.

Look for RP mentors whom you trust and who can help you figure out how, where, and when to engage in the kind of RP that works best for you. For more than 20 years, the TESOL International Association has had a Leadership Mentoring Program (LMP) Award. I was one of the first LMP awardees, in 2000, which eventually led to my becoming the 50th President of the Association 15 years later, in 2015. In the years in between, I have served as a mentor on the LMP, to help others prepare for leadership roles within the Association and beyond. What makes the LMP Award unique is that it is specifically designed to support groups that are 'under-represented' in the Association's membership and leadership. It is not clear, after more than two decades, what 'under-represented' may mean today, and if it still means what it meant when the LMP was created two decades ago. The LMP arrangement is a one-to-one, one-year professional relationship between a mentee (who is the applicant/awardee) and a mentor (who is often, but not always, a past president of the Association, or a past member of the Association's Board of Directors). Having started off as an LMP mentee and now having been an LMP mentor, I can confirm how tremendously rewarding this kind of mentoring can be for both parties.

Learn to set RP goals and to ask RP questions, in the same way as you do in your regular lesson and course planning and preparation. Although I am happy to admit my bias, I believe language teachers may be especially expert in classroom management and goal-setting. I have made that claim to non-language teachers, some of whom delude themselves with the line 'Oh, I don't teach *language. I* teach *content.'* Are you kidding? Give me a break! Have you ever tried to teach one without the other? Anyway, not surprisingly, those 'dis-content-ed' teachers have repeatedly, roundly rejected my claim! The basis for my claim is the fact that most of the language teachers I know are multilingual and multicultural, which enables them—like some kind of pedagogic superpower!—to comprehend and articulate something from multiple angles and points of view. That multi-perspective understanding may enhance their classroom management, goal-setting, and other language teaching-learning skills. Whether or not my claim is agreed with, it is very important that you have goals and questions in mind to help you focus your RP, and so you know how much progress you are (or are not) making towards achieving that particular RP goal, or to answering that particular RP question.

In your RP, balance seeing the moment-to-moment interactions in your classroom with seeing the big picture and thinking long term. As you have seen, the RTLs in this book make good use of metaphors and analogies to capture and convey aspects of their RP and LiLE experiences, for examples metaphors of 'moving' and 'seeing'— from the electron microscopes I refer to, to Neil's use of microscopes, telescopes, and kaleidoscopes as ways of seeing the detail, the big picture, and the relationships between the two, ideally at the same time, if possible. Sometimes the most memorable in-class moments are the unexpected ones. One of the more obscure Ancient Greek philosophers, Heraclitus is credited with the phrase 'expect the unexpected'; however, that appears to be some kind of self-cancelling tautological impossibility, making it of little use. Perhaps more helpful advice is: 'be ready to catch the unexpected moment.' That advice relates to the ideas of the teachable moment and the a-ha moment, which are not quite the same thing, but the latter can lead to the former, as an unexpected event can throw you off balance for a moment, but in a good way, that enables you to see what is happening from an entirely different perspective. RP can help us explore those moments in depth.

BRIEF CONCLUDING THOUGHTS

In Act 2, Scene 2 of Shakespeare's *Hamlet*, the character Polonius says:

> *Why day is day, night night, and time is time,*
> *Were nothing but to waste night, day, and time;*
> *Therefore, since brevity is the soul of wit,*
> *And tediousness the limbs and outward flourishes,*
> *I will be brief ...* (lines 88–92)

Of course, Polonius is being ironic (either deliberately or accidentally) as he is anything but brief, as he reluctantly leads up to telling the King and the Queen that their son is mad. Brevity has been one of the goals of this book, as we know how busy classroom language teachers are, and how little time they usually have for their own professional development. And even though this is not meant to be a witty book, I hope some of my narrative disclosure above did cause some of our readers to smile! Therefore, with brevity in mind, I will conclude with a few brief thoughts on RP and LiLE—which are as much hopes as they are thoughts.

As I wrote at the beginning of this book, I was surprised to see how many of the leaders in language education that I approached about contributing a chapter to this book replied that they were too busy, working on other things. When I inquired what those other things were, it turned out that those leaders were, ironically, often so busy meeting the demands of their leadership roles and responsibilities, they had no time to even think about—much less write about—their LiLE experiences. On the one hand, that is entirely understandable, as I approached some of the best-known and busiest leaders in our field. However, on the other, it is very unfortunate, and it may reflect the lack of institutional recognition of such writing, as a result of the pressure on university teachers to publish or perish. A related problem may that the kind of online newsletters published by the TESOL International Association, IATEFL, and other language education associations, which contain more experiential and less academic articles on leadership, are not valued in the hallowed halls of The Academy (Curtis, 2017). Whatever the reasons, it is my fervent hope that, in the future, leaders in language education think about, write about, and share more of their lived experiences of leadership. Those writings may score few, if any, scholarly points on the hierarchical scoreboard of academia, but they could be of great value to the next generation of leaders in our field.

A second point relates to what is known as the 'silo effect,' named after the large, vertical, grain storage containers seen standing tall in wheat fields. In the same way that those kinds of silos are not connected to each other, large storehouses of knowledge are also unconnected. For example, one of the first papers I presented and published, in the early 1990s, brought decades of clinical studies on autism together with decades of research on second language learning. In the end, my theories about the relationships between autistic children learning a first language and non-autistic children learning a second language were not supported by the data. But by bringing together two large bodies of work that had previously been 'siloed,' I was able to make a modest but nonetheless original contribution to the understanding of first and second language learning and teaching. Something similar happened when I left healthcare and started my MA in Language Teaching and Applied Linguistics. Because my head was still full of medical models, I took a well-known but quite linear description of a language lesson (teaching German grammar to native users of English in England) and rewrote the description as a metabolic pathway (called Krebs Cycle, after Hans Krebs, or the Citric Acid Cycle). Krebs is still one of my favorite cycles because it is a cascade of chemical reactions, each one linked to the next one, rather than the step-by-step, first-this-then-that description of the German grammar lesson. My second hope, then, is that the bodies of work on RP and on LiLE can be brought together far more often than appears to have been the case so far.

My third hope is that more systematic support is given to those language educators who are taking on (or who think they might one day want to take on) LiLE roles, starting with initial training and followed by ongoing leadership development, in the same way we now think of initial teacher training leading to teacher professional development. Those support programs could start with needs analyses, of the same kinds we have been using with our language learners for decades, and end with assessment of LiLE learning outcomes, just as we assess language learning outcomes, for example, with portfolios that document and demonstrate the learning process.

My fourth set of thoughts and hopes for the future of RP and LiLE involves the recent work being done to expand on the earlier work bringing non-Western belief systems to RP and LiLE. For example, in 2020, Charlene Tan presented a Daoist interpretation of Donald Schön's ideas, and found that 'A Daoist understanding of reflective practice offers a non-Western philosophical basis to Schön's ideas and adds to the existing theories on reflection' (p. 686). Tan (2020) agrees with Tao (2011), who stated that a Daoist reflective practitioner is someone who 'becomes supremely attuned to the complexity of the world and can thus navigate various domains of relationality with extraordinary grace, ease, and efficacy' (Tao, 2011, p. 463). For me, that kind of grace and ease is (much) more aspirational than actually achievable, but it is encouraging to see Schön's ideas being set in the broader, longer historical context of belief systems such as Daoism and Buddhism (Park & Mo, 2019).

Then comes the new technologies. In the two decades since the *Reflective Practice* journal was launched, new(er) technologies—and in particular mobile media devices and so-called 'social media'—have changed the way billions of people on the planet communicate. It is, therefore, no surprise to see recent reports on, for example, RP in virtual communities (Pow & Lai, 2021), and articles about RP using social media sites such as Twitter. For example, Kathleen Corrales and Trey Erwin studied 670 'reflective tweets' (2020, p. 484) from around 100 students taking English language courses at a private university in Latin America. However, although Corrales & Erwin found 'a correlation between deeper reflections and better performance on student exams,' they also found that the students 'tended to overestimate their abilities to write deep reflections as the majority of tweets were more superficial' (p. 484). No surprise there! Given that the 280-character limit on the length of a posting on Twitter amounts to barely a single 50-word sentence in English, it is important to see the limits of such platforms when it comes to RP and LiLE. Brevity may indeed be the soul of wit, but too much brevity can lead to a loss of essential detail. However, those who make billions of US dollars every year from such ways of communicating (if that can really be called 'communicating') would still have us believe that technology is *the* answer to all our problems— pedagogical, personal, and everything in-between. And while such claims are deliberate and knowingly made exaggerations for the purposes of inflating share prices on stock markets, some new technologies may be of some help. For example, Marilisa Birello and Joan Font looked at what they call the 'affordances of images in digital reflective writing' (2020, p. 534).

Based on a three-year study of the blog posts of 180 pre-service teachers of writing, in Spain, Birello & Font found that 'images in digital writing' can help such teachers 'in a meaningful way that can deepen their reflective processes' (p. 534). In other words, pictures helped, i.e., being able to incorporate digital images into their writing helped those teachers deepen their RP. For those readers who are, like me, 'artistically challenged' (and in my case, also diagnosed as being 'autistically challenged', Curtis, 2021), it is good to know that these newer technologies enable, for example, the incorporation of crystal-clear digital images, rather than someone trying to decode my squiggly-wiggly pencil-and-paper line drawings. Whether or not the inclusion of such images will really increase the quantity and quality of our RP, and if so to what extent, remains to be seen. But these new technological capabilities and possibilities have the potential to add some creative new dimensions to our RP in the future—perhaps especially in the post-pandemic (or in-between-pandemic) times ahead, when so much of our sharing may have to be done at a safe distance—separated by time (zones) and space, but maybe even more deeply connected through our shared experiences of RP and LiLE.

REFERENCES

Birello, M., & Font, J. T. P. (2020). The affordances of images in digital reflective writing: An analysis of preservice teachers' blog posts. *Reflective Practice, 21*(4), 534–551. https://doi.org/10.1080/14623943.2020.1781609

Bleakley, A. (2000). Writing with invisible ink: Narrative, confessionalism and reflective practice. *Reflective Practice, 1*(1), 11–24. https://doi.org/10.1080/713693130

Brookfield, S. (1995). *Becoming a Critically Reflective Teacher*. San Francisco, CA: Jossey-Bass.

Corrales, K. A., & Erwin, T. C. (2020). Twitter and reflection: Tweeting towards deeper learning. *Reflective Practice, 21*(4), 484–498. https://doi.org/10.1080/14623943.2020.1779048

Cunningham, C. L. (2012). Critically reflective leadership. *Australian Journal of Teacher Education, 37*(4), 49–61. https://doi.org/10.14221/ajte.2012v37n4.5

Curtis, A. (2017). Online professional development. *In The TESOL Encyclopedia of English Language Teaching* (Eds. J. Liontas & M. DelliCarpini). Wiley Online Library. https://doi.org/10.1002/9781118784235.eelt0653

Curtis, A. (October 2021). Living on the spectrum: The first 50 years. *Difference and Disability Newsletter*. TESOL International Association.

Park, S., & Mo, Y. (2019). Daily practice of Won-Buddhism: Insights from the mind diaries of early childhood teachers in South Korea. *Journal of Beliefs and Values, 40*(2), 246–263. https://doi.org/10.1080/13617672.2019.1597398

Pow, W., & Lai, K. (2021). Enhancing the quality of student teachers' reflective teaching practice through building a virtual learning community. *Journal of Global Education and Research, 5*(1), 54–71. https://doi.org/10.5038/2577-509X.5.1.1088

Tan, C. (2020). Revisiting Donald Schön's notion of reflective practice: A Daoist interpretation. *Reflective Practice, 21*(5), 686–698. https://doi.org/10.1080/14623943.2020.1805307

Tao, J. (2011). Two notions of freedom in classical Chinese thought: The concept of Hua— in the Zhuangzi and the Xunzi. *Dao, 10*(4), 463–486. https://doi.org/10.1007/s11712-011-9245-y

ABOUT THE AUTHOR

Andy Curtis (PhD) is a Professor in the Graduate School of Education at Anaheim University. From 2015 to 2016, he served as the 50th President of the TESOL International Association. He has (co)authored and (co)edited 200 articles, book chapters and books, he has presented to 50,000 language educators in 100 countries, and his work has been read by 100,000 language educators in 150 countries. He is based in Ontario, Canada, from where he works with learning organizations worldwide.

Index

Accelerated Leadership Learning (ALL):
viii, 16, 18, 162, 164

action research: 1, 6, 45, 56, 81, 154

advisor(s)/advisory: 29, 89, 97, 120, 132–
133, 142–143, 147

affiliates: 19, 27, 93, 117, 146

Anderson, Neil: 28–30, 57–59, 93–95,
147–150

anger/angry: 17, 80, 110

Aronson, Rosa: 26–27, 52–55, 88–90,
138–141

art: 44, 46–47, 89, 115, 127

attitudes: 37, 43–45, 59, 60, 86

Austria: 17, 18, 24, 83, 84

authentic/authenticity: 40, 55, 123

Bailey, Kathleen: 30–31, 60–61, 96–98,
150–154

Bailey, Curtis, & Nunan: 16, 34, 45, 51,
81, 94, 112

balance/balancing: 5, 10, 54, 73, 98, 110,
168, 170–171

bias/biases: 8, 37, 42, 70–71, 170

big picture: 38, 47, 59, 73, 81, 165, 167–
168, 170

Board of Directors: 20, 21, 27, 30, 92, 120,
125, 139–140, 146, 170

Brigham Young University/BYU: 28–29,
147–149

Broady, Christel: 20–21, 41–43, 76–78,
120–123

burnout: viii, 16, 18, 162, 164

California, USA: 30, 84, 147

CALL (Computer-Assisted Language
Learning): 21, 28, 92

caring: 104, 105, 123

case study/studies: 71, 81, 104, 107, 116

changing: 61, 89, 93, 109, 113, 133, 137,
140

China: 110, 128, 129–130, 144, 167

Christison & Stoller: 98, 109, 152

coaching: 71, 81, 107, 112

collaboration: 9, 26, 42, 80, 120, 121

color(s): 18, 59, 111, 162

communicate/communication: viii, 44, 78,
93, 137, 140, 153, 173

complex/complexity: viii, 21, 37, 54, 57,
88–89, 108, 123, 125, 146, 154, 167

conflict(s): 43, 75, 88, 126, 134

constraint(s): 28, 60, 68, 103, 152

continuum: 34, 48, 94

control: 58, 60, 84, 93, 98, 105, 113, 115

Covid-19: vii, 1–3, 8, 27, 120

creative/creativity: 28, 91, 93, 174

crisis/crises: 1–6, 28, 91, 143

critical reflection: 37, 44, 60, 70, 86

criticism: 89, 114, 139, 141

Curtis, Andy: 1–13, 14–19, 22–23,
34–38, 45–48, 68–73, 81–83, 103–116,
128–131, 161–175

data-driven: 37, 77, 78

data gathering: 38, 165, 167, 169

decision-making: 72, 77–78, 90, 109,
114–115, 123, 139

delegate/delegation: 98, 107, 115, 152–154

demands/demanding: 25, 56, 60, 88, 92, 169, 170

determination: viii, 18, 162, 163

Dewey, John: 41, 53, 55

dichotomy/dichotomies: 25, 47–48

differences: 43, 69, 82, 111–112, 137, 141, 165

disappointment/disappointed/disappointing: 22, 75, 106, 123, 138

distance: 37, 47, 76, 77, 82, 89, 94, 120, 174

distraction(s)/distract(ed): 52, 73, 83, 168–169

diversity: viii, 17–18, 20, 21, 74, 117, 120, 149, 162, 164–165, 169

downturn(s): 22, 143, 145–146

economy/economic: 28, 91, 143–144

educational leadership: viii, 15, 18, 27, 57, 104, 162

Effiong, Okon: 19–20, 39–40, 74–76, 117–120

emotions: 41, 49, 85, 134

empathy: 43, 107, 108, 164

empower(ed)/empowerment: 37, 40, 126, 148, 150

England: 2, 7, 19, 23, 36, 46, 128–130, 162, 166, 169, 172

enrollment: 22, 28, 91, 124, 142–143, 145–146

estrange/estrangement: 47–48, 82

Executive Committee: 20, 27, 89, 92, 117, 132, 139

experiential: 6, 9, 37, 50, 171

fair/fairness: 130, 132, 147, 151–153

falling: 22, 28, 13

Farrell, Thomas S. C.: vii–viii, 9, 55

fear: 110, 111, 112

feelings: 8, 29, 49, 79, 81, 85, 108, 167

finance(s)/financed: 21, 91, 142, 144

flexible/flexibility: 24, 92, 136, 143

fly/flying: 88, 131, 148, 165

France/French: 18, 26, 111

friend(s)/friendship(s): 9, 29, 43, 104, 118, 119–120, 129–131, 150, 164–166

Germany: 17, 18, 20

grants: 28, 91, 143, 145–146

Guyana/Guyanese: 17, 23, 128

happy/happiness: 53, 80, 85, 124–125, 135–136, 170

Harvard: 2, 4, 15

Healey, Deborah: 27–28, 55–57, 91–93, 142–146

health: 3, 59, 116, 132, 152

healthcare: 7, 36, 70, 169, 172

hearing: 6, 7, 42, 81, 82, 85, 97, 164, 166

heart: viii, 10, 41, 46, 76–77

hindsight: 10, 25, 74, 103, 116, 130, 132, 135

Hong Kong: 23, 127–130, 149, 165

honor/honored/honorable: 23, 75, 89, 164

hope: 3, 6, 7, 31, 71, 97, 169, 171–172

humble beginnings: viii, 15, 18, 162, 163

humor: 24, 115–116, 146, 165

immigrant(s): 15, 26, 144

inclusion: 20, 125, 174

Intensive English Program (IEP): 26–28, 51–52, 56, 86, 91, 144–145

Interest Sections: 89, 93, 139–140

internet: 8, 77, 133

interview(s)/interviewed: 17, 107, 128, 148–149

kaleidoscope(s)/kaleidoscopic: 58–59, 94, 170

language program administrators: 43, 45, 79, 109

Latin America: 29, 143, 173

listening: 19, 24, 78, 82–83, 97, 123, 136,
160, 166
loss(es): 1, 120, 131, 173
lost/lose/losing: 43, 47, 48, 57, 74, 76,
106, 117, 123, 143

MBA (Master of Business
Administration): 3, 6, 15
mentoring: 71, 81, 112, 169–170
Mercado, Leo: 21–22, 43–45, 79–81,
123–127
metaphor(s): 16, 31, 38, 46–47, 68–69,
127, 141, 164, 170
microscope/microscopic: 38, 46, 58–59, 94
mirror(s): 45–46, 83
mission: 54, 89–90, 138–139, 142
mistakes: 10, 26, 86, 110, 111, 113, 137,
141

narrative: 108, 144, 161, 171
Neuro-Linguistic Programming (NLP):
24, 49, 83–85
Nigeria: 18, 39, 75, 120
non-profit/not-for-profit: 23, 30, 54, 118,
122, 138
nursing: 36–37, 106–107

obligation(s): 20, 78, 138
option(s): 29, 55–56, 70, 97, 118, 148–
150, 151–152
Orlando, Rosemary: 25–26, 50–52,
86–88, 135–137

pain(s)/painful/painfully: 3, 143, 146,
163, 165
Palmer, Parker: 41, 51, 70, 135
pandemic: vii, 1–3, 8, 27, 36, 120, 163, 174
pathway(s): 11, 74, 117, 140–141, 146, 172
Pellicer, Leonard: 77, 104–105, 123
perseverance: viii, 15, 18, 162, 163
Peru: 17, 18, 21, 22
politics/political: 37, 39, 92, 104, 111,
126, 127, 131, 142, 154, 165

poor leadership: 1–3, 122, 163
portfolio(s): 45, 73, 81, 168, 169, 172
(post)colonial: 17, 129–130
poverty: 17, 20, 23, 123, 163
power/powerful: 9. 15, 39, 107, 110, 120,
127, 139–140, 141, 150
president(s): 5, 17, 19–21, 23, 25, 27–31,
48, 58, 75, 89, 90, 92, 93, 119, 120,
131–134, 146, 170
principal(s): 26, 28, 104, 107, 109, 112
privilege: viii, 15, 18, 76, 79, 126, 129–
130, 162–163
problem(s): 8, 24, 29, 42, 48, 52, 86, 87,
124, 127, 128, 153, 166, 169, 173

Qatar: 17, 18, 20, 74–75, 117–119

reflection-in-action/reflection-on-action:
60, 61, 96, 97
resilience: viii, 18, 162, 163
resistance: 113, 125, 139
respect: 24, 44, 80, 89, 123, 125–126, 129,
136–138, 140
revenue(s): 91, 138, 142–143, 145–146
Richards & Lockhart: 37, 44, 60, 61, 86,
88
Rosenberg, Marjorie: 24–25, 48–50,
83–85, 131–134
ruminate/ruminating/rumination: 60,
96–97, 150, 154
running: 24, 26, 30, 54, 69, 75, 83, 119–
120, 131–132, 134, 137

sad/sadly/sadness: 11, 75, 142, 166
Schon, Donald: 36, 50, 55, 60, 97,
172–173
self-assessment: 44, 54, 80–81, 94, 96
self-awareness: 38, 40, 41, 43, 107
self-doubt: 77, 110, 115, 117, 121
sharing: 10, 40, 79, 94, 106, 153, 166, 174
simple: 7, 10, 47, 49, 79, 87, 108, 167
solution(s): 51, 77, 87, 91, 97, 140
space: 4, 5, 21, 41, 88, 120, 122, 145, 174

Spain/Spanish: 1, 16, 29, 173
Special Interest Group(s): 24, 84, 89, 131
standing: 7, 9, 90, 129, 172
stepping back: 4, 38, 50, 52, 128, 134
stranger(s): 22, 111–112, 129
strategy: 85, 90, 140, 152
struggle(s): 30, 41, 146, 154, 166, 169

teaching assistant(s) (TAs): 21, 30,
    150–154
teaching/teacher(s) journal(s): 79, 81, 94,
    96
telescope/telescopic: 38, 58–59, 94
test(s)/testing: 21, 29, 60, 87, 142,
    147–148
time management: 24, 31, 98, 109
touch/touched, touching: 36, 48, 85, 121,
    124, 166
tradition(al): 89, 140, 145
travel(s)/traveled/traveling: 14, 16, 33, 46,
    67, 83, 88–89, 130, 135

trial-and-error: 23, 77, 127
truth/truthful: 3, 41, 114

uncertainty: 16, 111, 113, 136
upset: 76, 80, 114

values: 40, 41, 43, 53, 60, 70–71, 92, 123
video: 21, 45, 70, 71, 73, 81–83, 122,
    168–169
Vietnam: 17, 27, 135–137
visible minority: 15, 18, 123, 163
vision: 24, 29, 38, 40, 42, 44, 48, 56, 59,
    75, 117–119, 134
voice(s): 17, 21, 43, 45, 82, 83, 123, 131
volunteer(s)/volunteering: 27, 30, 49, 54,
    118–119, 133, 139–140, 146

water: 16, 38, 46, 49, 127
Wilde, Oscar: 9, 10, 13, 111

Zeichner & Liston: 60–61, 96–97

CPSIA information can be obtained
at www.ICGtesting.com
Printed in the USA
JSHW021600080222
22712JS00001B/23

9 781800 501386